SPORT IN THE AMERICAN WEST

Jorge Iber, series editor

Also in the series

Becoming Iron Men: The Story of the 1963 Loyola Ramblers,
by Lew Freedman

Our White Boy,
by Jerry Craft, with Kathleen Sullivan

More Than Just Peloteros: Sport and U.S. Latino Communities,
edited by Jorge Iber

Playing in Shadows: Texas and Negro League Baseball,
by Rob Fink

Remembering Bulldog Turner: Unsung Monster of the Midway,
by Michael Barr

West Texas Middleweight: The Story of LaVern Roach, by Frank Sikes

Wil the Thrill: The Untold Story of Wilbert Montgomery,
by Edward J. Robinson

SHOOTING FOR THE RECORD

SHOOTING FOR THE RECORD

Adolph Toepperwein, Tom Frye, and Sharpshooting's Forgotten Controversy

Tim Price

Texas Tech University Press

This book is typeset in Minion Pro. The paper used in this book meets the minimum requirements of ANSI/NISO Z39.48-1992 (R1997). ♾

Designed by Kasey McBeath
Cover photographs from Kenneth Toepperwein and Remington Society of America.

Library of Congress Cataloging-in-Publication Data
Names: Price, Tim, 1963-
Title: Shooting for the record : Adolph Toepperwein, Tom Frye, and sharp-shooting's forgotten controversy / Tim Price.
Description: Lubbock, Texas : Texas Tech University Press, [2016] | Series: Sport in the American West | Includes bibliographical references and index.
Identifiers: LCCN 2016005847 (print) | LCCN 2016018131 (ebook) | ISBN 9780896729773 (Hardcover : alk. paper) | ISBN 9780896729780 (E-book)
Subjects: LCSH: Shooting contests—United States—History. | Toepperwein, Adolph. | Frye, Tom (Exhibition shooter)
Classification: LCC GV1169 .P75 2016 (print) | LCC GV1169 (ebook) | DDC 799.3/1—dc23
LC record available at https://lccn.loc.gov/2016005847

Printed in Canada
16 17 18 19 20 21 22 23 24 / 9 8 7 6 5 4 3 2 1

Texas Tech University Press
Box 41037 | Lubbock, Texas 79409-1037 USA
800.832.4042 | ttup@ttu.edu | www.ttupress.org

In dedication to and remembrance of Bill Price, for his high hopes for this project, his steadfast actions throughout life, and unwavering love for his children, and their children. I'm proud he's my father.

"A man was his own creative force in the old days, and his own boss."

—**Fred Allen**, vaudeville performer and radio personality

CONTENTS

Part Five: The Spent Casings

ILLUSTRATIONS

PREFACE
Legacy Building . . .

"I move over now and offer my best wishes to Barry and his family on this historical achievement. My hope today, as it was on that April evening in 1974, is that the achievement of this record will inspire others to chase their own dreams."

—Hank Aaron, on the occasion in 2006 when his career record home-run total was surpassed by Barry Bonds.

Perhaps when that baseball flew off Barry Bonds's bat and kept going past the right-center field wall in San Francisco to become home run No. 756, Hank Aaron really meant what he said. Prior to that, in the months, weeks, and days that another Bonds home run took one more off the number he needed to reach the record, maybe there was not a hint of steam building up between Aaron's ears in those quiet moments when he contemplated what was bound to be true. His record was going to be surpassed by what might as well have been an android, a morphed being who was said to have lustily taken in a chemical to multiply his powers.

Aaron could have paced around with the thought and just got tired of it all, knowing there was no way a confession was at hand. Steroids are, as one scribe as noble as Jose Canseco has informed us, a sign of the times in professional sports. Yet, in his era, Aaron pristinely broke the record of all records when he swatted more home runs than Babe Ruth. It was a crowning achievement of a pure baseball life. Better, it became among the few moments that magnificently transcended sports even before the next pitch was thrown. In the first few steps out of the batter's box, when his trot rounded second, two white men were genuinely enthused and ran out to pat Aaron on the back. The roar of the crown continued, and play-by-play announcer Vin Scully broadcast clearly through the noise, ". . . what a marvelous moment for the country and the world. A black man is getting a standing ovation in the Deep South for breaking a record of an all-time baseball idol." In this context, there can't be anything that could rattle Aaron's mind from his time in the record book, not even the fact that a man suspected of cheating broke the record.

Was this the case? Or it could be Aaron's speech was legacy building. Perhaps he thought that his legend, built in large part by the class he showed while setting all those records, would turn into something petty in the view of today's what-have-you-done-for-me-lately audiences if he really spoke his mind. Aaron rightly could have uttered a line like, "You know, no one ever talked about me using steroids when I set the record." His record had been taken down, so why allow the personality, the image of high and esteemed character, the thing Aaron still possessed and the thing that would last, to crash and burn right along with the record? Political correctness, image, has gone so far, now, that it dictates what a man can or cannot say in a congratulatory speech.

I think we all have been told that there was more civility somewhere back there in a past generation, and perhaps that there also was more honesty, and that comments made as such were looked upon as just that. Honesty, not an agenda.

That line of thinking could be found in the storyline between Adolph Toepperwein and Tom Frye. These were two of the top-performing riflemen in the history of the shooting sports. Toepperwein was active from the 1890s to 1945, while Frye picked up after service in World War II to his death in 1982. Both men had a talent with the gun that was so fascinating they were hired by the major firearms brands of Winchester and Remington to perform sharpshooting shows in the days when the public still could be captivated without the assistance of the Xbox or reality TV. Show after show, easily more than a hundred performances in a year, typically would draw crowds past one thousand on each stop of a tour of the smallest burgs. Fancy shooting appealed to those rural crowds, but so did common-sense thinking like calling a spade a spade without being a jerk about it.

Toepperwein's turn to talk about a lost record came well after the days he sought to break through the door of the shooting sports that W.F. "Doc" Carver appeared to have latched. It was an outlandish, freakish, swim-the-Channel accomplishment—the world record for endurance target-shooting. Carver did it in 1888 when he spent six days shooting at 60,674 small, hand-thrown balls, not stopping until he hit 60,000. This was no small feat. Accounting for the weight of his rifle and the kick from the ammunition firing, Carver had to keep a cumulative 500,000 pounds lifted and in place for each shot and accept 515,000 pounds of pressure applied to his shoulder from the recoil of the firing weapon. Yet, this didn't scare away Adolph Toepperwein. He spent a lifetime longing to hold that record.

Then, years after Toepperwein's shooting career was done, when he knew that the rest of his life would more likely be counted in weeks than in years, a news report was brought to Toepperwein's attention. This news report appeared out of Reno, Nevada, in December 1959 with flabbergasting details of an attempt by Tom Frye to hit far more targets than Toepperwein ever tried.

Soon, Toepperwein was told and shown that there was something suspicious about the venue where it was claimed Frye shot toward the record. Toepperwein felt his response forming so strongly that he took his 90-year-old body over to the manual typewriter in his house. He slanted his head to the point he could make out the keys around what we believe to have been the macular degeneration that developed in his old age and blocked out much of his central vision. He composed an open letter to the shooting industry. He wasn't willing to miss an opportunity to be intimate with what he could see to be the truth. He would not make like Aaron would and "move over now." Rather, he specifically spelled out where he had the problem with the way Frye went about the record. It was in this way that Toepperwein formed a unique protest to an obscure sports record that was "sanctioned" and pulled toward the mainstream when it was published in the Guinness Book of World Records.

This little moment in time is an unlikely place to plot the source of a sports fan's quandary and sports-talk radio's easy call-in subject: How do the performers setting new records compare to their predecessors? People struggle to compare LeBron James to Michael Jordan, not to mention those separated by much more time, like pitchers Walter Johnson and Greg Maddux.

This book won't provide anything close to the end-all answer for such chatter. But there has been more than a couple of years of poking my hands through the dry cobwebs of history, so I know for sure I pulled away enough to inform myself of the lore of people like Ad and Plinky Toepperwein (the shooting team known as The Wonderful Topperweins), and Tom Frye and Newt Crumley. These are the lead principals in *Shooting for the Record*. Their names are connected in the world of the competitive shooting sports, and, perhaps haphazardly, we can see that one of modern American sports' first baby steps toward performance-enhancing substances and other newfangled monkey business as driving forces toward record-setting performances may have come on a dusty shooting range in Nevada in 1959.

Performance-enhancing substances? Take nothing from Frye, a gifted performer and a national champion among professional trapshooters. He has been inducted into trapshooting's Hall of Fame, yet when he shot toward the marathon target-shooting record outside Dayton, Nevada, he popped muscle relaxers. Wait, those are performance-enhancing substances? Hold your laughter. My mind did a double-take until I remembered sitting in a newspaper office one day around 1990 and I heard a colleague return from his assignment covering a hearing about performance-enhancing substances in modern pentathlon. "What are they using?" I asked. "Tranquilizers." I laughed at what I heard. "How do tranquilizers make you perform better?" I quit smiling when I was told that the type of drug they were using quieted the nerves and took away the shakes. Meanwhile, their competitors held the rifle in their hands during the target-shooting portion of the competition, suspicious of their competition's advantage. Adolph Toepperwein didn't have muscle-relaxers. His best stab at a performance-enhancing substance was the salt that was added to his bath water he soaked in after a long day at the firing line.

It appears Toepperwein knew nothing of pills as part of Frye's shoot. Toepperwein did have a beef over the stage for Frye's shooting. He believed it fell under the cliché of "cozy confines." Toepperwein produced a yellowed sheet of paper with hand-scribbled standards as to how far a shooter should stand from his targets when pursuing this sort of thing. This sheet contained unsanctioned, folklore stuff for a serious sports endeavor, but that sort of documentation is just about the same thing that organized baseball has to fall back upon when the dimensions of the playing field are plotted. It's ninety feet between bases, but it's pretty much open-ended beyond the boundary of the diamond.

Baseball must need such things. Home runs, offense, brings 'em in. Like the commercial with pitchers Maddux and Tom Glavine playfully suggests, "chicks dig the long ball." Baseball's team owners didn't pull the switch on the juice that was powering so many of those home runs that started flying in the '90s. And if androstenedione and trenbolone wasn't enough to do it, some willing owners would make sure that those outfield fences would be grabbed and pulled closer to home plate. The players certainly didn't bargain against it. I can remember covering the developments that led toward Alex Rodriguez signing his $250 million contract with the Texas Rangers. When he showed up in Texas, he took one last shot at what he left behind in Seattle. The Mariners never moved in the fences at Safeco Field, like he told them to. Baseballs just didn't seem to fly out of there. But they sure did at Fulton County Stadium, where Aaron played a significant portion of his career. It was a hitter-friendly venue to the extent that it had the nickname of "The Launching Pad." And they float kayaks past the home run fence where Bonds hit a lot of them into San Francisco Bay. The deepest part of the yard there is 420 feet. Sure, Ruth sailed more than a few over the close-in porch straight down the foul line at his Yankee Stadium. But his power alley was about 430 feet, if his fly ball didn't get lost in the 490 feet of center field.

The spirit of Toepperwein's hand-scribbled notes that related to the proper dimensions of an endurance shoot was caught by someone. The weirdness of this target-shooting record was saleable enough that *SPORT magazine*, the popular predecessor to *Sports Illustrated*, sought Tom Frye in 1962. They found him in Montana accurately blowing the heads off jack rabbits from long range. The article came away with no blaring negative judgment of Frye's work. And it did not obsess over the notion that the shoot was sponsored by a businessman, Newt Crumley, seeking to promote his casino business with the equivalent of towering home runs; Crumley, it must be noted, did have a reputation of fair-dealing and integrity. But the pertinent question, apparently, was asked of Frye: Was all of this legitimate? And Frye, in a story that was printed some ten weeks after Toepperwein's death, "manned up."

The additives to top-level athletic performance that show up now, compared to decades ago, walk through every doorway imaginable. This book encounters such things, but doesn't dwell on them. It was better to aim at storytelling, to celebrate lives lived well, or lived interestingly. Instead of solutions presented, yarns are. So, there will be some in the audience sitting there like a character from the motion picture *Ratatouille*, the critic Anton Ego, impatiently poking fingers into a table, eyeing down the waiter (OK, the author) and telling him that what he has written is "overheated puffery" and that some "fresh, clear, well-seasoned perspective" would, at least, go down well with a good bottle of wine. OK, I have provided the food (the narrative that makes up this book) and at least enough perspective here, I hope, to help sporting guns enthusiasts fairly place the accomplishments of Ad and Plinky Toepperwein, Tom Frye, and Newt Crumley.

ACKNOWLEDGMENTS

At some point in 2006, LeAnna Kosub of the *San Antonio Express-News* sports department called me with an idea. As a freelance journalist, I had been providing some copy for the newspaper, and she was wondering if I could knock out a package of stories for a recurring "how-to" on recreational sports. The topic for this one? Competitive shooting. "It would deal with target shooting, skeet and trap, gun ranges; that sort of thing," I remember LeAnna telling me.

So I researched the subject, and one name just wouldn't go away. When it came to successful shooting in San Antonio, I kept bumping into the name of Toepperwein, or was it Topperwein? Born in Texas to parents emigrated from Prussia, his given name was Adolph Toepperwein. But at some point prior to the World War I era, he became popularly known as Ad Topperwein. There are extended family and friends of Ad and Plinky Toepperwein who believe officials at Winchester Repeating Arms Company imposed the new spelling in order to avoid confusion over the Toepperweins' allegiance for America in the Allied forces fight against Germany. But Winchester's reference to the couple as Topperwein started as early as 1907. A company memo could not be found to support this, but Winchester somewhat "Americanized" a stage name for Ad and Plinky—The Wonderful Topperweins. Ad often was referred to as "Top," and Plinky as "Mrs. Top."

I was vaguely familiar with the Toepperwein story. There had been a display featuring the careers of the Toepperweins at the Hall of Horns Museum on the grounds of the Lone Star Brewery south of downtown San Antonio (the exhibit has since been moved to the middle of downtown and steps from the Riverwalk). Whenever anyone from out of town came in to visit, as quickly as I would take them to the Alamo, we'd also head over to the Lone Star Brewery. You got two wooden tokens that could be redeemed for beer.

I owe LeAnna, and many others, a beer. If only I could find those wooden tokens.

Hopefully, "thank you" will do for a number of helpful people.

Jerry Parsons, and his late brother Lynn Parsons, continued to keep the story of the Wonderful Topperweins alive.

Suzanne Toepperwein and her husband, Dwayne, led me to several of the Toepperwein clan, still proud of "Uncle Ad'ulf." Joann Toepperwein is the angel of this project. She was trustful while loaning a thick family scrapbook, helpful beyond words. She was a calming voice, too, and a patient listener. Ken Toepperwein allowed whatever time I needed to research the old files he has stored up on that peaceful ridge in the Texas Hill Country.

John Stein holds a collection of personal notes and effects from the hand of Ad Toepperwein and he spent an afternoon sharing it.

The manuscript of this book turned a major direction when I found Coni Wein. Coni's ol'der sister, Jan, married Tom Frye. I'm thankful to Coni's memory, and to her son, Justin, her cantankerous brothers Luke, now gone, and Dean. They loved Tom.

Peggy Drake, before and after our three-hour telephone conversation, opened doors to insights I found of her father, Newton H. Crumley. I saw that the loss of Mr. Crumley, so tragic to the young family he left behind, took from the rest of us the vast potential of even more public service.

There are people willing to be unsung to the researcher, and these are the accessionists, librarians, archivists, and historians I've come across. Of those, Roy Marcot and others in the Remington Society of America have been nothing short of heroic in their efforts to painstakingly preserve material that looked like nothing more than tedious company records. Among it all were a few things I found valuable that related to Tom Frye.

There was a lot of help and assistance, yet I imagine there could be things from the exemplary lives of Ad Toepperwein and Plinky, Tom Frye, and Newt Crumley that surely will bubble through the cracks that I thought were sealed. That's a shame, for I wanted to add everything I could from that esprit felt from the years of researching them.

If that esprit ever left this project, Tony Sapienza brought it back. It wasn't just the incredible research items he held. It was his willingness to step up and help in every way. He cheered louder and pulled for me more when things were down than when they were up. That's a friend.

The manuscript got a very helpful read from Kenny Ray Estes, and then great blessings upon acceptance at Texas Tech University Press. Thanks to Jorge Iber for his desire to include *Shooting for the Record* among the fine titles in the "Sport in the American West" series, and thanks to everyone Dr. Iber opened the doors to at TTUP—Joanna Conrad, Amanda Werts, and Rachel Murdy among others.

And there is someone in my life named Kathleen. She has given me the ultimate support: Time. Kathleen gave me the time I needed to do this project, and it was time well spent if it made our family—Khylee, Madison, Dwight, Texas, and Titus—proud.

Tim Price
San Antonio, Texas
September 2015

Part One

Defending a Mountain of 60,000 Wooden Blocks

Adolph Toepperwein, in a studio shot during his early days as the exhibition shooter for Winchester Repeating Arms Company around 1902, ready to throw a glass ball or composition target before firing upon it with a .22 caliber rifle. The hand-thrown balls were popular targets of the day. Collection of Kenneth Toepperwein.

CHAPTER ONE

His Dream

Ad's Haunted Mind

Darkness lifted, and the light came so Ad Toepperwein[1] could see the targets and start shooting again. The crackling from his .22 caliber rifle tickled the receptive chill of December air. The other noise was just as salient, yet as maddeningly monotonous.

"Hit. Hit. Hit."

Pronounced in the absence of excitement, profound as a sniffle, those words usually came just about every three seconds, steady, as long as Ad kept a bullet aligned in the magazine that pushed the ammunition inches from his mustachioed face. Another target, a little two-and-a-quarter-inch wooden block just like all those ones before it, was thrown into the air. With his long, slender arms bent in angles obtuse on one side and acute on the other, Ad aimed again and squeezed the trigger. The firing of the gun answered, and so did the judge.

"Hit."

By December 16, 1907, Ad's shooting had been going on for four days. Seven hours, every day, he'd been at it in front of the grandstand at the San Antonio International Fair Grounds. People trickled in to the fairgrounds in the winter off-season because word had gotten out that this local-boy-gone-big-sharpshooter was firing upon what was considered a world record for the most hits by rifle shot at hand-thrown targets. This young man, who grew up as the star product of San Antonio's schuetzen-crazed and vibrant German community, was known formally by his brethren as Adolph Toepperwein. The thought of the record had driven him even before his teenage years. His advance into adulthood and the progression of jobs that came with it refined those boyhood dreams into a desire to have his shooting fall under one bold, descriptive label: Legitimate. These jobs ranged from local newspaper cartoonist, to East Coast vaudeville performer, to the point where his livelihood became stamped as the exhibition shooter for the gun-manufacturing giant Winchester Repeating Arms Company. Finally, now age thirty-eight, Ad pushed his obsession over the edge, dangling out there for all to see. Could he really do it?

Plinky would do her damnedest to see that he did. Plinky was there, now, every time her husband, Ad, picked up a gun. When he was attracted to her bright eighteen-year-old eyes and red hair six years back near her family's Connecticut home, they soon married. She fell for him, and she also fell under the same spell that compelled Ad to put his grip on a gun. She wanted to learn how to shoot and perform those fancy tricks, and he taught her. She wanted to be a part of his shooting exhibitions, but not just an ornament who held a target while he whizzed bullets past her fingers. She learned to shoot and, judging by the fact that she could fire a bullet right through the playing-card edge of an ace of spades just like Annie Oakley did a few years before her, she could shoot well. When she plinked as many targets with her gun as Ad did with his, he took her along and saw to it that the Winchester company put their star performers' names on the bill as one, no matter what people thought about women firing a gun when they couldn't even cast a vote. With him turning somersaults and grabbing a gun and firing it through a target just before it fell to the ground, and her shooting chalk out from his fingers even though she had her back turned and aimed with a hand mirror, yes they were indeed everything the Winchester promotional pamphlets and posters said they were: The Wonderful Topperweins.

And now she was sending him off to an achievement that he sought long before he ever met her. She understood what it meant. So when the endurance shoot started four days earlier, as soon as Ad finished sliding the cartridges into the rifle, Plinky smooched him on the cheek. He smiled. It was time to start firing, and the count went up.[2]

"Hit."

Could he really do this? Well, he was the one who grew up bragging about how he would break the record of his boyhood idol, Doc Carver. He'd need at least 60,000 shots to do that, and so the local lumberyard sawed up enough wood to get him started. The cubes were so small that even the littlest hands could grab them. If Ad wasn't going to shoot a hole through them, they could have been sent to a toy manufacturer like Milton Bradley and have the rough edges sanded and painted to make a long train of alphabet blocks.[3]

Ad swallowed hard when he saw them at the fairgrounds, for they were everywhere. They tumbled and bumped. The sounds from such fashioned lumber were dull, of shuffle and muffle, and every side showed the blah of a pale yellow color. The only thing impressive about them was their number. The 60,000 wooden blocks it would take to put Ad in the neighborhood of Doc Carver, if they were placed next to each other with no space in between, would force anyone picking them up to walk a little more than two miles before they reached the end of the line. Once the horses got done tugging them out to the fairgrounds ring where Ad was shooting, a few "Mexican boys" swung large shovels from off their shoulders and scooped them into another pile about twenty feet in front of the firing line. Even when Ad shot them, they were coming down at such a rate that it was too much of a bother to move them very far out of the way. The record was still days out there. He had to keep shooting.

"Hit."

By the time Ad was finished on this fourth day, the judge hired to verify the proceedings saw that Ad was firing at more than seven thousand a day, about a thousand an hour—a breathtaking rate—for a total of twenty-nine thousand so far.[4] He had to aim those tiny bullets twenty five feet over and about twenty feet, maybe thirty, up to hit the wooden cube in the air. Yet only three times from twenty-nine thousand arm-cramping shots had the judge failed to repeat the same word.

"Hit."

Ad's accuracy clearly was honed through the first three days, thus his rifle shooting joined the work of the masters. These were the brushstrokes made essentially in quiet, seemingly not so appealing in the moment, but marvelous once collected after the skilled hand came to rest. The tense act of aiming a precise bullet at a distant moving target and hitting it was for Ad the mindless scribbling of his signature at the bottom of the painting.

Ad still was able to stand there tall, limber, lean, and angular, in a way resembling the coyotes that durably scampered through the South Texas brush not far from where he fired. With the fine walnut butt of the Winchester Model 1903 pressed against his shoulder, he struck a ready image.[5] He aimed, pulled the trigger, and found the target. But no matter how simple the task sounded, nor the aid of immaculate health alive in his Prussian-bred body, the stress of these simple actions mounted like the handiwork of a mason on cornerstone. The prototypes of the Model T that Henry Ford was working on in Detroit at the end of 1907 currently weighed about twelve hundred pounds. Considering that Ad was lifting a rifle of almost six pounds, or at least keeping it lifted and in a shooting position each time the wooden blocks were going up, by this time in the shoot his total workload of that six pounds was multiplied into a sum that had Ad hoisting just about the equivalent of one-hundred and forty-five Model Ts.

He was really feeling it, now four days in, another seven hours of shooting left behind in a thickening metal carpet of bullet casings and that Babelish pile of bullet-holed wooden blocks. Though he only missed two on that fourth day, it was twice as many as he missed all together the first three days.[6]

Something was up, and perhaps it was the tension. Shooting a gun required force-fed movements, and the positioning of the firearm was unnatural. Combined with the never-ending push of ballistics, this all spelled hell for the fellow who thought he could shoot a gun all day. The recoil of a .22 caliber, however muted compared to the kick of a shotgun, was amplified by the constant firing, and it began to label a purple bruise on Ad's shoulder. His trigger finger cramped and was cut by the thousands of squeezes. Anyone who gave this endurance shooting a try would see their trigger hand swell to the point that it could stamp in mud a bulldog's paw print. The constant focusing on a target flying against the backdrop of daytime sky was testing his eyeballs. Mental fatigue was expected from standing there and trying to concentrate on the accurate shooting of aerial targets for a full workday. But all that stress rode the skids to distress when the physical torment was thrown in. He was a master, but like the master facing the canvas while fighting obsession and madness, Ad also stepped into that dark, awaiting grip. And that's when he felt this new sensation, this scraping onto his scruff.

But time couldn't be spent figuring that one out. Another block went into the air.

"Hit."

Until he took his one hour for lunch, or quickly reloaded his rifle's ten-round magazine, the blocks kept coming just about every three seconds. Ad, however, felt like he could find some deliberation in all this rush. It actually opened to him when he found a rhythm with the target thrower and waited ever so routinely for that block to reach the apex of its rise. That's when he'd shoot it, when it was hanging there. Well, not hanging there, really, but at least when the block offered a short glimpse of slowing down. It was almost like the blocks drifted. Like his mind, drifting, drifting off. Another block went up. Another block went up!

Nothing. No noise. The judge was silent. Did he forget to shoot? No! There was no bullet! Was the gun jamming? Another block went up. And another! The bullet's just not coming out of the end of the barrel.[7]

The blocks wouldn't stop going up. And now maybe this was it: In his intention to make sure he toed a line twenty-five feet distant from the targets, as prescribed by his childhood hero Doc Carver, Ad's fixation on the distance requirement got out of hand. Or was the strain on his eyes playing tricks on him, because he was shooting again now. Yeah, the gun worked. But the blocks were a mile away![8] How was he going to hit those with a .22 rifle? It ought to be easy enough. The blocks were just hanging there. They were hanging there, in a circle, all around him. They wouldn't come down. This was nuts. And now it was the darn gun again. The rifle was firing off shots backwards.[9]

His mind was racing. This shoot clearly had gone wrong. What would be next? But there was a constant. It was the rub against the shadowy bristle on his neck. His body, his mind, was in fits. His hand cramped so badly that he couldn't handle a razor. His neck? His neck! Ad let out a scream!

Finally, he was awake. It was just a dream. He was dreaming, yet another one, and it passed with Plinky standing over him with a washcloth. With his hands and arms cramping so, Plinky took care of washing and dressing him. His neck? The local barber had just come in to shave Ad while he slept.[10] That meant it was just about time to head back out there, stand twenty-five feet away from those throwers, and pick up that gun again.

"Hit. Hit. Hit. . . ."

CHAPTER TWO

Why Don't You Just Keep Going?

Newt Gives Tom an Idea

His nose could have simply slipped off a falcon and fallen onto his face. The eyes could have, too, with their definitive, striking brows. And his shoulders, square and fit, could have been the platform for the launch of powerful wings so he could put a Peregrine's glare to use and spot prey from far above. Tom Frye's body, from what everyone could see, was put together as well as those handcrafted guns he carried. And when he was put to the test, Tom Frye's precise eye and steady hands produced marksmanship that filled a trophy room. Yet there was quarry still roaming out there, the sporting prize of a lifetime for anyone daunting enough to ever bring it down. This thing was so intimidating that the mere mention of it left him hesitant for one of the rare occasions of his life.

"I don't know if I could do it," Tom told the man. "Nobody would ever try to beat that record, let alone beat it."[1]

This was hardly the answer that would end the conversation. As impressive and talented as Tom Frye was, Newt Crumley had run up against bigger stars. Newt had Bing Crosby as a neighbor, and Newt's the one who sold the property to the crooner.[2]

"I think you could," Newt responded to Tom. "You shoot blocks in your shows, and you never miss. Why don't you just keep going?"[3]

Like it was that simple, to just keep going? This was 1959, some fifty-two

Tom Frye aims high at a target while an assistant grabs another.
Remington Society of America.

years since Ad Toepperwein had those tens of thousands of wooden blocks stacked in front of him and his rifle. As far as anyone knew there had been no other shooters bold enough to try it. By the sound of it, Toepperwein barely kept his wits when he did it. And now someone named Newt Crumley has the audacity to even mention it? Was he serious?

Definitely, the shooting world cowered in the face of the thing Toepperwein tried. But Newt shaded toward a good gamble. He always tried to put the odds in his favor, even if it was just by a few percentage points. He knew, if he kept playing that, over time, it would pay off. His mind just didn't seem to fold, and it sure wouldn't now that he had come in contact with Tom. Newt was drawn to the enthusiastic crowds that watched Tom perform—like Toepperwein had—as an exhibition shooter and guns demonstrator. The patches sewn onto Tom's shooting jacket were from Remington Arms Company, whom he represented when he traveled through the West from his Chatsworth, California, home. Whenever Tom made it back to his boyhood home in Ohio he beat that familiar path to Vandalia for the Grand American shoot, the biggest sporting guns competition in the country. He'd come back West with eight trophies in the decade that was coming to an end with Newt telling Tom he was so good with the gun that he didn't understand why he didn't just keep going and put his own name in the record book.

Yet, with the solid image Tom struck, there was something inside that shoved a little peg of reluctance into the gears Newt wanted to engage. It made Tom, a forty-three-year-old, feel older than he looked. It stuck there, many times painfully, even though Tom knew the glory that would come from pursuing Toepperwein. Tom remembered Mr. Toepperwein. He was this larger-than-life figure in the shooting sports. He was a gentleman, easily approachable. Like Ad's father, Tom's father taught him how to shoot. Vested in his son's future in gun shooting, Sam Frye made the one-hundred-mile drive down the Ohio road from their home in Findlay to Vandalia for the Grand American. And when Ad Toepperwein was in the crowd, Mr. Frye saw to it that teenage Tom shook the hand of a legend.

When other boys were off playing ball at the neighborhood diamond, Tom shot targets.[4] Then, Tom imagined himself breaking the endurance-shooting record. He could have gone at it like a junior golfer: This putt to beat Bobby Jones in the US Open; this target to beat Ad Toepperwein. But it might have been a boyhood infatuation, because it wasn't that long before other things, more practical events, started calling on his expertise at sharpshooting. Still more things worked against his athletic body, and took drips from his wellspring of a focused mind. To stand out in a field and fire for days on end at little wooden targets flying through the air? There were other ways to lay claim to the title of the best marksman on the planet. Didn't that shooting jacket, with the All-America emblems stitched on and awarded to him annually from *Sports Afield*, prove that? Besides, this world was now about to send rockets to space. Life was speeding up. The very face of firearms was about to change. Things were a lot different from the still-pioneer America that Mr. Toepperwein inhabited.

Newt Crumley knew that. He appeared to embrace change, to track it, even went so far to invest mightily in it. Newt had spent a lifetime keeping the neon of vacancy glowing above his comfort zone. He was lucky enough to be born to a father who built a fortune on top of desert scrub. And although Bing Crosby, often a hunting partner, would ditty a wisecrack line about "Newt sitting on his fanny,"[5] Newt showed no complacency, no pampering, and he wasn't willing to kick back and prop his feet upon that lucky birth. Once his father opened the doors to a casino in Elko, Nevada, the young man Newt showed anticipation that made the best card counter jealous. The Commercial Hotel had never before made Elko an entertainment capital, but when Newt booked big-name acts into the property's newly built theater, the dusty village became a fun, vibrant way station. Newt made sure people heard about it, and they drove roughly two hundred miles from places like Salt Lake City and Boise to see the stars—and fall into the action.[6] Las Vegas started peering beyond the bare expanse toward Elko. And what it saw made Vegas move. Newt Crumley could do that.

Apparently, Newt did learn plenty from his father, who had started with a saloon to refresh silver prospectors rushing in to desolate Nye County. The quick, big money that the senior Crumley made was turned into the Commercial. And when Newt took control of the Commercial he made a move to bigger trappings. The developers of the Holiday Hotel in downtown Reno were looking for a partner to start the casino business there. Quickly, Newt was the primary owner, and he ran the entire operation. And, as he did at the Commercial, he was unwilling to sit around and count easy money from losers. He ventured out, he met on equal footing with talented, ambitious individuals, and he tried to make his gambling business a part of the sporting landscape.

It appeared he didn't blink when it came time to climb out on the wing. He'd done it before, literally. He left Nevada at the calling of his country, and he served in the era of the world wars. He was recognized for meritorious service. He continued to fly after his discharge, but, even then, daring was needed. There was the troubled flight with his friends that Newt was able to land along a mountain ridge despite a snowstorm.[7] The experience didn't ground Newt.

Newt had often beaten death, and he beat most with whom he sprayed lead at gun competitions. He fired well, and he won several of Nevada's state championships in trap and skeet.[8] The shooting community around Reno was avid. And when one of the city's other casinos operated a sporting guns facility and shooting range, Newt also launched his Holiday Hotel and Casino into ownership of a game ranch south of town and near Dayton. It promoted hunting excursions for hotel guests and casino high rollers, but any sort of shooting competition could be conducted there—even an endurance shoot if Tom Frye was willing.

Newt could fit it into his schedule, for he played as hard as he worked, and there were no out-of-bounds markers between the two. He attended meetings as a regent at the University of Nevada, and he golfed. He played and taught squash and built the first courts in Nevada; he campaigned for state senate and won. He bought into a hydroplane race boat that had won a national championship, and with his civic mind christened Reno's name onto it.[9]

But perhaps it was the gun more so than the other pursuits that caused Newt's mind to look for glory days, an old school. How could a mind not think back whenever that smooth-finish wood, crafted by hand, slid back along the arm and propped against the shoulder ready to fire, the feel of cold steel gone warm as shells propelled through that barrel, and the smell of powder burnt? There was power in those blasts, in the sight of pulled clay disks flicked to grit in air. It was the gun, after all, that won the West, the home of the Crumley family past and present. Newt could bring the past alive, he could re-create the great endurance shooters, the big names like Doc Carver and Ad Toepperwein, and he could do it right there in Nevada. So he talked to Tom about it. Tom Frye, this visually able-bodied, keen-eyed, fine-handed triggerman, could make the connection from yesterday come alive in the present.

Newt tossed the idea out there, a target thrown by hand, but that was all for now. He'd leave the idea hanging there like a wooden block at the apex of its toss, because he thought it was the right time to fire it out of the sky. Setting the world record for hitting the most aerial targets was not on Tom Frye's radar. But with Newt in the picture, Tom finally started making blips toward the record.

CHAPTER THREE
Most Wonderful Shooting
Visiting Ad, the Old Master

Most everyone usually wanted to talk about those days he spent pursuing the record, even now, with fifty-two years passed since Ad finished his endurance shoot at San Antonio. Those dreams of Ad's, the nightmares with the wooden blocks always flying through the air, were as persistent as they were fantastic. Certainly Mickey Mantle, or any other sports figure at the peak of his career now in 1959, couldn't come up with an experience he could part with like that in print. Yet when journalists streamed over to the Toepperwein house next to San Antonio's Brackenridge Park and partook in the figurative sitting at the knee of the old master, they didn't have the easiest time directing Ad's thoughts to December 1907.

Their hopes could be boosted upon arrival. Even before they walked up the steps to the front porch of the wood-framed house, the guns motif was in clear view. At the Toepperwein mailbox was a list of the six rules from his Shooter's Code. A press of the doorbell came under a sign with "Keep Your Powder Dry and Don't Let Your Trigger Finger Get Rusty" printed on it.[1] After the welcome-in-take-a-seat, the entrant saw a room where guns veined from the walls. Before he went off on his fateful war reporter's trip to the South Pacific, Ernie Pyle knocked on that front door of the Toepperwein house in San Antonio. He walked into the den and found "a remarkable, helter-skelter, gun-infested room. There were guns everywhere—in cabinets, hung on the walls, standing in corners. And from under the couch Ad

Adolph Toepperwein, who lived alone in the years following his wife Elizabeth's death, signs a "bullet drawing." From some twenty feet away, he could "draw" images of Buffalo Bill, Uncle Sam, George Washington, and many others, into metal with bullets. Collection of Kenneth Toepperwein.

would pull suitcase after suitcase, each one full of six-shooters; there must have been scores of them."[2] Most sentimental were the rifles crafted by his father, the immigrant from New Ruppin, Prussia, whose gunsmithing and design contributions to the prototypal American craftsman John Marlin after the Civil War were sought after by hunters on their way to plains overrun by buffalo herds. If Arnold Palmer's career was just beginning to thrust exhaust back onto the runway with his first Masters win in 1958 in large part because his greenskeeper father stuck a golf club in his youthful hands back in western Pennsylvania, Ad had risen to the top of professional gun sports because his father taught him how to peer through the sights. Guns were, had been, and always would be, Ad's life.

On the weekend there would be no interviews conducted at the center-of-the-city Brackenridge Park duplex where Ad resided. To find him you'd have to drive more than thirty minutes northwest up Fredericksburg Road to the beginnings of the Texas hills at Leon Springs. This is where Ad tutored and counseled those with hopeful trigger fingers, those who knew straight-shooting instruction from a legend would remain on the vine only for so much longer. So out came the airmen from San Antonio's squadron of air fields based at Brooks, Kelly, Lackland, and Randolph, soldiers from Fort Sam Houston and then more from Camp Bullis and Camp Stanley, which was just right down the hill and across the road from Ad's shooting camp. And then there were the young folk who wore the dusty britches and boots of a ranch hand, or those junior clerks buttoning down the stitched and starched shirts as they apprenticed at businesses back downtown.[3]

If rural neighbors around Leon Springs didn't know any better they'd have thought an insurrection was afoot in those hills. They'd come to know it as a shooting lodge, though members of the Toepperwein family smiled at that thought because they regarded it, more aptly, as "the shack." Spare, it only could be considered well-appointed whenever the firing line was drawn and the unloosed had the room to lustily propel pellet and bullet to a quickly worn target. If Ad could catch a shooter just right in the only angle of vision that remained to him in advanced age, he could make that one a pupil and offer lessons to correct and improve. "Learn to shoot with both eyes open. Always come up in the target you're shooting from the bottom so you can see where you're holding the gun at all times. Shoot the instant you get the sights in the proper position, just as soon as you get the sight immediately under the lower edge. Get a good gun and stick to it."[4] He didn't even have to see to offer that advice, for it was his mantra to anyone wanting to become a better shooter, which Ad thought everyone could do.

There was a point when Ad thought the clouds in his ninety-year-old vision could dissipate and he could take up firing arms again. The medical knowledge of the day thought they were cataracts, but surgery didn't work. There was no misdiagnosis of what had happened to his hearing. It was muffled by the millions of shots he triggered from the chambers of rifles and shotguns just inches away from his ears. Anyone who sat in the Toepperwein apartment had to stand next to Ad and shout their questions.[5]

They didn't have to ask many after introducing one subject: Plinky. Fourteen years after her death, Ad seemed to talk of her like they'd just put down their guns with yesterday's setting sun. And while a first glance at the house confirmed the love and life with the gun, a closer look would reveal images of Ad's companion wearing a smile. The pictures of Plinky outnumbered the guns on some walls. In the haphazard setting of an old man's house, a few of them were left to hang there crooked. There were so many that an edge of one photo was slid in the paper-thin space between door jamb and wall. Proper frames and glass that topped one picture also pressed and held fast another shot of Plinky. The weight of paper stock forced one corner downward in another askew presentation of the wife and fellow fancy-shooting performer. And a bulletin board that could have displayed a calendar, or reminders of bills to pay, would have none of that. Plinky and her husband were tacked down as the headliners there, too.

They had found the magic that sprinkled happiness onto life after the vows were taken, and until death it was a union never knuckled under by careers conducted elbow to elbow. Marriage and profession together lasted about forty years, so those pictures on the walls captured Plinky wearing the reversed bib of a sailor-inspired outfit from the era of their first shows together. A clip of hair fit nicely under an abbreviated bonnet, the short brim of the hat curled up to let shine a smile not distant of the teen-age years. Photographers caught them in middle age, serious faced, firing at targets during one of innumerable sessions of practice. And in clearer, more focused and tighter view, Plinky's wrinkles warmly smile out with a shotgun propped on the shoulder of a print dress. A grandmother could have worn it—though Plinky, tragically, never was one.

Not all the story of Plinky could be held upon those walls, but the still-present energy of her faithful old mate contained the rest of the information like the best stitched leather. Surely some of those guns up there were her favorites. During these advanced years, Ad's mind could dawdle in interviews, and it could stop here with her shotguns because they were the weapons she used to stand down her own action and blast her name into shooting history. The old promotional posters and handbills, which would have been pasted in towns that managed the smallest dot along the railroad where the Winchester shooting tour could stop, had their spot now on the Toepperwein walls and in desk drawers. Ad knew where he had them kept, and he showed them for others to flip through the booklet pages and read for themselves. As they rode the rails across the country, Ad and Plinky left behind countless small buttons for their followers to wear on lapels and clip to rifle straps. The faces of the sharpshooting couple smiled out, Ad higher on the placard and Plinky lower, but snug.

THE WONDERFUL TOPPERWEINS . . . The portrait of the snappy-dressed pair was contained in a circle that was scooted upward to reveal a bottom line on the button . . . WHO ALWAYS SHOOT WINCHESTER GUNS AND CARTRIDGES.

"The Famous Topperweins," Ad said, recalling one version of the promotional blurb. "Man, those were the days."[6]

It was this period of his life that dominated the interviews, until the visitor wanted to go forward to the grit and determination and away from Ad's sensitive side.

How about shooting those blocks here in San Antonio back in 1907, Top?

Nothing. Did he hear? Seconds would pass. Was he awake? He was a nonagenarian, so surely it was understandable for him to nod off from time to time inside that stuffy apartment and not even help it. No, his hands were moving, running along the smooth finish of walnut stock and heavy metal barrel of one of the battery of guns he had pulled down from his wall moments ago. Was he off in deep thought? Inside which frame from the gallery of memories, supplemented by the annexes his shooting career had built since the time he could hold a gun his father hand made for him, was the old man peering, taking in, lost in thought? Ask again, about the shooting record.

"Oh. That!"[7]

Despite the dimmed eyesight and hard hearing, Ad knew when he took that first old man's step off his porch that the thick woods and chirping birds populating Brackenridge were just a few more steps away. The place looked much as it did when a general donated the land to the city of San Antonio at the turn of the 19th century. Through there, then, Ad would start off on his daily three-mile walk. If he was going to have his Shooter's Code attached to the mailbox, he might as well live by it. Rule Five: No marksman ever made champion and remained on top very long without keeping himself in top physical condition. This ninety-year-old man remained engaged in life, and whenever the still-functioning fringes of his eyesight captured in their periphery the image primal to Ad—weapon aimed at target—the antenna in his mind would crackle and tune. So when his walk took him by the Witte Museum he'd manage to spot one of the young girls of the Toepperwein clan during her archery lessons. The walk came to a stop, and Ad offered up a few pointers aimed at hitting the bull's-eye.[8] His pep talk done, Ad meandered along the green curves of the San Antonio River that cut right through the heart of this peaceful park.

Out the other direction of the Toepperwein yard was a different story. By the autumn of 1959, the vice president's kitchen debate with Khrushchev still was on the mind of the world, and the encroachment of postwar urban sprawl rolled along. A new terminal at the city's airport still lacked a major highway from downtown to serve it, so Broadway Avenue handled some of the uptown traffic out past the Toepperwein backyard. On its trundle north from the city center, the roadway ran between Brackenridge Park and Fort Sam Houston. The military post kept its importance from the time in 1886 when Geronimo was imprisoned there in the Quadrangle, and officers from the US Fifth Army headquarters often would drive up Broadway when business or home life dictated time away from the base. Ad had friends at Fort Sam, and also from downtown where Ad and his brother owned a sporting-goods shop.

Increased commerce and new developments rolled along the avenue, and in the fall of 1959 Ad's friends read newspaper accounts to him that offered more proof that the world was changing. The door had just been opened to the Space Age, and it sounded like Remington Arms Company—not Winchester—was stepping through it with some new ideas applied to guns for even the most down-home, basic use. One of Remington's regional field reps, in fact, was conducting a high-profile test of the latest product. News had been coming from Reno, Nevada, where that man was taking aim at thousands of wooden blocks similar to those Ad had shot out of the air almost fifty-two years earlier. To Ad, to anyone, the proceedings sounded legitimate. This fellow—name of Frye, Tom Frye—was at it for coming up on two weeks.

The blessings of a long life still had rainy days, and this one for Ad Toepperwein had come with the astonishing possibility that someone else could put their name on a record that Ad had always wanted to possess. Plinky was gone. No son, either. And when no one in the family would take Ad's offer to learn how to shoot well enough to follow in his footsteps and give up their passion for his, the show went to other hands. And, now, someone else was staking a claim to World Record Holder for endurance shooting with a rifle. A lot of people wanted to know how Ad received the news.

Pretty well, apparently. Local outdoors writers made that drive up Broadway and talked to Ad about it. Any regrets? None, he told them. He sounded congratulatory, if certainly resigned, that someone cared enough to follow his trigger pulls.[9] The three-mile walks went on, and the extended family and circle of friends would gather at "the shack" for birthday parties they knew probably could be counted on one hand by now even if, as was the case, Ad still possessed a sharp mind.

There was plenty of critical thinking left to be done, and it was engaged when this news came from Reno. Photos were released from Frye's shoot. How much Ad could see of them wasn't clear, but his friends could narrate if Ad couldn't get the angle just right from what was left of his vision. The camera caught Frye sitting atop the wooden blocks with gun in hand. It was a pose that had been unique to Ad about fifty years ago, except there were more than 25,000 extra bullet-holed blocks for the prospective new champion shooter to sit upon. That wasn't all. The still photos caught images of the event in progress.

So, this shooter—with mind-boggling accuracy—is the man who has come along to challenge the old record? Well, no wonder, judging by what was going on in those photographs.

If the coming blindness made it impossible for Ad to fire his old guns accurately, or get a clear vision of photographs that were handed to him, it could not stop him from maintaining a dialogue with people he knew in shooting circles. He'd stay in touch, even if it meant a typewriter had to be produced and a letter pecked out, the swooping, cursive Ad Toepperwein signature at the bottom. Would Ad write a letter for Remington and Tom Frye to see? Yep. The open letter concerning this new shooter was delivered with Ad's salutatory tongue placed in his cheek.

"Most wonderful shooting, I would say," the letter read, "and I don't believe he could have hit more if he had set them on a fence post."[10]

That was just a preamble. The words that left the house alongside Brackenridge Park grew more direct. The last gasp of endurance shooting, it was turning out, was exhaling controversy.

Part Two

The Shooting Stars

The young performing Adolph Toepperwein, before he grew a trademark mustache, prior to 1900. Courtesy of Tony Sapienza.

CHAPTER FOUR

"World's Champion Rifle Shot"

Ad and His Idol

Local newspapers from 1880 through the turn of the century had a habit of running glowing stories of Wild West shows presented by Dr. W.F. Carver, and one reporter was headed out to the local exhibition grounds for another glad-handed interview with the show's notable proprietor. Doc Carver though, had a different message for the reporter this time around:

Get your newspaper to run a correction of the story that appeared earlier this week, Doc wildly threatened, or you will be shot![1]

This was typical of the way William Frank Carver busted through his adult life. He was six-feet, two-and-a-half inches with innards that pushed his body weight to about 250 pounds.[2] His attitude and personality stood as tall and weighed as much, and their bile could be aimed at either a partner in a business deal or a skilled competitor sporting afield. The exchange with the reporter became just another bar that Doc graphed upon so many of his personal relationships. One day spent in cohort, the next in confrontation.

There were days when those backstage rants would spill over in front of an audience once the curtains were lifted. There was word that once, when his part of the show went wrong, Doc became so upset that he took it out on his horse with a whip applied by the butt of his gun while at least some of the audience was in view.[3]

Yet the sensational stories of bluster weren't the things that attracted a ten-year-old boy to join up with his cousin to make a trip out of the rugged hills surrounding San Antonio when Doc Carver came to town. Legitimate ability with a gun, and innovative ways to showcase it, captured a lanky kid named Adolph Toepperwein. He saw Doc shoot bullet holes through silver dollars that had been thrown into the air, he saw him shoot accurately from horseback, and he could see a sort of rapid-fire exhibition upon feather-filled glass balls quickly thrown in succession by hand. It was a segment of the show that had enthralled newspapers in London when Doc toured there the previous year. "The Doctor now kept up an almost continuous stream of fire," the report read, "and the balls were shattered in all directions, (his assistant who was throwing the targets) existing for the time being in a perfect storm of broken glass and feathers."[4]

Beyond the visual effects and body-shaking gun blasts, there was enough about Doc that would draw attention to him even if he kept his manners in tow. Before Doc's tour made its way to San Antonio in 1880, he had made a breakthrough with a shooting exhibition two years earlier on the East Coast. His raw physical nature appeared to be on display as much as his gun shooting according to a *New York Times* reporter: "He is as fine a specimen of fully developed manhood as ever walked on Manhattan Island. . . . [H]e is exactly the man that ordinary people wouldn't put themselves out of the way to pick a quarrel with."[5] Doc had a solid build on top of his head as well, a flow and flash of auburn mane that draped to his shoulders. Though he could give his ever-present mustache a hint of a handlebar, mostly he kept it brushy and thick in the way of a walrus. The rich color contrasted sharply and effectively from the pastiness of his face, where he also sported smooth, pudgy cheeks and the beginnings of a double chin.

It was a perfect time for a striking, talented performer with a gun like Doc Carver. There was that feeling in the 1800s that gun ownership in America was a common part of life; the popular use of firearms was growing beyond the battlefields of the Civil War.[6] Spectator sports still were an unplowed field during the last quarter of the 1800s; baseball had no consistent season-end series to determine a champion between leagues, football looked more like rugby and had no professional leagues or major-college associations, and James Naismith was still putting peaches rather than balls into baskets. Faced with such paucity, people often craned their necks to see what could be done with the sort of guns they had for themselves at home.

So it was that Creedmoor became one of America's first venues for sports competition. Its popular draw boiled down to the rivalry between Old World and New. A shooting team from Ireland was regarded as the best in the world when it set records in competition against the English and Scots at famed Wimbledon in 1873. About a year later in September 1874, the Irish shooters had crossed the Atlantic and competed against an upstart team of American amateurs. That rural field at Creedmoor, past the East River from New York City, was pounced upon by a crowd of more than eight thousand people to watch Ireland vs. the US.[7]

The Americans' defeat of the Irish was pristine and sanctioned shooting skill, but theater managers overlooked those details when they placed shooting acts on their stages to capitalize on the craze generated from Creedmoor. The shooters inside those theaters, in fact, had a pitch that lacked nothing compared to some of the traveling salesmen out on the main street. If the benefit of snake oil was barked out there, the guy with the gun was not to be outdone with his slogan:

"World's Champion Rifle Shot."

By the time Doc made it to New York for his breakthrough in 1878, he needed two hands to count the times he saw "World's Champion Rifle Shot" printed on theater handbills. Some chroniclers thought there might have been as many as seven shooters making that illegitimate claim at one time.[8] Just about the only way to score the shooting came when the ashes fell off the cigarette that was shot at, or the button that fell from the vest—never mind that there was a wire hidden inside the cigarette that could flick away the ashes at the twist of the tongue,[9] or the faulty thread that couldn't keep hold of the button at the push of a diaphragm. No referees. No governing body. Not even a competitor to fire against. It was smoke and mirrors compared to what happened at Creedmoor.

Every time Doc heard a shooter's boast or saw from someone a claim to be "World's Champion Rifle Shot," Doc was looking at a world that was flat. But he thought he could bring some sense to it; he could make it round. So, from his home at Oakland, California, he wrote a manifesto, and it appeared December 13, 1877, in the pages of the *San Francisco Chronicle*. He claimed, "I can break 1,000 glass balls faster than any other man living, and that I will go to any part of the world to shoot."[10]

Doc was a dentist, but he left his chair for good and shot his way through matches and exhibitions across the continent. Finally, wearing Western garb that made him look as funny to East Coasters as Columbus did to the natives, Doc arrived at New York City on the sunny morning of Sunday, July 13, 1878, and figuratively rushed ashore to unfurl his flag and plant it into the land. He was ready to claim a new world.

Adolph Toepperwein was mesmerized, and all it took for the trance to get started was the site of a workbench studded with clamping vices and hand-crank drill presses. Hung up about the shop's walls or vectoring along the top of the bench would be flat mill files, screwdrivers, saws, and a hammer with its punches ready for use. These were the rude implements of fine craftsmanship, and this was the shop that Adolph's father kept in the town square of a Texas Hill Country community with the often-mispronounced town of Boerne (it's BURR-nee). Ferd Toepperwein's line of work was exacting. Gunsmithing was all done by hand, with no aid of power derived from electricity, diesel, or compressed air. The carving of a wood gun stock—the placing of metal plates, springs, and screws—was precision stuff, and Ferd Toepperwein's firstborn was impressed.

"[It's] my greatest delight . . . to hang around my father's gunmaking shop and watch him at work," Adolph said.[11]

It was indicative of the creativity that already was flowing from the family line. Ferd's father, Lucian Toepperwein, was a schoolteacher at Neuruppin, Prussia, and the author of at least six published books in Prussia featuring tales for children. But with revolution on the rise throughout Europe at the end of the first half of the nineteenth century, Lucien Toepperwein gathered up a family that included a ten-year-old son formally named Emil Albrecht Ferdinand Toepperwein and sailed for a fledgling North American republic known as Texas.[12]

Two decades later, Ferd gained experience with light artillery while serving in Dege's Battalion on the Confederate side during the Civil War.[13] His hands-on experience around guns earned him a nickname: "The Mechanic," and upon his return home he opened a gunshop on the city square between Blanco and San Antonio streets in Boerne. The home he built along with his wife, Johanna, of the large Bergmann family in Boerne might have been on the edge of the frontier, but it was a well-crossed edge. It was on the route between San Antonio, almost thirty-five miles to the south, and the federal forts garrisoned to supply Indian fighters with armament. And the High Plains of Texas still were teeming with bison. A hunter on his way to the slaughter could be outfitted and his sights expertly set with a short stop at Ferd Toepperwein's gunshop.[14]

Ferd had a handy testing ground for his work, and a ready place to show his wares. He was listed along with his younger brother Paul as one of nine charter members at the founding of the local Schuetzen Verein. The bylaws for this shooting club were written in German,[15] and their competitive gatherings were creative. Schuetzen matches often featured wooden targets that were carved into eagles, and the competition required that shooters clip off wings and other parts of the eagle before piercing the small explosive-filled cavity of what was left of the target.[16]

Every Sunday at one in the afternoon—as long as it wasn't hunting season—Ferd could walk past the balloons and banners that flew overhead and take his practice at the firing line. By the time he got up there a keg usually was rolled up alongside the shooters so they wouldn't have to wander off to quaff down a stein if their nerves needed calming—or not. Yet competitions were so finely contested one year that a finalist shot out the center brad that held the target to its post. When the black-disk bull's-eye fell to the pit below, the crowd watching roared its approval. The target was reaffixed, yet it fell again when the next competitor fired his shot through the new brad. Another resounding roar went up.[17]

The family Ferd and Johanna planned had begun to sprout. Adolph Toepperwein was born on October 17, 1869. A year later his sister Clara was born, and Ferdinand Jr. (Fred) came along five years after that. The women and kids picked wildflowers from the surrounding fields, which were made into garlands to be draped around the winners at the shooting competitions. But flower picking wasn't the keen interest of young Adolph.[18]

Ferd's shop kept Adolph supplied with the proper armament. He started with a hand-made crossbow. Though Ferd did give his son a shotgun, he toned down the blast a bit by giving him a 14-gauge muzzleloader. He also kept it light by getting him a .22 caliber Flobert rifle.[19]

Ferd had plenty of work and a fashionable enough income. Ferd was a landowner, including prime property that fronted South Main in Boerne. After Adolph was born, Ferd sold it to a French architect for $1,200 in silver coins.[20]

Ferd didn't just rely on the basic gunsmithing skills. He tinkered. He figured. He created, and the inventions of E.A.F. Toepperwein became stamped. He signed patent applications, and one of the three that were granted made its way to a desk in New Haven, Connecticut. John Marlin set up a shop there after cutting his teeth on pistol making in Samuel Colt's plant over at Hartford. Into late 1879, a full six years after Winchester debuted its highly successful '73 model, Marlin patented a repeating rifle design. It flopped, and he never put the prototype into production. Marlin stuck with it, even if he had to push back from his own design desk and fish the patent office. By the early 1880s, he showed that he could streamline various ideas into an intriguing product. He acquired the rights from the patents of three inventors to make what he would years later call the Model 1881, the first repeating rifle he had taken to market.[21]

One of those patent applications was signed by E.A.F. Toepperwein, and he claimed to have "invented a new and improved Repeating Fire-Arm" by using an "apparatus [that] is very simple, cheap and reliable."[22] Marlin followed the design to implement a cranking lever that would transfer cartridges from a magazine to a chamber and eject the spent shell, and he reasoned away the sticker shock from the high price of $32.[23]

"Being a higher price than any other repeating rifle," Marlin said, "this, with the fact that the factory cannot keep up with the orders, is the best testimonial." He pointed to an advertisement claiming "Dr. Carver and Buffalo Bill use Marlin rifles in all their exhibitions, finding them quicker and more accurate than any other."[24]

Doc Carver met William Cody—"Buffalo Bill"—not long after a letter dated May 10, 1868, passed from Gen. William T. Sherman to fellow general Philip Sheridan. Sherman had encouraged Sheridan "to invite all the sportsmen of England and America there [to the West] this fall for a Grand Buffalo hunt, and make one grand sweep of them all."[25] Doc was so excited about the prospects that he began cutting all ties to his proper life. He'd been handed down the practice of dentistry by his father, but he parsed words when confronted with the direct question of whether it ever had been his profession:

"You are a dentist, are you not?"

"No," he replied. "I went into an office in California and in fact became one of the profession, but never practiced it at all."[26]

Yet people remembered reading about a "Dr. William F. Carver, Dentist" from advertisements in newspapers circulating through the North Platte, Nebraska, area, where they placed him doing business at Ray's Drugstore.[27] Further, the trail of pulled teeth extended west to a two-week stint at Fort Sidney, then on to Cheyenne through some point in 1875.[28]

Doc took the plunge to the outdoors and was noticed by an adventurous scout with an eye for the acting stage—William F. Cody. That their initials were the same appears to be coincidence, but Doc's aspirations to follow the way of Buffalo Bill Cody were not. Cody reported that Doc had "recently acquired considerable notoriety as a rifle-shot" as both of them headed out along the Republican River in a hunting party with the wealthy Thomas P. Medley of London.[29]

Close to a decade after they first met, Cody and Doc bumped into one another on the East Coast where Cody had been performing Western stories on the stage and Doc had returned from shooting exhibitions in Europe. They began talking about parlaying their experiences on the buffalo ranges into a traveling show. Cody felt compelled to contact the proven entertainment agent Nate Salsbury.

"I do not want anything to do with Doctor Carver," Salsbury told Cody. "Of course, I turned them down."[30]

The Wild West, Hon. W.F. Cody and Dr. W.F. Carver's Rocky Mountain and Prairie Exhibition, opened at Omaha Fair Grounds on May 17, 1883. It wasn't long before nerves frayed. Doc's temper flared, and it showed as he and Cody displayed their marksmanship by firing at glass balls thrown into the air. Doc chided Cody for using a rifle loaded with shot that would spray fine pellets about two or three inches across the target.

"A four-year-old boy can break glass balls in the air using shot," Doc said.[31] Doc told everyone that, for his part, he used bullets, which demanded more precision upon the target. And so it came that when it was Doc's turn to shoot the glass balls during a show at Coney Island, he missed one and people saw him take out his frustration. They said he slammed the gun over the head of a horse. Then they said they saw him punch one of the show's hired hands.[32]

Salsbury had been watching. He had seen what happened at Coney Island and, in his mind, termed the whole proceedings a "ghastly failure."

"Cody came to see me," Salsbury said, "and said he was through with Carver and that he would not go through another summer for a hundred thousand dollars."[33]

Salsbury took over the show with Buffalo Bill and took it to heights never seen with Doc (by 1885 more than one million people attended Buffalo Bill's Wild West).[34] Doc started his own Wild West show, and he continued calling out anyone claiming to be a World's Champion Rifle Shot. As he did with the one he thought was aggrandized as Buffalo Bill, Doc singled out one he thought was a poser. By going back to New York, he would capture the attention of everyone who thought Captain Adam Bogardus was indomitable. Bogardus had wowed the New York press on January 4, 1878, at Gilmore's Garden, by endeavoring to shoot five thousand glass balls thrown from a catapulting trap he manufactured, and now stood to promote. Though Captain Bogardus would give himself five hundred minutes, or eight and a half hours, to do so, he came in with about twenty minutes to spare. His scorers estimated that he needed 5,163 shots to bust the five thousand balls.[35]

"The accomplishment of the great feat of skill and endurance was, of course, loudly cheered," a reporter for the *New York Times* noted.

Captain Bogardus had used the shooting sports, as one of his daughters remembered, to go from a "poor, struggling carpenter" to "one of the most prosperous men of town, a leading citizen."[36] Doc sniffled at the substance of Captain Bogardus's shooting. Captain Bogardus used a shotgun. And Doc played with the style, too, hearing that the dour-faced man with the receding hairline drew applause for having to shoot, exhausted by the end of it, from a chair.

Doc's retort came when he told everyone to show up at Deerfoot Park in Brooklyn on the morning of Sunday, July 13, and starting at 11 o'clock he'd fire his rifle—not a shotgun—and break 5,500 glass balls in five hundred minutes. That's five hundred more glass balls than Captain Bogardus did, yet Doc said he'd do it in the same amount of time. With six Winchester rifles to rotate, and at least three assistants to load and cool the guns and throw the targets into the air, Doc got busy.

He fired so quickly that three of the rifles soon overheated, even though they had been dipped into water.[37] The trace of water that was left in the barrels of the guns that were still working served as an agent to spew the powder from the firing of the ammo into the air around Doc's face. The glass balls, filled with feathers to better confirm Doc had hit the target, sprayed glass fragments through the air, unavoidably into his own eyes, and the white down feathers even dusted the spectators. And, with the advent of smokeless powder still years off, how else could have Doc responded to the combination of all this?

"For God's sake, boys, how much more have I got to do?"[38]

With eighteen minutes to go, he had one hundred left. He shot those one hundred in eight minutes, and they served as broadsides to Bogardus. Doc needed 6,208 shots to hit 5,500, and he did it with ten minutes to spare. He let down in the days after the shoot by resting with a handkerchief, filled with ice when possible, to bring down the swelling around his eyes. He didn't perform for more than a month.[39]

But Doc wasn't done badgering Bogardus. He wanted a head-to-head match, and he felt he had the support of the public to keep pursuing it. Frank Butler, the Irish-born sharpshooter who was touring through Ohio in April 1881 just days before his fateful meeting with Phoebe Anne Moses (Annie Oakley), could sense the enthusiasm for good shooting when he walked through the lobby of a Cincinnati hotel.

"I was tackled by one who wanted to know what I could do," Butler said. "I told him I could beat anything then living, save for Carver or Bogardus."[40]

Finally, Carver and Bogardus met in February 1883 for $500 a side. They proceeded in a match where each would shoot at one hundred live pigeons. Doc won, 83–82. But most of the matches were blowouts. Doc finished it off by winning nineteen, losing three, and drawing in three.[41]

The young boy in Texas handling the rifles and shotguns his gunsmith father crafted for him was scooped up by the virility of Doc's shooting. And all Adolph Toepperwein had to do to follow after his hero was to walk outside and scoop up the hundreds of rocks lying around in the Hill Country and throw them into the air to shoot.[42]

His father had reason to wonder if his son was following the right example. The Civil War veteran, the craftsman, had dark, thick hair. His eyes pierced forward from either side of a straight nose and under a strongly shaped forehead. His son was a spittin' image, take away the dad's thick beard.

"Son," the father would say to the Doc Carver–inspired boy, "if a job's worth doing, it's always worth doing better. You can do better." Adolph knew there was something different about his father; he had been sick lately. So this conversation would last in his memory for a lifetime. "I will do better," he replied.[43]

By 1880 the Toepperweins had left their country life in Boerne for an address listed at a busy location of 41 Alamo Street in downtown San Antonio.[44] Ferd Toepperwein had fallen into a malady that nastily manifested itself as digestive disorders. It would not go away, and before his eldest son Adolph became a teen-ager, Ferd Toepperwein was dead at the age of forty-one due to "exhaustion from chronic disease of bowels."[45]

Adolph Toepperwein had learned about guns from a genuine practitioner, his own father the gunsmith and inventor. So if he was going to keep learning about guns, a phony "World Champion Rifle Shot" wouldn't capture his imagination.

Nor would Buffalo Bill. William F. Cody's little secret of using shot cartridges—sprayed pellets—rather than bullets to break his targets flamboyantly while riding horseback, would bring a sneer from Adolph: "[A]ny marksman, with ordinary skill, could perform the same stunt with a week's practice. I know of three women who did this stunt and did it very successful [*sic*], so there was nothing wonderful or outstanding about this kind of work. . . . As a showman Cody held four aces, as a shooter just a pair of deuces."[46]

Adolph's head followed his father, but his soul was revived with that charismatic figure preaching gun stunts, performing seeming miracles when he laid his powerful hands upon that rifle. Doc Carver was on tour again, making a swing through the South. Adolph would have to get away from work—with his father gone he had to work in a crockery shop in downtown San Antonio—to go to the show. He brought along Rudy, and he turned to his cousin. "I will be," Ad said, "a better shooter than Doc Carver one day."[47]

CHAPTER FIVE

Shaking the Hand of a Legend

Tom Comes of Age

By the time Sam Frye moved into his house on Liberty Street in Findlay after 1910, the western Ohio town was gridded into tight, straight-line rows of mostly two-story homes. It was fifty miles south of Toledo. Mr. Frye was a draftsman at a planing mill, and the oil and gas production of Findlay was falling off from its peak when drillers tapped onto the Trenton limestone formation looking for natural gas in 1884. They found gushers of black gold near Findlay and Lima. A dozen years later, John D. Rockefeller's men had almost 6,500 wells dotting the northwestern Ohio countryside, which made the state the nation's yearly leading producer of oil.[1] This type of oil stunk to high heaven when it burned in kerosene lamps, so Rockefeller hired the first petroleum engineers to scrub the foul smell off it.[2] This became a breakthrough moment.

But in the final few days of 1915, Mr. Frye didn't get a piece of the action out on the oil fields. Still, a breakthrough moment came for him and his wife, Mabel, with the birth of a son they named Thomas Richard Frye on December 28, 1915.[3] With the first child in their family, the Fryes were free to ponder what might come of little Tom.

Mr. Frye had some ability in his hands. So did Mabel. That was proven out by the fact that at the planing mill he could turn sketches into the technical drawings better suited for the design of streamlined production. And she became respected as a milliner, a designer of beautiful women's hats.[4] Away

13th Ohio State Highway Patrol Training School
Graduation ~ 21 August 1941~ Ohio State University Tower Club

Left to right: Robert A. Schmittauer, Thomas R. Frye, Henry W. Barber, Clarence E. Brookmyer, Paul H. Stansbery, David M. Hartsock, Olin J. Simmons, Bernard L. Hopkins, Mark S. Trees, Paul R. Arnold, John C. Botte, Ohio Governor John W. Bricker, Ohio Department of Highways Director Hal G. Sours, OSHP Colonel Lynn E. Black, Judge Reynolds, John M. Relac, William H. Vinning, William F. Harrell, James C. Mansbarger, Charles L. Curran, Paul S. Kinsey, Glen C. Patterson, Howard A. Jackson, Charles E. Wallace, Harold C. Tidd and Minor C. Mobley

Tom Frye, standing second from the left, in his graduation picture from the Ohio State Highway Patrol Training School. Ohio State Highway Patrol photo.

from work, he made it to the shooting ranges and became one of the better target hitters at his gun club.

And with his son, there might be the same sort of talent contained in those hands. But talent, particularly when it's with the accurate aiming and firing of a gun, doesn't always just burst through the surface of the shooter at its own whim. There might be promising signs, but like the oil or natural gas of the fields near Findlay, it has to be tapped. The right tool has to be placed in the right hold. And the bit has to be situated at the right angle. Even then, most leads turn out to be just ordinary. But there are some that perform beyond expectations.

Sam Frye, the draftsman, designed a way to find the talent hidden inside his son. Besides Mr. Frye's own leanings toward sporting gun shooting, there were other factors that could push any boy growing up in Ohio down the same path. The Buckeye State, particularly its western half, had become sports-shooting country.

Not too long before Tom was born, businessman Frank Chamberlin moved the production of his trap-sprung targets from the big town of Cleveland to Findlay because he believed the clay that existed in the ground there was of top quality to make the sporting disks. It didn't hurt that his company was able to negotiate with the local utility to pay $100 a year for all the natural gas it needed. Chamberlin's company hired fifty people who were able to ship out 24 million targets (480,000 made per employee, or 9,000 per week by each worker) the first year.[5]

If that wasn't noticed, more seismic events in shooting circles took hold. One of the very first superstars of shooting, Annie Oakley, grew up in Darke County north of Cincinnati. By 1885 she broke through to the top of the lineup of acts in Buffalo Bill's Wild West.

By 1904 the state began to feel the influence of its adjutant general, the portly Ammon B. Critchfield, and teams from Ohio won matches associated with the National Rifle Association. Critchfield was in office when the state legislature appropriated $25,000 to develop a rifle range for the National Guard within sight of Lake Erie and between Toledo and Cleveland. By 1907 the NRA competitions moved to the location dedicated as Camp Perry.[6]

This was less than sixty miles from the Frye family home, and in time Findlay would be bookended by major competitions that drew people from across the country. The American Trapshooting Association moved its Grand American to a location just north of Dayton at Vandalia in 1923, and it soon became the world's largest shooting event with more than one thousand competitors in 1927.

It was a one-hundred-mile or so trip from the Frye house, and Sam Frye made it enough that family members bragged how he "won honors" at Vandalia.[7] When he thought Tom was ready, he gave the young boy an air rifle to use for his first experience in shooting.[8] It was a father-to-son hand-me-down that already pitched an echo from earlier decades in America, the sort of passing that led hopefuls to shooting stardom. Tom was like most boys in enjoying sports such as baseball.[9] But Tom didn't feel like he was missing out on anything when his friends kept playing catch, or shot pool, while he shot clays.[10]

Tom was a rangy, athletic-looking sort with long arms that made easy work of cradling a gun. At Findlay High School, Tom showed at least a passing fancy for hunting and gunwork. He was president of the Outdoor Club his senior year in 1935.[11] With his smooth boyish face beginning to firm into adulthood, and topped by a raised clump of tight-waved hair that resembled a washboard that was leaned back against a wall, Tom joined his father at shooting competitions at one of Findlay's gun clubs. Tom outperformed the old man. Vandalia wasn't too far out of the way for the Fryes. So they headed down there in 1932, after Tom's sixteenth birthday.[12] They shot, but what they did at Vandalia when the guns were not in their hands came with more importance.

Tom Frye needed a break, a chance to prove himself as he moved beyond the influence of his father. He wasn't a senior at Findlay High School until he was twenty, graduating with his younger brother James. He made no mark in the shooting world as the Great Depression puddled around the country over the next five years. He enrolled right there in town at Findlay College, and along with taking up study in coaching and biology,[13] Tom joined the school's football team that was equally struggling to make a mark. Findlay College had six winning seasons in the forty-three years prior to Tom lacing them up. When Tom played as a freshman in 1936, the team finished with a 0–7 record and was outscored 224–19 for the season. But they improved over the next two seasons when Tom played and won three games each year.[14]

Tom could notice that cadet training for Ohio State Highway Patrol had been moved to Findlay when a flood of the Ohio River caused widespread destruction through Cincinnati and other portions of the state in 1937 (some 100,000 were reported as homeless, 385 killed, and massive property damage estimated beyond $500 million).[15] It was a ten-week session, and nine of the thirty men who entered did not complete training. It testified to the demands of the patrol's expectations. This was, after all, a job not without danger. Far from it. By the end of the 1930s, five patrolmen had lost their lives in vehicular crashes, and there was the murder of Patrolman George Conn, who had been shot by fugitives in 1937. But Tom could swallow the risks. The life of a patrolman fit Tom. It would keep him outdoors, and he could train often with a gun.

So Tom, when he reached the patrol's minimum admission age of twenty-four, signed up and started training in late June 1941 at The Ohio State University in Columbus. The training included "boxing week," which apparently became one of the patrol's ways to weed out cadets. This allegedly included tactics applied against the first African American to sign up for the Ohio patrol when, according to patrolmen who were there, Sanford Roan "was asked to demonstrate much more often than average," for "several rounds in a row without a break"—a departure from normal procedure where boxing was concerned. The fights were conducted in the summertime outdoors on a lawn, and combatants went at it without mouthpieces to protect their teeth, and had no other such headgear either. Broken noses, worse, were the norm, as was a staredown from a lieutenant to any cadet who showed signs of passivity. When Tom saw the end of the two-month training, the original class of forty-six cadets was hammered down to twenty-two. That's a forty-eight percent pass rate.[16]

Thomas R. Frye made it—but not for long. He saw the newsreels roll following December 7, 1941. In a four-month period before the summer of 1942, forty-two patrolmen, out of a force of almost three hundred, went into the military.[17] That included Tom, who in February matriculated to Lockbourne AAB in Columbus and enlisted in the Army Air Corps.[18]

He quickly showed his ambition by applying for officer training school. While waiting for that to come through, homesickness set in. After being assigned to Camp Williams in Wisconsin, the man identified at that time as Thomas R. Frye, PFC, had written back to colleagues at the Ohio patrol and told them he missed them. "He said he likes it," patrol's newsletter read, "but he sure would like to get back on patrol."[19]

He finally was granted admission to officer training school, but in less than three months Tom showed the Army his skills extended beyond writing citations. They saw how he handled a gun, so they shipped him to a swamp that had just been drained outside Fort Myers, Florida, named Buckingham Field. Tom soon would swat mosquitoes, and teach airmen how to fire high-powered guns.[20]

At least one person at Buckingham was glad to see Tom had been averted from further law enforcement. Hardly anyone could touch Joe Hiestand when he started hitting the shooting ranges out of Hillsboro, Ohio, just east of Cincinnati after 1930. But Ohio state patrolman Frye did; years back he wrote Hiestand a citation for speeding when their paths haphazardly crossed. Hiestand certainly was speeding through the Grand American Handicap at Vandalia by winning All-American honors four of five years starting in 1934. Hiestand could pull rank on Frye in shotgun circles, and he could do it at Buckingham Field as well. Frye came there as a lieutenant; Hiestand was captain.[21]

But reporting to Captain Hiestand with a shotgun across your arms was good duty. "Pilot cadets were required to shoot skeet as a part of their basic training," said Bob Allen, who was a pigeon-shooting partner with Hiestand on trips to world-famous competitions at Monte Carlo. When Allen was stationed as a gunnery instructor in Arizona, he was invited to come out to see what Buckingham had developed to train its cadets.[22]

Hiestand gave Allen a tour of the gunnery school at Buckingham, where one of the exercises was called "moving base." A gunnery student would sit in a custom-built seat in the back of a truck, which would be driven around an oval track and past trap stations that would throw clays at different trajectories. Remembering all the action from gamblers surrounding their shoots at Monte Carlo, Hiestand bet Allen he could take his gun from his shoulder, prop it on his hip, and shoot the course while being spun around on the back of that truck. He hit twenty-five straight.[23]

While waiting for that truckload of cadet shooters every morning, the instructors could practice their own shooting. Tom could fire shot after shot until it was time to teach. He wasn't noted for "moving base" like Captain Hiestand was, but other things influenced him to make his first notch as a competitive shooter. The trapshooting associations couldn't register it, but everyone took note when Tom hit 1,134 consecutive skeet targets at Buckingham, an incredible mark when two hundred straight could be considered to be expertly accurate.[24] Another gunnery school instructor, tall and personable D. Lee Braun, was allowed to compete for the first time in the 1943 Grand American to shoot on an Army five-man team that won the Team Race. He clearly was a rising star, and he was headed for a career with Remington Arms Company when World War II would finish. Maybe the legendary firearms maker, based in Ilion, New York, since being founded by Eliphalet Remington in 1816, would dip further into the Army crackshots for expert representatives.[25]

Tom wondered if there might be room for him. "I can remember as a kid when gun and ammo makers fielded whole squads of exhibition guys, fellows who brought gasps at sporting clubs, corporate gatherings, and meets," Tom said. "They did the impossible with firearms and did it sometimes seven days and nights a week."[26]

Tom remembered one in particular. This "exhibition guy" was legendary in shooting circles. Indeed, his tours for Winchester Repeating Arms Company made Ad Toepperwein a household name in many parts of America. And when Tom was being introduced to the shooting sports while he was a teenager with his father's trips from Findlay to Vandalia for the Grand American Handicap in the '30s, Sam Frye made sure his son approached Mr. Toepperwein. The Fryes could see something more than an "exhibition guy." They knew he was a man who challenged the shooting records of old by firing tens of thousands of shots at targets in unthinkable endurance events. The teenage Tom could see there was a professional air about this man, a personable sort who "would always take time to shake a hand." And young Tom did so; he shook hands with Ad Toepperwein, and thought of Toepperwein's mammoth body of work, "figuring nobody would ever touch it."[27]

CHAPTER SIX

Because T.R. Said No

Ad Takes Aim at the Big Time

Teddy Roosevelt apparently didn't consider himself to be a good shot, "But I know how to shoot often."[1] And with such comments the minds at gun manufacturers went spinning. What a competitive advantage it could be for a firearms company to be associated with a rising, charismatic public figure rough cut from the frontier. The wheel landed at Winchester Repeating Arms Company because Roosevelt fired off positive comments almost as rapidly as he spent shells from his Model 1876.

After two years of hunting on the prairie, Roosevelt wrote *Hunting Trips of a Ranchman* in 1885, stating, ". . . the Winchester is the best gun for any game to be found in the United States, for it is as deadly, accurate, and handy as any, stands very rough usage, and is unapproachable for the rapidity of its fire and the facility with which it is loaded."[2] Later, when T.R. returned from his post-presidency African safari in 1910, he wrote in *Collier's* more praise of the Winchester gun. He noted that the Model 1895 with the .405 chamber "is, at least for me personally, the medicine gun for lions."

Winchester ad men had to wring their hands to keep from throwing those words into the font of the company's print advertising. But, famously and progressively wary of big business, Roosevelt expressly forbade the company from using any of the comments he made in his correspondence to the company in their advertising from the 1880s onward.[3]

At thirty-one, Adolph Toepperwein performed for the Orrin Bros. Circus that toured mostly through Mexico in 1900, the year before he accepted a position with Winchester Repeating Arms Company. Collection of Kenneth Toepperwein.

William Clark, the advertising manager at Winchester, knew the company had been embargoed from using the president's name in all advertising. But Henry Brewer, who was a superintendent of the cartridge operations at Winchester, could see Clark was in fits over the embargo.

"This was a great disappointment to Clark who felt this was one of our great opportunities for advertisement and it almost broke his heart not to be able to use the president's name in connection with it," Brewer said.[4]

Clark weaseled his way around it. He knew Winchester could respond in the affirmative if, by some chance, the media asked if the company had helped in outfitting the president's hunting trips. Roosevelt was soon due back from an African expedition when Clark peppered a display ad with big bold letters: COMING EVENTS CAST THEIR SHADOWS along with a drawing of a Winchester rifle imposed upon the outline of the African continent. This was too close for comfort for Winchester president T.G. Bennett. He called Clark into his office. Bennett was a stout fellow, a former soldier and youth wrestler around whom no one made small talk or jokes. When anyone blew it, Bennett turned a pair of piercing, steel-gray eyes onto the delinquent he had called onto the carpet.

"The advertisement did not mention Roosevelt's name in any way, which had been his instructions," Clark hedged.

"[You] might have followed the letter of the instructions," Bennett told Clark, "[but you] certainly had not followed the spirit of them."

So Bennett quickly wrote an apology to the president. It got to Brewer that Bennett threw Clark under the carriage. Bennett's letter informed Roosevelt that he had personally given instructions that the president's name could not be used in advertising, and while following the letter of the instructions "the pressure had been greater than our advertising manager could stand" and he violated the spirit of the agreement.[5]

Even with Bennett's caution, the minds in the main offices of Winchester's plant at New Haven, Connecticut, could not stand still. There had to be a way to capitalize on someone's good shooting, get Winchester products in his hands, and let him have at it. Perhaps there was an opportunity to get William Cody or Annie Oakley. They were at the forefront of popular shooters, and Buffalo Bill's Wild West still was generating big crowds. But how dependable would Cody be; would he consume more ammunition or booze?

There was Doc Carver. But as perilous as it would be to hire a heavy drinker, it would be just as big a problem to hire someone with a heavy temperament. Doc never would be confused with a team player. Doc, in fact, had bad-mouthed Winchester products in the press: "I want to squelch some stories," Doc would huff, "which are being circulated to the effect that the Winchester company paid me for my endurance shooting. Nothing is farther from the truth. I did try to get some guns from them, but they said that their guns could never stand the strain, and actually preferred that I use some other make."[6] Bridge burned.

So, what shooter was out there? Who, among the sober, even-tempered set, still possessed enough magnetism—the performing dexterity—that could legitimately move the brand forward? One of Winchester's regional representatives chimed in. Jim Hildreth worked the southern region for the company. Some years before 1900, he bumped into a lanky fellow with a pretty good shooting act down in Texas. This young performer by the funny-looking name of Adolph Toepperwein was beloved by his German kindred who were the hardy backbone of San Antonio. When spectators at the city's July 4 parade in 1898 had a choice of celebrations to attend afterward, most of the German crowd chose to hop on the electric streetcars that ran to a park where fireworks would be shot. But before dark, the crowd of 2,500 listened to a concert by the Carl Beck's Band and settled in for an exhibition by the twenty-eight-year-old Adolph.[7] Hildreth decided he had to find him.[8]

Few major cities in the civilization expanding through North America were witness to savagery on Main Street as was San Antonio. Even when some of the early settlers slapped up an adobe façade on a recognizable sloping bold centerpiece and opened it as a church, eventually it was taken over as a fort. It became the bookmark for San Antonio's defining moment—the Alamo. It was an early edition of urban combat, a stream of Mexican soldiers clamoring wooden ladders onto the church's walls and scaling over with rifle firing and bayonets stabbing a bunch of insurgent Texans. That was 1836.

Four years later, the arrival of a Comanche peace council was to meet with the new Republic of Texas government. It was hardly peaceful. The town folk were enraged when they saw the Indians parade one white hostage taken from a previous battle. It was a teen-age girl who was missing her nose and had bruises all over her body. Inside the dirt-floored, limestone-walled courthouse, negotiations were short and misunderstandings were outnumbered only by the shots that soon rang out. The doors of the courtroom busted open, and the surviving Indians, women and children included, tried an escape. More than forty people died. This was the Council House fight, right there in the main plaza of San Antonio.[9]

The German immigration would soon build. These Europeans brought industry, the urban order of something as seemingly small as neat cottages, shuttered windows and gardens, social clubs and the incumbent parades and theater or things otherwise cultured, and ample drink known as beer.[10] By 1880, San Antonio was the largest city in Texas, and the Germans the largest ethnic group.

But they couldn't curtail all the violence; miscreants roamed the countryside as plentiful as varmints, and they entered the burgs hungry for something, even if it wasn't theirs. In San Antonio the vice had a way of ending up back at Main Plaza, often around a place known as Jack Harris's Vaudeville Theater. Though some onlookers were impressed with the interior dressings of an oak bar with dark stain and a mirrored-back bar fully stocked with cork-top whiskey,[11] the exterior could not have been gaudier. That the cigars were sold by Sim Hart in the saloon's tobacco room was advertised with a paint job right above the side door to the establishment. It was a graphic artist's laughable depiction of a man's smiling face—chubby, sloppy, triple-chinned look with mottled hair and eyes that were asymmetrically set.

That was where Ben Thompson came to drink. Thompson was known to have shot and killed a handful of men and gotten off the charges, yet at this present time he was duly elected marshal of Austin. During his reign the crime rate was said to have gone down around the capitol.[12] But trips to San Antonio were a different story. He had quarreled with one of Harris's dealers over the conduct of a card game at the Vaudeville and left while pointing a gun at the dealer—and scooping up all the cash that was lying on the table.[13] Upon Thompson's return in July 1882, Harris was tipped off and waited for Thompson with a shotgun. But Thompson, from outside the saloon, fired inside and struck Harris. He was carried home and died. Thompson was placed under arrest, but acquitted at trial.

About two years later, on-again-off-again friend and overall bad guy King Fisher convinced Thompson to stop off in San Antonio, and they stumbled down to the old Vaudeville. Another fight broke out inside when the establishment's principals took offense to Thompson's presence. Shots fired amid the wrestling, and when the bodies were pulled away, two stayed down. Thompson was reported to have nine bullet holes in him. As many as thirteen were counted in Fisher.[14]

Over the next days there would be a kid in his early teens—one recently forced into finding a job—walking along the same street that fronted the place of Ben Thompson's and King Fisher's deaths. He needed the job because his father had died and left two other younger children and a widow. Adolph Toepperwein would hear about the gunfight, and if the brawl had erupted a few hours earlier during work hours, Adolph quite likely would have heard the shots. The job he took to support his family was located at the crockery shop along Commerce Street. So here was Adolph, living in a city such as this, with no father; instead he was idolizing a man such as Doc Carver. What would come of that?

It had been a little more than thirty years since Adolph Toepperwein's grandfather brought his family to Texas. There was no slowdown of German shipping companies keeping up with the traveling demand of immigrants to North America, and the Norddeutscher Lloyd Company out of the port of

Bremen was one of the top liners crossing the North Atlantic. A man by the name of Jacob Servaty was ready to sign up and give a new life a try abroad. At the age of forty, he arrived on the East Coast of the United States in 1882. An engineer, he eventually made it up to New Haven, Connecticut, found work, and sent for his family. On May 25, 1883, the NDL ship *Oder* finished up the sail to the New York wharfs. That included a group of five from the Servaty family, and among the group was Matthew Servaty, age four, and a sister named Elise. She was red-headed and about two years younger than her brother.[15]

Settled in New Haven, the Servaty family of Jacob and wife Catharina grew over the next decade. The immigrant daughter, now called Elizabeth, had seven brothers and a sister. When the census taker of 1900 walked up to the house on Davenport Avenue, he was told Elizabeth was a nineteen-year-old and was working just a few streets down at the huge plant built by Winchester Repeating Arms Company.[16]

That the firm was operated by an entrepreneur who was not a firearms designer and inventor—Oliver Winchester started making money through designing men's shirts—gave it nimbleness in business most gun shops lacked. Mr. Winchester knew how to take a product to market and sell it. A holder of a patent himself (he authored a process of shirt fitting), Winchester was comfortable with innovation. He procured the work of designers like B.B. Hotchkiss to land a US military contract, and this line of thinking carried over into the company after Winchester's retirement when T.G. Bennett, as president, struck an association with John Browning for notable work on shotguns.

There was no doubt the Winchester people knew how to produce a quality firearm and were cranking them out from the production line. But with major guns manufacturers dotting the East Coast, particularly through New York and Connecticut, the people at New Haven did not feel comfortable that the guns would just fly off the racks. They wanted to push it, so they'd need the sales force to do it. They would need that, and a star.

He was without his father. And he only saw his big, masculine idol Doc Carver infrequently on tour stops in San Antonio. Further, Adolph Toepperwein couldn't get his best friend interested in trick shooting. Rudy, his cousin, thought it was a waste of ammunition. The few bullets anyone could afford would be better off fired through the neck of a deer. Louie Heuermann and Pete Hehn became friends, and they indulged Adolph's shooting.[17] They reported that "Tep" was giving marvelous performances with his rifle, and by the time he was sixteen Adolph claimed he could do everything Doc was doing.[18]

Pete also was gaining note around San Antonio as an amateur boxer. But the lanky "Tep" didn't spar. He hung around Pete and was listed as a timekeeper during the bouts.[19] It was October 1896, and the Bexar Athletic Club mixed in sparring with bag punching, wrestling, and "exhibitions of strength" onto its entertainment agenda. But there also were musical presentations, recitations, and charcoal sketches. And that's where "Ad. Toepperwein" was listed as a participant.[20]

He was a natural artist.[21] He was so skilled that his drawings got him out of the crockery shop. He landed a job as a cartoonist for the *Express* newspaper in downtown San Antonio. Like his father, he was creating things with his hands. This job required accuracy, flair, and creativity. He would do things with his pencil that Doc Carver did with his gun.

And while Adolph may not have been bothered by the spirit of his cousin Rudy's chiding about wasting ammunition, there was truth behind it. Fancy shooting came attached with a fancy bill. Bullets weren't cheap. And so the job as a newspaper cartoonist brought in some money. He'd practice his shooting constantly away from work. Using his artistic mind he'd create shots he hadn't seen anyone else doing, certainly not Doc, Adolph thought. So, he kept his day job but broke out on his own and started a shooting act around town.[22]

By December 17, 1896, the city's newspapers were reporting that Adolph Toepperwein was offering shooting exhibitions. When Adolph gave a fancy shooting exhibition on June 6, 1897, at Aue's Park, his act was placed between a morning dance and orations and an afternoon of sporting events (races) and then a dance.[23] Adolph quickly worked on ways to help in the promotion. Again, he followed what Doc did. Endurance shooting. By the time his twenty-sixth birthday rolled around, people were claiming Adolph had surpassed a mark set by Annie Oakley around 1885 when she shattered 943 out of 1,000 glass balls tossed into the air. It was ten years following Oakley's shooting that Adolph hit 955 out of 1,000 clay pigeons in 1895.[24] And two years later, not long after the Aue's Park exhibition, Adolph broke his own world record by hitting 979 out of 1,000 clay pigeons flying through the air at the city's centrally located San Pedro Springs Park, which brought out a crowd of "several hundred people" according to newspapers. He did it with "remarkable ease and little fatigue." The targets were thrown by hand twenty to thirty feet high at a distance of twenty-five feet from the shooter. There next to Adolph during the entire shoot was his pal Louie Heuermann, keeping score. He tallied up a perfect 100 during the fifth hundred set and had his best run of 141 consecutive hits during the seventh and eighth hundred sets.

The word that this young man from San Antonio was shooting with such flair put him on the radar of a guns-manufacturing power no less than Winchester. The company sent him a new .22 caliber with a highly polished English walnut stock as a gift. He took the gun up to land his family held northwest of San Antonio near Leon Springs, where his father counseled him to "do better," and went to shooting. "Out of sight," he said, which people took to mean that everything he shot vanished.[25]

Big ideas were rolling into Adolph's head. In July 1898, Adolph started telling people he would leave for New York, "at an early date," and give an exhibition of fancy rifle shooting up there.[26]

His father was only in his memories. Doc was busy with other stuff, mainly trying to wrestle out of the shadow of Buffalo Bill. But there was another person entering into the life of Adolph Toepperwein, and this person knew the way to New York and the East, the big time off in the distance.

CHAPTER SEVEN
Your Friendly, Neighborhood Gun Shooter
Tom Wears the Remington Green and White

It all started in 1948. A car would drive up, tires deliberately crunching down on gravel through some of the unpaved parking lots in front of shooting ranges throughout northwest Ohio. Upon stopping, out through the door stepped up a tall, broad-shouldered man with the new, yet-to-fade fabric of vibrant green sleeves that broke out of a gray vest. Keys still jingling in hand, he walked around to the back of the car and unlocked the trunk. And when he did so, it was the treasure chest for any trapshooter, for it was jammed with beautiful, glossy shine of new shotguns straight from the factory.[1]

Tom Frye's appearance as the field representative and exhibition shooter for Remington Arms Company came during an electric time to attend a gun range. America had been taken up by the rush of the postwar years. The economy was booming, and gun ranges weren't left out. Far from it. Military men came home and, after training in the handling and shooting of guns of all nature, found a safe place to keep their interest piqued. Participation in trapshooting events like the Grand American Handicap at Vandalia, Ohio, had doubled from the wartime years and had broken participation records set before the war by 50 percent.[2]

Trap was one of those sports where the average guy could come out on weekends to watch the pro shoot, then try with his own hands what he'd seen the pro do with maybe the same equipment and the same conditions the average guy had. The pro had done it right there at the range where the

Tom Frye was considered to be flamboyant in his dress. He covered a good portion of his shooting vest with pins and buttons and wore a trademark Western bolo tie. Remington Society of America.

average guy paid his membership dues. Tom Frye, wearing the green and gray of Remington, was a budding star. Within a year of commencing his employment as a field rep, Tom was noticed by Jimmy Robinson, the one-man committee that named the All-America Trapshooting Team for *Sports Afield* magazine. Robinson was an unlikely star-maker—a cigar-chomping Midas in tobacco-stained country-boy clothes. Robinson named Tom to the All-America professional trapshooting first team in 1949. Tom had made a splash at the 63rd annual Ohio State Trapshoot on June 10, 1949, at Middletown when he was tied for top honors in the professional class with the proven Cliff Doughman of Morrow, Ohio. Doughman, who had just turned pro as a field rep for Winchester, won in a shoot-off.[3] Doughman was the national leader of shooters registered by the Amateur Trapshooting Association that year from the 16-yard mark in doubles. This all added to his credentials that included a seventh-place finish as an amateur at the Grand American seven years earlier. In '46 he was runnerup in the Doubles Championship and the next year won the North American Clay Target Championship. He had been named to the *Sports Afield* team by Robinson, either as an amateur or pro, for three consecutive years by the time he and Tom met in the shoot-off.[4]

When he wasn't competing, Tom was asked for pointers at the shooting range. He delivered, even if it often came in a matter-of-fact way. "Shooting is like any other sport," he told people at the range. "The man who practices is the man who becomes proficient." In time, he'd expand his advice, particularly if he bumped into someone who loved hunting as much as he did. He started by telling them to keep their head down on the stock of the gun and lead to the target. "Become familiar with your gun," he told them. "In the off season shoot some skeet or trap. Use hand traps if necessary, but get that practice in. The hunter who does keep his hand in by some off-season shooting will be amazed at the amount of game he'll bag the following year." Sometimes words didn't get the job done, and Tom would see shooters allowing the sprung trap to fling its target into a long glide and a gradual ease downward. Those were difficult to hit. So Tom faced the traps and locked in on the targets right out of the release and with one trigger squeeze shot them to pieces while they were on the rise.[5]

The black-and-white photos used to promote his shows presented a well-dressed man, his thick chest stuffed underneath the gray breast of that Remington shooting jacket. He was a handsome image, a square-jawed face looking assuredly straight ahead while a shotgun rested comfortably but ready to be raised to the target by those long arms. He had his admirers.

At the '49 state shoot in Middletown between Dayton and Cincinnati, there was a young shooter who always seemed to finish with high marks. At Middletown, in fact, Fred Waldock Jr. won a Class A state title by hitting 199 of 200. Waldock, a twenty-year-old at the '49 state shoot, was studying law at Ohio State University. He'd come home every summer to the family home at Sandusky, located on Lake Erie midway between Cleveland and Toledo and some fifty-five miles northeast of Tom's native Findlay. He shot a Winchester pump, but he preferred loading it with shells from the Remington family of ammunition companies. This put him regularly at the Remington tent and in the company of Tom. Despite there being about fifteen years' difference in their age, both men quickly bonded.

Tom, the boy who took up the gun back in Findlay, clearly enjoyed seeing young people interested taking up the gun sports. At the Erie County Conservation League at Sandusky, Tom helped launch a free "junior rifle training school" there. At the end of the class there would be rifle shooting competitions to qualify the contestants for the National Rifle Association "Ranger" badge.[6]

Tom invariably would accommodate Fred's college-student eagerness to go shooting. They arrived at the shooting range and Tom surprised Fred when he said he wanted to shoot skeet.

"Hey, I thought you said, 'If you want to shoot skeet you're just a broken-down trapshooter,'" Fred retorted. But the target disc would go up, and Fred got wide-eyed when Tom fired with one hand on the gun. Tom preached safety with the gun, and Fred could tell Tom wouldn't pull a trick if it came without safety. Tom's one-handed shot was sure and true, his vice-grip hand keeping control of the weapon while the shot removed the target from the sky. So the slim Fred felt like he had to step up. It was a pull, and fire. Fred barely managed to hold the gun; his arm was in shock. "I feel like I've broken every bone in my hand," Fred said through his grimace. "I'll never do this again."

Fred tried to share the appreciation Tom had for rifles when he bought a .30-06 and had it ready when he came home from university during Christmas break. Even if it was freezing outside near the home the Waldock family kept at the Cedar Point area of Sandusky, both Fred and Tom knew where they could shoot if it was too cold for anyone to open the gun range. They headed out to the edge of the water along Lake Erie. No sunbathers, no sailboats. Just an expanse of white, blue, and reflections and glare from an amply sunlit day. A gull broke into the air, and Tom grabbed the .30-06 from Fred and pointed the mean barrel out over the lake.

"There's no way in God's green earth that you'll. . . ."

Bang. Fred stopped talking and saw the bird, what was left, make a feathery plummet to the lake. Two wings, nothing in between, made their clumsy drop down. "Bingo!" Fred yelled.

Tom had met Fred's sister, Sara Jane, and the two started dating. Tom asked her to marry, and when they did, Tom moved in with the family at

Cedar Point. It was a good arrangement for Sara Jane, who preferred to stay close with her parents. Besides, Tom was traveling often in his duties as a gun-manufacturer field rep who liked to compete as well.[7] It was good for business to compete, and with Cliff Doughman setting the pace and taking a job with Winchester that was similar to Tom's, Tom had a standard to chase and some amount of pressure to make Remington look good against its major competitor. In 1952 and '53, Doughman led the nation both from the sixteen-yard mark and at doubles.[8] Fred, as a twenty-three-year-old, won the 1953 North American Clay Target Championship at Vandalia with an impressive performance. He hit all two hundred in the main event, plus fifty straight in the shoot-off.[9] Tom won the World Professional title at sixteen yards in trap in 1950.[10]

At the Grand American Handicap at Vandalia in the summer of 1954, part of the trap competition had Fred in an amateur squad that collectively fired at 1,000 clays. These five gunners, each shooting a set of 200, hardly missed. Fred hit 199. His father, Fred Waldock Sr., just let one fewer get by. Two others in the squad, Bob Allen (a budding retailer of clothing designed for clay shooters) and the 1952 Olympic gold medalist George Genereaux of Canada, matched Fred Jr. As good as they were, they couldn't match the score of Marvin Driver from Missouri Valley, Iowa.[11] It was quite a round, and Fred Jr. was going to let Tom know about it. He wouldn't have to wait long, because Tom and his green-sleeved jacket had busted through the crowd and were headed in his direction. Before Fred could brag, Tom told him and the other four shooters squarely, "You just broke the squad record." The squad record for what? The world record. Tom thought no one else had hit that many in an amateur squad.[12]

Tom recorded a rarity as well, a perfect run of one-hundred in doubles reported in 1956 at Fennwood Shooting Park a few miles south of Sandusky at Bellevue, Ohio.[13] Frye progressed through the industry class at the 1956 Grand American and reached his final day in late August by winning a shoot-off with Bill Adkins of Louisville, Kentucky.[14] Tom's shooting that summer as measured against Doughman, heralded as "one of the greatest professional shooters now in action" while leading the nation's industry shooters with a .9888 average on 2,500 targets, was described as "thrilling" by the hometown newspaper in Sandusky. The report was that Tom outshot Doughman 956–951 in the overall and 384–380 in the all-around to win both of those titles.[15]

If Tom wasn't shooting in competition, he was showing the product. He wasn't home much. Sara wanted to keep living at her parents' home. Tom had a common interest in shooting with the Waldock men, and clearly had the respect of Sara's mother (she also was named Sara). But he expressed uneasiness about the living arrangements.[16] There was one thing that was obvious, however. Tom and Sara had no children. They divorced. Tom thought about leaving Ohio. With an Indian head sewn onto the shoulder of his jacket, Tom had a strong admiration for the Indian brotherhood. Remington had an open spot for a field rep out West.

When Tom's banner year of 1956 against the likes of Cliff Doughman was up for awards, Jimmy Robinson gave Tom the stamp of approval. Robinson had the All-America lineup printed in *Sports Afield* in 1957, with Tom on first-team and named captain for the first time. It was a co-captaincy with Doughman. The news release sent out to bring attention to the teams noted Tom's hometown: Denver, Colorado.

CHAPTER EIGHT

Here Comes the Texas Triggerman

Ad Shoots His Way to Fame

On the last day of the calendar in 1900, Adolph Toepperwein opened his mailbox in San Antonio and found a salutation from Winchester Repeating Firearms Company. It wasn't an English walnut-stock rifle, like the one the company sent him a few years back. The executives at Winchester wanted him to come to New Haven and talk about a job.

Adolph got on the train within days.[1] It didn't matter that he now had a steady job as a sharpshooting rifle performer with an established, big-name circus.

"I traveled with the circus and had a barrel of fun," said Adolph, now a seasoned performer who felt like he was working toward the class of gunman that was his idol Doc Carver. "We played most of the United States and Mexico too—wherever there was a railroad track or even a good road. Those folks (in Mexico) really appreciated good shooting. They looked upon a fine marksman as a respected personage. I got my share of shouts of *¡Ole!* during my tours with the circus south of the border."[2]

His cousin Rudy could tease him about the ammunition that was wasted by showing off with the gun, but Adolph was making a career out of it. By the time he received Winchester's letter, he had left San Antonio and performed on the major stages of the East Coast. He felt he'd taken his show to the next level after that at the auditorium the Orrin Bros. circus owned at Mexico City.

Elizabeth "Plinky" Toepperwein, known formally as Mrs. Adolph Toepperwein in the press, in the early days of her shooting career, likely prior to 1910. Collection of Kenneth Toepperwein.

He headed to snowy New Haven by mid-January 1901. This was the chance he'd been seeking all along. He was around guns at almost every instant. He saw the new models coming off the assembly line, and the company executives encouraged him to wander about, ask questions, and get hands-on with the product by taking the firearms apart and putting them back together. After a day of touring the plant he took the company catalog back to his hotel room and memorized every page.[3] When Winchester president T.G. Bennett, just beginning his second decade at the helm of the company, brought Adolph into his office and offered him a job as a traveling representative in the sales department, the decision was easy. "Of course," Adolph said. "Where else could a man shoot all day and get all the ammo he needed and get paid for shooting it all up? I'm tired of riding these rails in Mexico. I quit."[4]

Adolph struck a different image around the halls of Winchester. He was fit looking. Clean cut, he kept his mustache neatly clipped and never let it

Ad and Plinky Toepperwein were married and performed together as a team for about 40 years starting around 1905. If they weren't performing, they practiced almost every day with rifles, shotguns, and handguns. Collection of Kenneth Toepperwein.

fall into the form of a walrus that Doc Carver wore for some years. He wore fashionable vests and could sport one of those different, stringed Western ties. His wide-brimmed hats also could tip him off as someone from the West, a Texan perhaps.

That women would notice him at their workplace was not far-fetched. Even though they weren't guaranteed the right to vote, plenty of women were working on assembly lines in large manufacturing plants like Winchester's. Even as early as the Civil War era, women were abundant in the assembly rooms. With their long hair drawn back by pretty bows, their neck-hugging blouses sleeved to the forearm and their skirts no higher than the calves, women sat and loaded the small ammunition cartridges while men hovered around them—to do the heavy lifting of stacking crates of bullets and shells.[5] And there, a nineteen-year-old girl with red hair was working the pistol cartridge-loading machine in one of the ammunition rooms. Adolph passed through the room on one of his walks through the plant. The girl noticed. "I'm going to marry that man," Elizabeth Servaty told her workmates.

Company rules would not allow her to approach the exotic-looking visitor, or vice versa.[6]

If teen-age "Lizzie" were to ask questions about that man, she'd hear about a legend that already had been growing for a few years right there on the East Coast.

George H. Walker knew his way to New York. That's where the big-name talent could be found, and for the right price Walker knew that a good entertainment manager could lure the stars to Texas. During his stint as manager of the well-funded, Harry Greenwall–owned Tremont Opera House of Galveston, he was able to secure a performance by famed actress (and suspected W.F. "Buffalo Bill" Cody mistress) Sarah Bernhardt.[7]

But he knew the local folks liked to see home-grown talent as well. And Walker would not restrict his bookings to actors. In San Antonio, the German community enjoyed the shooting sports, and thousands were drawn to see the twenty-something Adolph Toepperwein break no less than Annie Oakley's shooting records starting in 1895 and his performances at the July 4th celebration parade in 1898.[8]

The quick-thinking Walker was keen to hustle sporting events. When professional baseball arrived in Texas in 1888, San Antonio bid to have a team. So Walker hopped the train to Galveston to meet with the Texas League. Even when his shoes had been—as a wiseacre reporter euphemistically put it—"appropriated" while he slept on the Pullman, Walker managed to put his best foot forward. The selection of replacements at the local cobbler must have been limited because he was sporting a pair of new patent leather dress shoes with high ankles and pointed toes. Walker didn't fret it. He immediately started boosting San Antonio. "It is the greatest town in Texas," he told the team owners. "He continually repeated his boom talk" and was insistent on San Antonio being in the league. He was enthusiastic, until his new shoes came to someone's attention. "Every pair of shoes in the sleeper had been stolen during the night," Walker told them before redirecting his pitch for San Antonio's inclusion into the league.[9]

Walker booked talent for the city's most respected venue for entertainment, the Opera House, which opened on December 20, 1886, steps from the Alamo.[10] Walker would instruct the design of new sets and changes to the interior before heading off to New York to make talent bookings for the next season.[11] Back in San Antonio he brought in Adolph and saw that his shooting act could work indoors. And when Walker saw Adolph was a talented artist, he found a way to showcase his work with "crayons." Walker billed Toepperwein with another local boy, banjoist Con Boyle, for a benefit show.[12]

"The people sure seemed to go for the shooting part of it," Adolph said to an excited Walker. Though Adolph expressed some hesitations about show business, Walker thought his boys' talents had legs.[13]

Boyle would go on to play up East with the Jack Haverly Minstrels, a large entertainment troupe that performed in blackface. On August 1, 1898,[14] Adolph showed up at the International & Great Northern Depot on West Houston Street in San Antonio's Cattleman Square, where trains departed for Waco, St. Louis, and Kansas City.[15] Adolph sat and nervously waited for his train to take him to his stop at St. Louis, then on to New York. At the station, Adolph had time to notice the images of a five-pointed star made from holes punched through the back of the benches where people waited for their trains. He had started with simple images like that when he used his rifle as a pencil to "draw." He drew any sort of images that came to his head by placing a piece of paper about twenty-five feet away and shooting, the collection of bullet holes forming the pictures. His Indian head, with its feathers and war bonnet, was different, striking.[16]

But he was totally unsure of himself upon arrival in New York. He found the theater office where the auditions were conducted. He opened the door at the end of the dark hallway and peeked through to see a room teeming with strange-looking characters. One man was ready to perform with his trick dog, another with a guitar. There were musicians, dancers in costume, and a juggler taking up room in the corner. Adolph showed up carrying his gun case, wearing a hat that made it pretty obvious he was from out West, or some other bumpkin-filled place on the sawdust trail. The room started clearing out, and Adolph, too, got his call backstage. With his rifle out of the case, the backstage chatter included him. "I understand they hired him to shoot us," a showgirl said, "instead of firing us." Adolph laughed with everyone else.[17]

That's the sort of thing that could break the nervous tension. Yet no matter how legitimate he or Walker thought he was, his act would have a difficult time standing out from the line of people who shot guns on stage—and cheated. These guys would shoot at candles set upon a wooden box set on its side. The other side of that box hid an assistant who would pull on a string and extinguish the candle's flame. When the assistant snuck out from behind the box during the applause, he could come on stage with a cigarette in his mouth. The shooter would fire, but the assistant insured a "hit" when that little wire he had running through the cigarette was tapped by his tongue, causing the ashes to fall.

"In vaudeville and sideshows the shooters used mechanical gimmicks," Adolph noticed. "Anybody who's just a fair shooter [can] make a good show."[18]

Adolph had his audition. Now it was time to talk, and he'd have to do it in the halls of the giant of the industry. B.F. Keith clearly was one of the top, if not the top, purveyor of vaudeville theater at the close of the nineteenth century. In the 1890s when Adolph showed up, Keith productions were showcased in more than thirty theaters through the East Coast.[19]

Keith formed a partnership with E.F. Albee through their lease of a theater in Boston. Albee was notorious for showing little love for actors, and his style made actor Marion Spitzer churn after one negotiation. "Scarcely anyone mentions E.F. Albee," Spitzer fired off, "without intense bitterness."[20]

"When you were eventually ushered into his august presence, the stage would be all set," Groucho Marx noted. "In his private lair his carpet was all thick and silent. His desk was about eighty feet long, or so it seemed, and on it there would be nothing but an expansive vase containing a single rose. The only chair in the room would be the one occupied by the master. The poor actor, trembling with fear, would stand there before him, shuffling his feet like a schoolboy who had just been caught redhanded swiping the teacher's lunch."[21]

Albee, however, was too busy for another trick shooter and had a secretary shoo him off.[22] Walker wouldn't let the opportunity pass. "A stubborn cuss," Adolph thought. "I was ready to call it quits right off."[23]

Walker knew Gentleman Jim Corbett, who was dabbling in vaudeville and had property in New York. Walker took Adolph there and, in the presence of sportswriters keeping tabs on Gentleman Jim's boxing career, touted Adolph as the "Texas Triggerman." The talk touched on the shooting galleries at Coney Island. If Adolph was "the best shot the world has ever seen," as Walker said he was, he could go out there and prove it. The sportswriters would go, and if the "Texas Triggerman" could make a show with his gun, a booking agent for Albee would catch wind of it.[24]

So the hotdog stands, rollercoasters, carousels, and other amusements lined along south Brooklyn at the burgeoning Coney Island might have distracted Adolph from thinking that he could be walking toward the break of his life.[25] Something had better happen; Walker's bankroll was dwindling. It cost good money to try to win prizes in the shooting galleries, and the only thing tangible that Adolph could win—to quote the sign affixed next to a three-quarter-inch bull's-eye about thirty feet away in the first gallery they visited—was "a ten-cent cigar every time you ring me." Adolph didn't even bring his own gun. He went through the ones lined up at the gallery like he would if he were to look for a cue stick that wasn't warped among those on the racks at a pool hall. Easily noticing the unset sights, among the shoddy guns' other maladies, Adolph thought, "If I use one of these guns, I'll be lucky to hit the backstop." His hands finally lighted on one that was acceptable—what else, a Winchester, a Model 1890 .22 caliber. He lifted it to his shoulder and started firing on the duck targets moving at the top first. The targets toppled left and right. There were no misses among Adolph's initial volley. He threw in some trick moves. No misses. Plaster birds were decapitated. Stars formed with clay and small clay pipes were busted, easily raining fragments onto the gallery's cluttered floor. Adolph started pouring it on, and he made the proprietor of the shop start to dig. The bell up there by the sign? A newspaper reporter recounted the action: "[H]e kept the bells ringing like a perpetual alarm clock."[26]

There were others shooting in the gallery, but they stopped and saw how this skinny fellow was doing it. Amazement covered the crowd that already was there. And when Adolph accepted the cigars, he turned and gave them to the impressed New Yorkers. The man running the gallery had lost count of everything. How much did Walker owe him? Walker gave the fellow $5, but the man was out of cigars and out of ammunition. The crowd, once buzzing, now whooped and hollered, and all the man at the front of the gallery could do was bring down the shutters and call it quits for the day.

It was quite a turnaround, for Adolph was not unlike many others who had gone to New York for the first time. "I didn't feel right," he said. "But the first time I felt one of those rifles up against my cheek, I forgot where I was. I just started firing. . . ."[27]

People followed Walker and Adolph to the next booth, and the fellow running the place apparently had no clue. Adolph gave that fellow's targets the same treatment, and the cigars popped out of the place like felled logs. Adolph had no use for the smokes.[28]

"The less you drink and smoke," the "Texas Triggerman" told the crowd as he accepted the cigars, "the better shooting you can do. And if you wish to become really expert," he continued, handing the cigars to the men surrounding him, "avoid tobacco and liquor entirely."[29]

The suggestion made by the sportswriters to Walker at Gentleman Jim's could not be going better. The buzz his "Texas Triggerman" was creating now was easily noticeable—not just the usual midway chatter. It was so much so that operators of shooting galleries down the line started shutting their awnings before the sharpshooter came down to clean them out of prizes, too. The sportswriters were there, and they had the wild story splashed in the city's dailies. Someone had informed them that this young man once hit 979 out of 1,000 targets thrown into the air, not just sitting there like they were at the shooting galleries, and that he had hit 241 straight. Word got back to San Antonio. They knew all about Adolph's shooting records, but their favorite son was making them proud with his exploits on the big stage.

The San Antonio writers heralded:

> 'Tep' is shooting his way to fame in New York. He has created a sensation with his rifle at Coney Island.
>
> Adolph Toepperwein, the young Texan who enjoys the distinction of being the most skillful small calibre [*sic*] rifle shot in the world, is in New York. Mr. Toepperwein, incidentally, visited Coney Island recently and with his six-shooter, which he twirls as a pastime, he put the shooting galleries of the Midway out of business. He peppered all the small targets with .22-calibre [*sic*] bullets and in half an hour got himself barred from the ranges.[30]

Beyond their own reporting on the Coney Island incident, the *New York Journal* accepted Adolph's letter with advice on the proper handling and aiming of a gun, to benefit "those who are anxious to become skillful rifle shots. I aim to instruct." This was signed, "Yours, Adolph Toepperwein—Champion Rifle Shot of the World."[31]

It was the first publicity Adolph received in the East.[32] One of the booking agents took Adolph back to the Albee offices, saying, "This man didn't miss a single shot—not one." A contract was drawn up, and the "Texas Triggerman" signed.[33]

"I was offered jobs making $75 a week," Adolph beamed, "[and that's] more than I could make back home in a month."[34]

It was an incredible break, but the hard work wasn't over. Adolph's first performance on Albee's stage would be critical. Vaudeville managers were results driven, and Albee's men were known to give up on a performer after one week. When the "Texas Triggerman" ventured beyond sniping the props that had been set up for him, the audience loved it. Adolph remembered the hole-punched benches outside the train station when he shot out the designs with his gun from across stage. His rifle-bullet drawings of an Indian chief in profile were an immediate hit. He'd create it from twenty-five feet away and use 152 shots. To keep it feasible in a fast-moving vaudeville performance he could get it done in less than five minutes. And Adolph kept it fresh by sniping out images of current public figures. He perfected an image of Adm. Winfield Schley, who just that summer of 1898 was a Spanish-American War hero after directing the decimation of Spain's Caribbean fleet at Santiago, Cuba.

"I find that picture shooting—that is to say, forming a portrait by a series of shots—attracts the public greatly," Adolph said. "One must picture in his mind the portrait he wants to form out of bullet holes then proceed to follow the imaginary line with a swinging motion, beginning at the bottom and shooting with both eyes open, so that the growth of the picture may be watched carefully on both sides."[35]

Albee's office, where Adolph was a nuisance in his first visit, now stamped him. In the Albee operation terms, he was given "the route," and Adolph made the trip out of New York to other principal vaudeville theaters in Baltimore, Boston, and Philadelphia.[36] By late winter of 1899 Adolph's act hit the news wires. The drawings he did with his rifle were the centerpiece. The *Portsmouth Herald*, with a cutline of "Latest Rifle Wrinkle," actually printed one of his drawings done of Admiral Schley, full with walrus mustache and Van Dyke beard. The article referred to Adolph Toepperwein being the "champion shot of the world" and "expert picture shooter, and with his rifle can draw a man's head in less than five minutes." It took nearly two hundred shots to get the likeness of Admiral Schley.[37] After quoting from a *Philadelphia Record* article about Adolph's Indian head shooting taking 152 bullets in rapid fire, a writer with the *Reno Evening Gazette* stated, "It is not clear whether or not this marksman is a member of Roosevelt's regiment of rough riders. If he isn't he ought to be."[38]

Yet this schedule was grueling. Adolph performed three times a day and six days a week.[39] He spent most of his time indoors, dimly lit no matter the newfangled electric lights. So, by 1900, Adolph left vaudeville. He quickly found work again. He signed a contract to tour with Orrin Brothers Circus, mostly in Mexico. He wouldn't be there long. The people at Winchester wanted him.

The work week would end at Winchester Repeating Arms Company. If the coming spring weather would make an early appearance, much of the workforce in 1901 got outdoors for a stroll in the main park, just like people would in any major city. In New Haven, Connecticut, that meant walking out to the Green. It was a square city block smack dab in the middle of town, lined by churches and butting up to the campus at Yale University. Thick, tall trees lined the streets along the Green, and benches could be sat upon where footpaths crisscrossed the park.

Adolph, the spindly Western-looking fellow now walking the halls at Winchester, made it out to the Green; he could sit in his hotel and study the company catalog and manuals for only so long. It was a pleasant place to walk, a nice diversion while he waited for his first Winchester assignment. In fact, when would he shoot?

Finally, his thoughts of shooting were diverted. The trip to the Green had done it. Among the strollers he might have found a familiar face getting a drink of water. Had he seen this woman before? Had she seen him? In Adolph's mind, she was as distinctive as he must have been to her. She had kind eyes that became vibrant when she smiled. Even when she grinned she showed a firm jaw. Her wavy, fluffy red hair could not be well contained under any hat, it seemed. She looked so young. And when she stood her wasp waist, quite noticeable, was accentuated by her blouse and long flowing dress pinned down by a tightly tied belt.

Who was this? It seemed she noticed him as well. So Adolph Toepperwein got up the nerve to introduce himself. She worked at Winchester, too, over there with the new assembling machines in the pistol cartridge-loading room. That girl, what was her name?

"Elizabeth Servaty," she said.

"Elizabeth Servaty," Adolph repeated. "Music to my ears."[40]

CHAPTER NINE

Car Wreck

Two Tons of Lead Come Back at Tom Frye

From his place in Sandusky, it wouldn't take much more than thirty minutes for Tom Frye to drive straight down Highway 4 and make that one right turn onto Route 20 to get to Fennwood Shooting Park. This was the site of one of his bragging rights in the shooting world—the word that had circulated that he had accomplished a rare trick of hitting one hundred consecutive hits on double targets in 1956. This also would be the place where friends would throw a going-away party for Tom. When he showed up at Fennwood in March 1957, everyone knew Tom had decided to take a transfer to new territory for Remington with headquarters in Denver, and several hundred people came by with their farewell wishes. They thanked him for spending a great deal of time helping shooters in the region improve, and they appreciated that he had given many demonstrations to sportsmen's and civic groups.[1]

Now, moved to Denver, there would be few straight drives to anywhere to go shoot. One of the first competitions Tom entered out West, about a month following his departure from Ohio, required a seven-hour drive to Ogden, Utah. The Weber Sportsman's Gun Club in Ogden finished up a competitive trapshoot on April 7, 1957, and Tom hit twenty-one of twenty-five in one short round of singles and forty-two of fifty in another before he went twenty of twenty-four in doubles.[2] It was far from the sort of performance he claimed at Fennwood, but people also heard that Tom had a

As an eighteen-year-old student manager and lover of aviation, Newt Crumley accompanied the University of Nevada football team on a flight to the Los Angeles area to play USC on November 8, 1929, the first report of a college football team traveling by air to play an opponent. From right, Carol Cross, Crumley, Fernando Ambrose, Tommy Thompkins, and Dick Tupper. University Archives, University of Nevada, Reno Libraries.

girlfriend.[3]

There was a vibrant shooting community in the West. It just wasn't as compact as it was in western Ohio. The Pacific International Trapshooting Association conducted registered competitions through much of the region. But a lot of the shooting was done informally, and the gun clubs proliferated. The clientele was, in some cases, as high profile as one could get. Movie stars, politicians, and public figures were flocking to the shooting sports, and there were two hot spots in particular. The biggest names in Hollywood found a spot in Los Angeles County, a location where some Western movies had shot scenes near the Aqua Sierra Gun Club at Chatsworth. It was not unusual to show up at Aqua Sierra and see Roy Rogers, Clark Gable, or Robert Stack toting a shotgun and firing accurately at clay targets.[4] And away from

Hollywood, up the coast at San Francisco, just as star-studded a crowd was forming at Pacific Rod & Gun Club along Lake Merced. Ernest Hemingway was on the list of notables who shot at Lake Merced, and when Tom swung by he ran into his former fellow Army Air Corps shooting instructor Lee Braun, who was his manager at Remington.[5]

The networking Tom could do through Lee at Lake Merced was rather impressive. Lee shot often with Alex Kerr, who took some of the money from the family fortune that his parents built through the Kerr Glass Company and opened a sporting goods store in Beverly Hills that attracted its own group of stars. Kerr was the one with the blond hair and matching stubbly mustache, but just as easy to notice at the firing line was the portly, dark-haired fellow who chomped on a big cigar while he looked over the sights and shot. It was General Curtis LeMay, who in the postwar years was in charge of the Strategic Air Command. One of the officers who reported to him had gone on after his service to operate his family's growing casino and hotel holdings in Nevada.

This General LeMay protégé was ready to open a casino in Reno, a gambling market that seemed to go out of its way to complement its casinos with the gun sports. In 1950 at the Western-themed Harolds Casino at Reno, another casino operator named Raymond "Pappy" Smith and his two sons bought the Jabberwock Gun Club and turned it into what officially was known as Harolds Trapshooting Country Club. It was site of the Golden West Grand shooting competition, the largest in the country next to the Grand American Handicap. It wasn't a mundane affair. Members of the Smith family would wear a New York Yankees baseball uniform and drive a yellow dune buggy up and down the shooting line, giving away thousands of Stetson cowboy hats, bottles of Jim Beam, and gold-coin belt buckles as trophies to winning trapshooters.[6]

Their casino soon would have a competitor that had ingeniously attracted large crowds to gamble at casinos located in some of the most out-of-the-way places. The new man in town had a promotional flair that rivaled Harolds, yet he brought an operation that reflected the efficiency, order, and respect for discipline of a General LeMay operation. Newton Crumley was one of General LeMay's colonels, and Newt made such a reputation in Elko that *LIFE* magazine came to town and reported that this fellow with the decorated military background was a "crack rifleshot and big-game hunter." The magazine article included a photo of Newt smiling at a money-strewn table;

the story claimed Newt had won a $10,000 pot in a poker game.[7] Newt took over a hotel in Reno and installed a casino operation that quickly would make money. Yet he made time to shoot, like his commanding officer General LeMay did, at places like Lake Merced. Tom Frye would make it out there, rumbling along in another one of those long car drives through the West. But Newt Crumley went at a faster speed, and he satisfied his desire to get on top of it all.

Newton Hunt Crumley grew up as an only child as his father and mother kicked around the mining towns of the West. The father—Newton Crumley—opened a saloon in Nye County, Nevada, to refresh prospectors during a silver rush in 1913.[8] In the next ten years he leased the big Goldfield Hotel.[9] Crumley was the proprietor when a devastating fire ravaged Goldfield in July 1923.

As that fire roared and reporters sought to describe a town burning to death, Crumley was contacted for his description of the scene. He said the estimate of losses had reached $1.5 million, even with the fire not yet extinguished. With access to water in a place like Nevada always a challenge, people trying to put out the fire tried to break the blaze from devouring what was left of the town by blasting sticks of TNT.[10]

This was not the first time a Crumley male had been challenged. Newton Crumley, who settled into the West with his brother J. Grant Crumley, was one of eleven children of Sarah C. Crumley and Benjamin J. Crumley—the Reverend Benjamin J. Crumley. Rev. Crumley lived in Georgia, but his religious visions led him to enlist in the Union Army after the outbreak of the Civil War in 1861.[11]

The Crumleys could not have been the most popular family on the block there in Georgia. So they moved westward and raised cattle in Kansas.[12] If the cowboys the Crumley boys worked with there weren't a rough enough lot, they eventually would be surrounded by cutthroats upon their arrival in Cripple Creek, Colorado. It got particularly dicey for J. Grant Crumley one evening in the summer of 1901 when, as the owner and operator of the Newport Saloon in the mining district, he got into an altercation with a newly rich prospector named Sam Strong. When things became so heated over Strong's losses at the roulette wheel, Strong pulled a pistol.[13] Grant, described as big and chubby,[14] would figure to be imposing in a barroom brawl.

Quickly, Sam Strong was lying on the floor of the Newport with part of his head blown off and Grant standing there holding his sawed-off 10-gauge shotgun. Grant got off the murder charge, on the grounds of self-defense, and he and Newton soon were rushing in on the reports of gold and other minerals around Tonopah.[15]

Grant Crumley had a reputation to outrun. Even before his killing of Strong, he took a beating from the press. A newspaper account credited him with being worth $2 million, yet also referred to him as a "noted bad man . . . [reputed] to be in many scrapes, and is believed to have been concerned in the kidnapping and tarring and feathering of General Tarsney at Colorado Springs."[16] Thomas Tarsney, an elected adjutant general in Colorado sympathetic to union miners, indeed was tarred and feathered by masked men who tricked him out of a Colorado Springs hotel room while he was in route to a labor dispute at Cripple Creek in 1894. Tarsney could not identify his assailants.[17]

Unlike his brother, Newton managed to not get caught up in such controversy. He had married someone from Belmont (forty-five miles north of Tonopah) named Lee Hunt. And on February 3, 1911, in Tonopah she gave birth to a boy. He was named Newton Hunt Crumley, and even though there was no "Junior" in the name he would often affix it anyway just to make sure there was no confusing him with his father. Eventually, the young Newton would attend high school in Reno. He would visit his grandmother, who continued living in Belmont. When the mining rush ended there, the courthouse would soon go empty. Yet, like ghost town buildings often do, its doors stayed swung open, and passers-through would stop and follow a tradition: they'd sign their name on walls inside. A thin high-school boy with pleasing waves and curls of bright blond hair, Newton found that much of the room to scrawl any sort of name upon the courthouse interior walls was taken. He headed toward the upper floor and signed along the stairs, Newton Crumley, Jr.—8/21/25—R.H.S.[18]

In less than three years, Newton Hunt Crumley would graduate high school in Reno in 1928. He stuck around and attended the University of Nevada nearby. He matriculated as a scrawny local kid. In an effort to bulk up, he joined the boxing team. But he still had trouble filling out a winter coat a year later when he experienced a life-changing moment on November 8, 1929. He looked out of place alongside bigger men—he was a student manager of the football team—indeed everyone looked out of place as the football players walked alongside a fleet of airplanes with the dark-colored fuselages and silver wings of the Nevada Airlines Company. With their single propellers pointed northward at Reno's Blanchfield airstrip, the University of Nevada football team became the first squad that anyone knew of to fly in airplanes and travel to a game.[19]

Thus, people seemed more nervous about climbing aboard those whirring, single-engine Lockheeds than they were to play the powerful, defending national champion: the University of Southern California. The Nevada coach, George Philbrook, in fact "could not convince his family that air travel is the safest method for a football coach with a family to annihilate space and time so he went to Los Angeles last night on the train," a news story read.[20] Yet without incident, or anything serious—"[I]n a few instances [the flight was] disastrous to their digestive organs," someone deadpanned, "otherwise there were no fatalities"[21]—the planes landed at a field around Glendale, California, in time for the next day's game at the six-year-old Los Angeles Memorial Coliseum against the national-power Trojans.[22]

The team's plane trip to L.A. was said to cost $2,000, which was about $350 more than the school would have spent to send the squad by train as usual. Newt had a hand in planning the trip, because a newspaper reporter was told that "the student managers assert the publicity received will bring in more than $350 in additional revenue at the gate in Los Angeles."[23] But the crowd at the majestic coliseum was scant, an estimated 20,000, and USC beat Nevada 66–0.

The team came home to much less fanfare, and their sports stories were replaced with business dispatches of the stock market crash in New York. Newt's wavy blond locks, his grinning and youthful face, his fashionable sporty overcoat draping around his sharp tie, would be replaced by Army discipline. He graduated from the University of Nevada in 1932. While plenty of his football friends were mortified by flight, Newt's spirit got caught up there in the clouds. He joined the Air Corps, and he earned his wings shortly after basic training in San Antonio. He made a promise to his fraternity brothers back at Reno. Upon his first parachute jump, if he ever needed to bail out, he'd send them a box of cigars.[24] A lighthearted joke among frat brothers could come to a mean test in the wide-open spaces in the West, and beyond.

Tom Frye had his new girlfriend in Denver. But something else was missing. That shooting jacket with the Remington colors had those All-America trapshooting team patches from *Sports Afield* for five straight years. But he didn't have one for the 1957 shooting season. James Joseph found out why. As a writer for *Guns & Ammo* magazine, Joseph made it a point to see Tom Frye shoot. But, as Tom was known for choosing his words carefully before saying anything, he didn't have the easiest time finding out the reason for the hole in Tom's shooting resume when he was prompted to ask about his absence from the shooting circuit.

"Automobile accident," Tom answered directly.[25] "In [the hospital] again . . . out again . . . back in traction again."[26]

It had happened when one of those drives around Denver caught up to him. He was by himself at the wheel and the next thing he knew he was across the seat on the passenger side of the car, pushed up against the door.[27] He had been sitting at an intersection, ready to pull forward, when the driver of another vehicle ran his red light and t-boned into Tom's car.[28]

The aftermath left Tom in excruciating pain. He spent months in the hospital immediately after the accident because doctors mandated traction. Jacobs looked at Tom, thought about the hellacious impact of metal coming upon Tom as he drove once through the streets of Denver, and wrote this sentence for *Guns & Ammo*:

"Through 30 years of shooting—ever since he was gunning afield with his dad back in Findlay, Ohio—Tom had likely got off a couple of tons of lead and shot. In Denver that day, all two tons of it—on wheels—came back at him. . . ."[29]

Tom had fired upon so many clay discs with his gun, yet when the doctors looked at the X-ray from his back they could look at his own discs lining up in his back and make the same statement as the judge out at the shooting range: Hit! Luckily, his spinal cord remained intact underneath those few crunched vertebrae. Tom could remember an old line he once used to joke with his former brother-in-law and friend, Fred Waldock Jr. What did broken-down trapshooters do? They shot skeet. Tom could use a trip to the skeet range. He was broken down. He needed something to get his career going again.

CHAPTER TEN
Plinky!
Elizabeth Toepperwein Learns to Shoot

Adolph Toepperwein, the newest field representative employed by Winchester Repeating Arms Company, no longer had to idle his time roaming the halls and assembly lines in the big New Haven manufacturing plant. His nights no longer had to be filled with going back to his hotel room where he could sit by himself and read the Winchester catalog. He had taken advantage of one of those weekend strolls to the Green in downtown New Haven, and it brought excitement to his life. After all, it was uncanny that the young woman he met, this German-born teenager, worked at the same place he did.

And now, Adolph knew what his first assignment in the field was going to be. It was a trip of about 450 miles from New Haven, and when Adolph arrived around May 1, 1901, he got an intense look at the firearms marketplace at the lavish Pan-American Exhibition that would run through October in the country's eighth-largest city, Buffalo, New York.[1] Winchester firearms were placed alongside the products of fifty other ventures in the overall outdoor sports/military goods sector. In particular, Winchester armament was sharing a sales floor with every other giant stalking the guns product line. There was American Ordnance Co., of Bridgeport, Connecticut; Colt's Patent Firearms Co., of Hartford, Connecticut; Driggs-Seabury Gun & Ammunition Company, of New York City; Lefevre Arms Co., of Syracuse, New York; the Peters Cartridge Co., of Bridgeport, Connecticut; Remington

Lawrence Toepperwein was born in 1904. He was the only child of Plinky, shown here with her son, and Adolph Toepperwein. Photo courtesy of Tony Sapienza.

Arms Co., of Ilion, New York; Savage Arms Co., of Utica, New York; Smith & Wesson of Springfield, Massachusetts; and Union Metallic Cartridge Co., of Bridgeport, Connecticut. Winchester and the others displayed all sort of small arms, sporting arms, and ammunition, including the latest offerings of smokeless gunpowder.[2]

Guns were everywhere, much like it was back in New Haven. But it looked like this would be no time, nor place as Adolph could see, to entertain. The exhibition grounds, popularly tagged as Rainbow City, did offer a 12,000-seat stadium, a fancy place designed in the Greco-Roman flair. It looked like Chicago's Soldier Field in miniature, but the cowboys and Indians engaging in a Wild West show over there shot blanks. Besides, it was made clear to Adolph that he was in Buffalo strictly on business. His manning of the booth was a directive from company president T.G. Bennett.[3]

This was not what Adolph had envisioned from a company that already had employed the idea of exhibition shooting. In the 1870s, James E. Stetson was working for Winchester as a gun-barrel craftsman. But when he demonstrated he could accurately fire bullets out of the barrels he made, the company moved him out of the barrel shop and onto the road for full-time shooting under the Winchester banner. He was said to have competed against Doc Carver and won a diamond belt awarded to the champion marksman of the country.[4] That sort of lore would bother Adolph, for he clearly demonstrated his talent in front of large crowds in Texas, New York, and Mexico. Used to, he shot every day. He hadn't done it since he arrived in Buffalo, and he had a hard time imagining he could make it through the entire six-month stay without shooting a gun. Perhaps his mind could be eased by corresponding with Miss Elizabeth Servaty back in New Haven, which he did regularly.[5]

Work continued, and the crowds picked up on September 5 when President William McKinley and his wife and traveling party arrived at the Exposition. Estimates had it at more than 100,000 people walking through the gates the day of the president's arrival. McKinley, who had started his second term after the country was on the high of being victor of the Spanish-American War, wore a top hat and got out openly among the crowd.[6]

The president got out to the exposition for a second day, but instead of a speech that brought loud cheers the day before, Adolph could not mistake what he heard this time. It was a gunshot.[7] People had scurried about, and they actually reported hearing two shots. Word got out that a man had approached the president with his right hand wrapped in a handkerchief, and that's where the shots erupted from a concealed pistol. The newspapers reported that McKinley had survived the assassin's bullet, though doctors could find only one after the other one fell out from the president's jacket. In about a week, President McKinley was dead from the complications of the bullet wound. Adolph returned to New Haven. He met the Servaty family, the parents and brothers and sisters of Elizabeth. Then he packed for another assignment for Winchester back down in Texas.[8]

If this was the man Elizabeth Servaty would marry—he had come over to meet "Lizzy's" parents and the family—she'd better get to know about shooting. It seemed that's all Adolph Toepperwein wanted to do. She knew all about packing cartridges for pistols at the Winchester plant, but she didn't want anything else to do with guns. If she was interested, she could find out more, and she could find a like-minded set even if the shooting man she found attractive wasn't around—and he wouldn't be for a while because of his assignments away from New Haven.

Social restraints considered (women did not have the right to vote guaranteed in the Constitution, among other things), it was not farfetched for a woman to be taken by the idea of shooting. Annie Oakley was at the height of her fame; her spot near the top of the bill in the widely popular Buffalo Bill's Wild West made her one of the few female entertainers to be a household name. Annie was only five feet tall, but she and W.F. Cody were considered to be America's first personalities to dabble in superstardom after their smashing tour went through England and onto the European continent.

Annie broke the barriers, and the grass roots took hold. If Elizabeth got hold of *Rifle* magazine, published monthly not far away in Boston, she could read what other women were up to with guns. A letter to the editor of *Rifle* stated, "We also have a day set aside for the ladies' shoot, as we have a 'Ladies Rifle Club,' which is an auxiliary to Capital Rifle Club," a shooting club secretary penned. Within two years of publishing the letter, *Rifle* did make the bold step of heading a front-page article with the words "Ladies' Day at the Rifle Range": "It is no uncommon sight to see ladies at the rifle range, and that many of them are becoming capital shots." The skill of some, the story went on, is "surprising" and "they often surpass the efforts of some of the sterner sex. Ladies are rapidly becoming interested in rifle and pistol shooting."[9]

Adolph returned to New Haven, to the Elizabeth who had his heart, and in January 1903 they were married. Adolph was directed by Winchester to travel, to represent the gunmaker and provide hands-on expertise to the customer that could be found in no other way. He was able and trusted, so when thirty-three-year-old Adolph planned to set up camp back in San Antonio, twenty-year-old Elizabeth went. She always had lived in New Haven, and San Antonio was not like New Haven. With Adolph getting out on the road so much, they would keep a residence with his mother and younger sister Clara just east of downtown and blocks from the Alamo on Starr Street.[10] Her in-laws greeted her warmly and appeared to like her.[11] She started referring to her husband as "Daddy." And she wanted no part of being away from Daddy, him off giving exhibitions and her staying at home. So she wanted to know: Could he teach her to shoot?

When she voiced her intentions to others, her family included, she was greeted with dropped jaws, no matter what was going on at places like the Capital Gun Club and the reassurances offered in the pages of *Rifle*.

"I have been asked many times how I became interested in trapshooting," Elizabeth said. "The answer is very simple. My husband is a shooter, and I concluded that I would like to do the same things he did." She did, despite the snide comments and slanted gawks from people who thought women should be squeezing a wash rag, not a trigger. "I [am] among the few women who [take] kindly to firearms. [I am] looked upon as a freak."[12]

Really? But Adolph figured, why not? "It sure pleased me when she took an interest in my shooting," he said. "Most women are scared of guns."[13]

"Nine out of every ten Americans are good shots. The knack is born in them; . . . a rifle comes into the hands of an American as handily as does the spear into the clutches of a Zulu. A man who is a good average shot from his own instruction and natural adaptability can become a skillful marksman if he will apply himself to a few simple rules that I have found advantageous in my work."[14]

These were the words that Adolph used to start instruction to the hundreds of men hopeful to become expert in shooting. But now he would start the shooting lessons for Elizabeth Toepperwein. Adolph was ready to take his "Lizzie" to the shooting range. What he found when they got out there didn't surprise him.

She was awkward. She lacked poise with a loaded firearm in the grasp of her palms and fingers. She was nervous. She evidently was paying no attention to where she put her feet to help her position her body, and ultimately her aim, comfortably toward the target.[15]

Lizzie admitted that she shared with most women a "natural horror of firearms," and she was "too timid to try simply because [I] have never been encouraged in that line," she said.[16] She was hesitant, and it was showing up in her first few uneasy pulls of the trigger. It's easy to let the bullet get away from you.

But she found a simple key early on in her shooting. "The first important thing for the beginner is to have a gun of the proper fit," she said, which was in full agreement with her husband when Adolph said, "Get a good gun, and stick to it." After time, Lizzie articulated it quite well: "The mistake often made by the novice is to try some gun, which, as a rule, is not suited to his particular makeup. If a lady, the borrowed gun is almost certain to be too long in the stock and as a rule too heavy; the result is that it is held in an awkward manner, the recoil received by the shot frightens the shooter, and she loses her enthusiasm then and there. Have someone 'fit' you with the proper gun [and] teach you the way to stand and hold."[17]

Lizzie was lucky. Her "Daddy" had access to the complete line of a major manufacturer. And he placed a small .22 caliber in her arms. She picked up on Daddy's instruction on foot position. And then they mingled in the shooter's dialogue, his instruction in words and motions, and her response in rimfire and target puncture. These were moments that came to be as important to their marriage as those spoken in courtship.

"When beginning your marksmanship," Adolph began, "shoot at a bull's-eye say twenty feet away, firing just as soon as you get the sight immediately under the lower edge of the disk. Shoot the instant you get the sights in the proper position, always coming up in the object from the bottom, so you can see where you are holding the gun all the time."

Crack.

"In a few days you will find you can hit the mark ten times out of fifteen." Normally, he'd direct new shooters to fire at a bull's-eye measuring two inches. Once success was achieved, he recommended decreasing the size of the bull's-eye to a half inch and increasing the distance of the range.[18] He did something different with Lizzie. He had her shoot a bullet into a blank sheet of paper from about thirty feet. Daddy told Lizzie to fire ten shots as close as she could to that first bullet hole. Her first groupings made for a wide spread, but Daddy was encouraging.[19]

"You will be surprised to find that you can pump bullets into it at a surprising rate."[20]

Crack. Crack. Crack. Crack crack crack crackcrackcrack—and so with time her groupings around that first little bullet hole became smaller and smaller. It wasn't long before Adolph could walk over to the target area and place a buffalo nickel over it and cover all of the bullet holes from Lizzie's gun. It amazed him how quickly she was picking this up.[21]

"Learn to shoot with both eyes open. It will be difficult at first, but in a week or so you will find it the most reliable way to attain accuracy. You will see the advantage of this method by pointing your finger at an object, sighting over it with both eyes open. It will be evident that you can not only see the object itself, but all around as well. The effect is startling at first, but you will profit by it."[22]

Crack.

"Just as soon as you are able to hit stationary targets," Adolph mentioned, "[we'll] try flying objects."

She wanted to go forward, and Adolph obliged, for in Lizzie he found a woman who loved to shoot, and she relished the practice.[23] She was ready to try her hand at aerial targets.[24]

". . . get your aim just as they have risen to their fullest height and then begin to return to earth. Always hold under them and take a full sight. For flying targets coming across your aim, place your gun so that they will be obliged to come into the firing zone. Never follow an object you want to hit. Let it come to you in all cases."

Crack.

"I have found in all my shooting experience that the first sight is the best. It is only a matter of time before your finger will work in unison with your eye, and the moment your sights find the object your finger will press the trigger, automatically, so to speak."[25]

Crack-plink. Crack-plink.

It was an odd sort of sound. But it was the unmistakable sound of success. It got more distinct, more "plinkier." Adolph had started throwing large tin cans into the air for Lizzie to shoot. As she kept hitting them he switched to smaller ones.[26]

She keenly followed everything her Daddy had told her, working from the feet on the ground up to her hands on the guns. "I [have] discovered that there [are] so many interesting points to learn," Lizzie said. She was hooked, and she demanded more.[27]

"Throw up another one," she said in an excited voice, "and I'll plink it!"[28]

Adolph thought about that. Plinky. Plinky!

CHAPTER ELEVEN

A Sharpshooter and the Movie Stars

Tom Catches the Eye of Newt—and Others

As changes of scenery go, it could be much worse than to go to 9584 Wilshire Boulevard, Beverly Hills, California. Just a couple of streets over from Rodeo Drive, and with the Beverly Hilton Hotel a few blocks in the other direction, this looked a heck of a lot different from an intersection in Denver where Tom Frye with multiple back injuries was painfully pulled from a totaled vehicle. The block lettering upon the storefront at Wilshire read Kerr Sport Shop, and it had to be one of Tom's best stops on his sales route through his new territory as field representative in Southern California for Remington Arms Company. He'd be reporting to D. Lee Braun, his old colleague as a gunnery instructor during the war and friend at shooting stops through the West. Braun was a regional sales representative for Remington, and he was close friends and a shooting competitor with Alex Kerr, the man who opened his eponymously named sporting goods shop in Beverly Hills.

To open the doors at Kerr's, on occasion, would be to see Hollywood's elite engaged in outfitting their favorite pastimes. It was said that Gary Cooper, Bing Crosby, and Cary Grant were a few of the hallmark names from the movies who shopped at Kerr's. Cooper, it was claimed in a 1958 edition of *Preview* magazine, "visits Alex Kerr's sports shop, browses in the gun department, always hefts a pair of matched Purdy's and murmurs, 'Wish I could afford these.'"[1] Tom did more than just bump into Cooper at Kerr's.

Tom Frye presents Remington's breakthrough Nylon 66 .22 rifle to *High Noon* motion picture star Gary Cooper (right), circa 1960. Notice the .22 caliber bullet he tosses above his right hand. Collection of Dean Dunlap.

"He [is] a wonderful man, [and] he [is] a good shot and did his own shooting in the movies," Tom said of Cooper.[2]

Tom didn't need to assist Cooper's gun shooting on the set. But studios had employed exhibition shooters to fire from positions off-camera while the stars simultaneously were aiming at targets during action on-screen. In this manner James Stewart was seen shooting a rifle and "hitting" targets thrown into the air during Universal Pictures' filming of *Winchester '76* at its release in 1950, yet Winchester Repeating Arms Company exhibition shooter Herb Parsons was the one actually picking off those flying coins for Stewart.

So, when Tom got away from his sales route for Remington, he had occasion to head off to the movie lot. He appeared on the set of *Gunsmoke*, and he broke out a bolt-action rifle and placed it in the arms of actor James Arness. Wearing his Western vest and Marshall Dillon sheriff's badge, Arness was one of the few people who towered over Tom's height of some 6-foot-3.

The relatively new bachelor, Tom's thinned chest and shoulders weren't filling out his Remington shooting jacket like they had in Ohio. He wore a felt, medium-brimmed Stetson hat and looked to be trying to get Arness's hands just so on the rifle.[3]

It was reported that Tom was doing "considerable shooting for the movies and TV commercials" while in Los Angeles.[4] If he wasn't on the set with movie stars, he still found time to shoot with them. One popular spot for the high-profile shooters was Aqua Sierra Gun Club, up along the escarpments north of Los Angeles. Roy Rogers was said to own it, and he certainly spent plenty of time there aiming his gun at the trap-thrown targets.[5] Tom thought Rogers was the best of the gun-shooting Western-themed actors. "He's proficient with handguns, rifles, and shotguns," Tom said.

Life was becoming sweet out West. It apparently so suited the Frye thinking that much of Tom's family followed him. His younger brother Jim and his wife were living in Kalispell, Montana, and Tom visited them on occasion.[6] His mother made the move to Los Angeles County and brought her hats and millinery work with her. So did a sister, who was gifted with her hands and was working on paintings, illustrations, and other artwork.[7]

His family stuck with him, yet so did other things from the past. What happened in Denver, even the last few days of his marriage back in Ohio, kept a cloud over Tom. The girlfriend he had in Denver did not stick with him. Tom could get his mind off that back at work, though making his rounds while driving between the shooting ranges and gun shops took him longer than usual. He'd stop more frequently so he could get out of the car and stretch his back.[8] Tom already was reluctant to wear hearing aids to help with his shooter's hard-hearing.[9] He remained content to let a few words pass by and just say nothing in conversations among large groups if it meant he could keep the hearing aids at home. After the accident he was fitted for a back brace. It hugged his back, sunk down below his trousers. It was not the sort of thing a competitive shooter would enjoy wearing.

When he walked back into Kerr Sports Shop on Wilshire Boulevard, the back brace wasn't noticed. He was with the likes of Clark Gable, Gary Cooper, Roy Rogers, and Bing Crosby. The collection of people at Kerr's was attracted to what Tom Frye could do.

Bing Crosby became a giant in the entertainment industry when his version of Irving Berlin's "White Christmas" sold millions of copies starting in 1942 and led to a motion picture of the same name. Crosby won the Academy Award for best actor in 1944 for his role in *Going My Way*. By this time, Crosby started pointing his getaways from Hollywood toward Elko, Nevada. He was interested in purchasing ranches where he and his sons could dally alongside the hired hands at the ranch to know the value of hard work and the outdoors.[10] One of his neighbors around Elko County's North Fork Valley was putting a PX brand on the cattle that were raised at that collection of ranches.[11] It was Newt Crumley, the son of the man who emerged from the dusty saloons of the Nevada mineral rushes and bought the Commercial Hotel in downtown Elko.

Crosby started talking to Newt about buying some land, and the two struck a deal for multiple pieces of property. Crosby wrote a song about his experiences there, "Comin' to Elko," and he comically (and seriously) referred to the deal with Newt:

> And now comes the time when we were really put on the block.
> We met a high-class operator, a fella named Doby Doc.
> He told us of some ranches belonging to the Crumley clan.
> He said we'd get them for nothing, or at least that was his plan.
> But when our kids are ten and twenty, we will still be paying plenty.
> I'll be singing sweet little Annie while Newt's sitting on his fanny,
> counting up my dough.

The transaction was worth a reported $221,000.[12] But Crosby's lyric about Newt sitting on his fanny was a bit of playing around, for Colonel Crumley had a distinguished military career as a pilot, yet he also seemed a forward-thinking visionary out there on the desolate Nevada ranges. Newt was a risk-taking businessman who actually used the entertainment business to leverage his entrepreneurial success.

It came when the elder Crumley spent $70,000 to acquire the Commercial back in 1925.[13] Gambling was legalized in Nevada in 1931, but it was daunting for casino owners to get people with discretionary income to travel to middle-of-nowhere Elko during the Great Depression. Up-and-comer Newt had an airman's spirit, and he wasn't about to let a Depression keep him or the Commercial Hotel down. His idea to bring in business was so simple, so almost ready-made, it was hilarious. The train tracks from the old Transcontinental Railroad's line made by the Central Pacific route were spiked through the ground just a few blocks from the Commercial. Performers in the entertainment industry, still hoppin' even in the Great Depression, could make an overland route between their prime money-making gigs—the burgeoning film business of Hollywood and the respected theaters along Broadway. How could Newt not hear the talk caused when some movie star or big-band leader was spotted at the train station? The light bulb in his head shined, and it illuminated a dark gap in the casino business. No one, not even Las Vegas, was bringing in big-name entertainment acts as a way to attract people who normally wouldn't come in to gamble.

But this light going off in Newt's head would ring up a huge bill. Newt took the math to his father. That $70,000 that the family spent to buy the Commercial? What would it look like to add another chunk of change to get someone to come in for a week and entertain? If Newt were able to land a headliner like "King of Jazz" Paul Whiteman for an extended run, it would go into a five-figure contract. Whiteman, just three years earlier, was commanding one-nighters for as much as $5,000,[14] and he soon would be a new co-star on the long-running Tuesday night NBC Radio show hosted by George Burns and Gracie Allen in Los Angeles. A new lounge would have to be built at the Commercial to do it right, and that would cost some money too. But the Crumleys would not charge admission. The hope was that the people who flocked in for a good show would drop a few coins in the casino.

Newt announced the engagement to have Whiteman appear late in 1941,[15] but the lounge at the Commercial was ready to go before then. Ted Lewis was somewhat in the same line musically. Lewis once had employed a clarinetist named Benny Goodman, and when he became the "King of Swing" in the '30s Goodman pumped Lewis as his influence.[16] So the deal was cut: Lewis and band would get paid $12,000 for a one-week engagement. Included in the week, at Newt's insistence, was one performance in front of Elko's senior citizens' community. On April 26, 1941, a spotlight cut through the darkened lounge at the Commercial to reveal bandleader Ted Lewis singing and dancing to "Me and My Shadow." The locals were agog. "We've never seen anything like that here in Elko," resident Morris Gallagher said after he attended opening night.[17] It was happening. In Elko.

The locals weren't the only ones caught by the action. Many cars were coming in on US Hwy 40. With the news out that Whiteman's orchestra would follow Lewis at the suddenly hopping Commercial, the nearby Stockman's Hotel started bringing in its own acts in order to keep up.[18] Visitors rolled in from places like Boise (191 miles away) and Salt Lake City (204 miles). And that's when this gamble became a shrewd, watershed business move. Those people weren't going to drive all the way to Elko and be satisfied to hear a musical act. They gambled while they were there. And they weren't the only ones.

"[The performers] might end up owing Newt before they left because they gamble," said Diz Pucinelli, who kept the accounting books for the Crumley family.[19]

The son figured out a new way to get people to his dad's card tables at the Commercial with an après betting buzz to complement its casino. They weren't doing this in Vegas. They weren't doing it in Reno. They would. The Commercial was on the map. It was more than a dot next to the rail line. Soon, Jimmy and Tommy Dorsey, Sophie Tucker, Chico Marx, Tennessee Ernie Ford, Spike Jones, Xavier Cugat—with a Mexican Chihuahua in tow—and a well-mannered young bandleader by the name of Lawrence Welk played there.

By 1948, Crosby was performing in Elko. He had convinced movie executives to premiere the motion picture *Here Comes the Groom* in Elko's downtown, and it generated about $10,000 to build a local hospital. CBS Radio had a live national broadcast, and afterward Crosby brought in his friend Roy Rogers for more fundraising.[20] His friendship with Roy Rogers also included a deep appreciation for guns, for Rogers was the owner of the Aqua Sierra Gun Club in the Los Angeles County bedroom community of Chatsworth, California.

A professional shooter employed by Remington Arms Company was looking at owning a house in Chatsworth by 1959. He had a sales territory for Remington that covered Southern California, and he often was a featured sharpshooter at the Kern County Fish and Game Protective Association Barbeque and Field Day in Bakersfield.[21] Newt still had friends out there from his days as base commander at Minter Air Field.[22] Newt, the shooting enthusiast that he was, and being the type of guy who was driven to do anything the best he could, wanted to see how the pros shot. So he watched as the shooter pulled oranges and other fruits off that green Remington Arms tablecloth and threw them into the air to shoot. This guy never misses, Newt thought.

Tom showed back up at the Remington home office at Bridgeport, Connecticut, for meetings with other field reps, and they wondered sometimes if his mind was wandering. It turned out, however, Tom wasn't wearing his hearing aids and always pegged a young rep to sit next to him and always answer when Tom leaned over and whispered, "What was that he just said?"[23]

Tom didn't have everything. But he did have a lot. He had looks. Talent. And to hear the talk of his fellow field reps at Remington, he had a way with women. And the word going around among the field reps meeting in Bridgeport was that Tom was seriously dating a very attractive young woman who was part of a prominent family. Her name was Carolyn Kerr, and everyone steeped in the shooting business, particularly on the West Coast, knew the family. Her father was Alex Kerr, one of the most talented skeet shooters the sport knew and the man who owned the Kerr Sports Shop, smack dab in the ritziest part of Tom's sales area, on Wilshire Boulevard in Beverly Hills. Robert Stack, the actor and accomplished skeet shooter, counted Kerr as a close friend and said Kerr's was the "fanciest sporting goods store in Beverly Hills."[24] It was regarded as the "gun shop to the stars."[25] Kerr's had everything outdoors, from fishing to hunting and camping. It also did well with indoor sports—a bowling alley was downstairs, and there was a putting green on the roof.[26]

The Kerr family's money came from the famous fruit jar company that Carolyn's grandfather founded on the West Coast before 1905. With the handy two-piece metal lids and gaskets that sealed over a clear glass jar that had the Kerr's name embossed in cursive on the side, people could preserve their own fruits and vegetables at home. It was a lucrative business.

Carolyn didn't devote her interests to fruit jars. She wanted a family, and she thought she found the man to share it with when she saw handsome Tom Frye. They became engaged, and the couple acquired a house on Devonshire Road in Chatsworth in anticipation of getting married. Their family grew when Tom came back from work one day. "It's the cutest little poodle," Carolyn remarked happily upon seeing her new pet.[27]

Tom could have a bounce in his step for another reason as well. After twenty months where there were more operations and more traction, the doctors appeared to have it figured out. In February 1959 they operated on Tom and fused four vertebrae. Once he recuperated from the surgery it was clear that things were back in working order. He had no trouble walking. He could sleep through the night. And, though he had not lifted a gun for the previous year, he was back at it. He and Carolyn took a trip to Hawaii, rode through the bumpy, back-jarring backcountry in a jeep, and Tom shot a boar. It was such a prized trophy he had the thing mounted and brought back home. And in April he was back in Bakersfield performing at the Kern County Fish and Game Protective Association Barbeque and Field Day. He was pictured on the front page of the local newspaper, aiming a rifle straight forward through the wind. He shot well enough to impress most everyone, as the newspaper noted he "proved his right to national honors."[28]

He shot through the lion's share of his normal show. He pulled the oft-used trick of an exhibition shooter, firing through the hole of a washer. When people disputed the shot, claiming that anyone could fire toward a washer and say they made it through the hole, Tom covered the washer opening with tape and fired. The washer came back down with a hole through the tape covering the opening. He told the audience standing to the left of him to be on the lookout because he would toss a silver dollar straight into the air and shoot it in a way that would deflect the coin toward them. Once he did that, he promised people to the right he would do the same for them. He'd have more objects thrown into the air, but he shot with the sights on his gun covered and still fired a hit. He also drew the Indian head with .22 caliber bullets onto a metal sheet. It took him fifteen reloads, or about 250 to 275 bullets to finish the profile.[29]

The word was out that this was the guy who, when he served in the military as a gunnery instructor during World War II, had set an unofficial skeet record by hitting 1,134 targets consecutively during a single session of shooting. He was one of three men, the reports went, who had broken one hundred straight trap double targets on two occasions. And now, since his shooting was going well again, maybe he could get back out on the trap circuit and shoot registered targets, and maybe make another trip back to Ohio for the Grand American.

With Carolyn, with the last surgery, Tom's personal life was swinging back up. And something else was at work that would push his professional life back to the top of the sports shooting world. He'd soon get his hands on it.

CHAPTER TWELVE

A Working Mother with a Working Gun

Ad and Plinky Billed as the Wonderful Topperweins

Why not? Why not have Lizzie join up and shoot with Adolph as a team promoting Winchester products? At the rate she was picking up instruction and turning it into refined fancy shooting, Lizzie would be pulling off the same stunts her husband had in his repertoire from a stationary position.

"There is much amusement in shooting at oranges and beets and tomatoes in flight," Adolph advised the nascent, promising "[i]f a .22-calibre [*sic*] bullet strikes an orange in the center the fruit will completely vanish in a cloud of yellow spray, as will also the beet, showering crimson mist in mid-air. When one becomes expert on flying targets, objects as small as marbles and empty cartridge shells can be smashed with ease."[1]

They already had done this before, but now they invited people to watch. Adolph walked down range from Lizzie. He stuck a crayon from out of his hands. She shot it out of there. He placed chalk between his lips. She fired and clipped a white chunk right off. His mother and sister Clara watched and couldn't believe it—that Elizabeth could do it, and that Adolph was fool enough to let her try. But Adolph saw that now, a month into her training, she had a sure trigger underneath an unflinching grip.

Though there was a cute and appealing story behind Lizzie's path to her nickname of Plinky, there were obstacles to get her involved in mainstream shooting. What shooting competitions were taking entries from women?

Plinky Toepperwein was the first woman to win the Texas State Shoot in 1908, competing against men. In this photo from the Grand American Handicap, Plinky can be found as the only woman competitor to the left. Collection of Kenneth Toepperwein.

And where were the women promoting guns, or for that matter where were women in the crowds watching sporting events? When photographers took their pictures of the grandstands at baseball's first World Series in 1903 between Boston and Pittsburgh, the images showed plenty of top hats and suits, but no bonnets or long dresses. This doesn't even mention the restrictions on women voting, the right for females to cast a ballot not guaranteed until the 19th Amendment was passed in 1920.

It is true that Annie Oakley enjoyed the peak of her career before 1905, and she showed an audience in her breakthrough performances that a woman could handle a gun as well. But her main employer wasn't the manufacturer of a conservative commercial product. She was, for all practical matters, a circus performer.

There were other obstacles. Adolph was calling her Plinky, but there was another name she would go by in about nine months. Mom. Pregnancy was

Plinky Toepperwein struck a pose as a sturdy representative for the Deadshot Powder Company that was an ammunition concern and subsidiary of Winchester Repeating Arms Company. Plinky told everyone that some of the shooting pouches she used were given to her by W.F. "Buffalo Bill" Cody. Collection of Kenneth Toepperwein.

not going to allow Lizzie into the public eye. So, with the birth of Lawrence Clark Toepperwein on February 12, 1904,[2] Adolph had a family to support. If Winchester was assigning him to duties as a "missionary" in its sales force in the Southwest, he took the task and did the best with it.[3]

Adolph's job now was to push the advent of smokeless ammunition along with the complete line of Winchester firearms. In 1905 Winchester was on its way to ramping up production from its list of one hundred smokeless cartridge models (one hundred and seventy-five would be available about ten years later). And in 1895, Winchester reported an annual output of 67.5 million factory-loaded shot shells, which grew to 243.4 million made by 1907.[4] Smokeless powder was an improvement for the firearms industry, yet this new brew that could contain things like nitroglycerine and ether sometimes tipped to the volatile, so it was not without its design mishaps. Ad's sales route in 1904 included a stop in Lockhart, less than seventy-five miles from

San Antonio and not forty from Austin. It seemed that the Reverend J. M. Purcell of the First Presbyterian Church was looking for a gun and came out to Ed Masur's Hardware Store while Adolph was in town. Adolph laid on a thick sales pitch for the smokeless gunpowder, and he identified Rev. Purcell as someone who might change over to it.

"Look, man," he told the preacher, "no smoke when you use this new smokeless powder in a newly designed Winchester rifle. Your gun not only will have Mr. Masur's guarantee, but the Winchester Repeating Arms Company also will stand behind this new gun for use with this new smokeless powder. You will help bring on the 20th Century new age for firearms."

Rev. Purcell bought a case of smokeless cartridges that would fit into his new .30–30 he bought from the Winchester line that retailed out of Masur's. Out on his farm two and a half miles east of Lockhart, Rev. Purcell had nailed a tin can to a tree to stand some rudimentary target practice. The preacher deliberately placed the cartridge into the magazine, then advanced it into the chamber. When it fired it blew off an ear-splitting roar. That wasn't the only thing that split, and that's not to mention the tin can. It was forgotten it had ever been nailed up there, for the breach of the .30–30 barrel split long ways nine inches. It was such a quick domino reaction after that. The hammer kicked back against the safety, which was thrown back into the spectacles the preacher was wearing over his now-gashed face. Rev. Purcell was a true shepherd of the spirit who offers eternal life, for only a man of God, truly not fearful of worldly death, could manage to keep his wits to the point that he slowly lowered the peeled gun away from his bleeding face and managed to keep his son from running off like he'd seen the work of the devil. "That's not what it's supposed to do," the reverend told his son. Mr. Masur paid the preacher's doctor bill to touch up his face. He made a successful inquiry of Winchester's insurance, as well. Ad caught wind of the malfunction, and the next time he was in town he searched up the preacher and personally apologized.[5]

Lizzie was at home with Lawrence. But that wasn't all she did. Living with her sister-in-law Clara and mother-in-law Johanna, Lizzie spent time every day firing away at targets and practicing her shooting.[6]

Adolph still was consumed with the dominant thoughts of his own childhood, those words from his dying father that if a job was to be done, it could always be done better, and his boast to his cousin Rudy that he would be a better shot than Doc Carver one day. So Adolph pressed those ideas, and he fit in some time to take a few cracks at some endurance performing. Just a year after his first assignment in Buffalo at the 1901 Pan American Exposition, Adolph was believed to have set a world's record shooting clay targets, breaking 986 of 1,000 thrown from traps while firing his .22 caliber on September 23, 1902.[7] Winchester ran an advertisement detailing Adolph's remarkable performance, making sure everyone knew he did it with the latest in Winchester greaseless ammunition.[8] "I am glad that you are pleased with my shooting," Adolph said, "but it was only the result of using the best ammunition I assure you." In November of the following year newspapers credited him with breaking 1,500 targets thrown into the air without a miss. The next month he got credit for shooting 5,000 targets tossed into the air twenty-five feet from him. They measured 1 ¾ inches, and he stood up there in a public park and had a go at it for about six and a half hours (332 minutes) without taking a break. By the time he was done he sniped 4,954 of the 5,000 objects, loading his own weapon. That meant he was firing off between twelve and thirteen shots per minute. True to his words, Adolph would fire at smaller objects like walnuts and marbles,[9] showing indeed they "can be smashed with ease."

Adolph's next big assignment was the Louisiana Purchase Exposition. It was becoming known as the St. Louis World's Fair, and Adolph and Lizzie were scheduled to leave San Antonio for St. Louis on the night of April 13, 1904, to be in charge of the Winchester display.[10] Lawrence, just three months old, would be able to stay with his aunt and grandmother.

The press credited Adolph with another record when he lined up with his rifle twenty-five feet away from a target tosser and hit 3,507 consecutive objects out of the air. They were 2 ¼ inch composition discs, and it took him four hours and ten minutes, or about fourteen shots per minute. The crowd watching Adolph shoot went into the hundreds.[11] They got a chance to see him shoot one of his Indian profiles and other characters that required 350 rounds done in twelve or so minutes (close to thirty shots per minute, or one every two seconds on average) from twenty-five feet away.[12]

Adolph's salary covered Lizzie's expenses. By the end of the Fair, she showed her progress was coming at warp speed. She endeavored to hit 1,000 clay discs from twenty-five feet, but Adolph took one of the new breakthrough small-bore rifles Winchester had recently introduced, the semiautomatic Model 1903 in .22 caliber, and had her use that one rather than get clobbered by the kick of the shotgun. It was an easy gun to use, the first semi-automatic rifle Winchester had marketed.[13] She proved accurate with the rifle, hitting 967 out of the 1,000 disks and finishing the job in ninety minutes (about eleven shots per minute).[14]

It was a stunning debut, a landmark moment, with as much riding on a woman's handling of the gun since the day in 1885 when Annie Oakley performed for the first time for Buffalo Bill's Wild West in front of 17,000 in Louisville, Kentucky.[15] In fact, this newcomer had outperformed Annie. Lizzie's 967 hits topped Annie's 943 of 1,000 hits on glass balls (usually sized similarly to the clay discs) when Annie switched once from her shotgun to the .22 caliber.[16]

But this was just a start. Lizzie was just twenty-one. It was time to shake up the establishment.

Sea Girt was a sports landmark, the first pang of frustration for New York fans who would continue to see popular events leave their aging fields, stadiums, and arenas for newer ones that the state of New Jersey would build across the Hudson. With the New York state government bickering with the National Rifle Association over the use of the Creedmoor range, the New Jersey State Rifle Association by 1890 had built an expansive shooting range on 148 acres along the Jersey Shore. Its target area was backed up by sand dunes that would break here and there and offer a view of the blue Atlantic. By 1892 the most important shooting matches began to move there.[17]

Sea Girt also was the grounds for the competition that awarded a marksmanship medal for the military-issue rifle. The standard gun was the Krag-Jorgenson. The hard-kicking models could weigh as much as nine pounds, and the .30 caliber was adopted by the US military in 1892.[18] It could easily handle the distances for the military competitions of anywhere from two hundred to five hundred yards. So on September 5, 1906, as it happened every year, a long line of men arranged in the queue to take their shot with the Krag to score the fifty points needed for certification. Someone saw a skirt in that line a ways back, but as the line moved along, the unthinkable was becoming apparent. A woman was in line and thinking she could compete with the men.

The organizers of the event, all men, huddled. Someone had been told that "Eyebrows were arched, cigars were chewed, and officials drew together in heated consultation."[19] A reporter covering the event for a Philadelphia newspaper saw what was going on. "This position of the young woman is just now puzzling the executive officers of the National Rifle Association, for in the past none but men had been so honored. Even the representatives of the United States government are in a quandary."[20]

Adolph was there; he had participated in a rapid-fire contest where he drilled fifty shots within a minute at a target three hundred yards downrange. With Adolph hovering around, officials contemplated the wording of their rules. The NRA's executive committee in 1903 had passed resolutions about training "young men." But there was no language that barred women. In fact, the directive stated that the association sought to enable "citizens not connected with any military establishment an opportunity to qualify" for the Marksmen's Medal. They tried, but the hard-liners in the NRA establishment could not get a consensus to give the woman the boot.

Lizzie took the nine-pound Krag. Her long dress covered her legs, yet her hair flowed Annie Oakley–style and was uncontained by a sporty creased hat with medium brim. She got to work. She kneeled, as was the requirement at two hundred yards, and fired. The distances would progress to five hundred yards. At the required prone-forward position, she fired. She clipped away, working quickly with the required five shots at each position while some of the men she competed against did something completely unexpected: They cheered her on. A lot of them had failed to qualify in the hot weather. Not Lizzie. She scored a 61.[21]

People were eager to talk to her, including the Philadelphia reporter who now had a huge story on his hands: "One of the surprises . . . is a clear-eyed, handsome young woman who, four years ago, had never handled a gun," the story in the *North American* read. "[G]oing above the average requirement, she was entitled to enrollment." She was asked how she came about such shooting, especially with the big Krag-Jorgenson. "[U]ntil four years ago," she answered, "[I] was like every other woman—mortally afraid of firearms." For her work at Sea Girt, she would be awarded the Marksman's Medal.[22]

This was an America that had slapped around the land, dominated it, and made the fierce finally succumb. Now, from the 1880s onward, the country wanted to find a few playthings. And the things the country fought with and killed with now had become the toys. Guns. Why not a few tricks? The ramrod that once was used manually to stuff the ammo load down the throat of a musket now had been imaginatively pretzeled into a lever that could be clicked and clacked along to make that ammo repeat and ready to fire in a second.

Women had been joining in on the entertainment. There was May Lillie, wife of Gordon Lillie, who was billed as a sharpshooter for her husband's Pawnee Bill's Great Wild West Show in 1887. The show deemed her "the greatest Lady Horseback Rifle-shot of the World" until 1889. There was Annie Oakley and her rival Lillian Smith, proving a chronicler's contention that while women weren't noticeably attending baseball games in the early 1900s, "exhibition shooting was a wildly popular sport and maybe the first sport that was open to women on equal terms with men."[23]

And now Elizabeth Servaty—Lizzie Toepperwein—stepped out into the shooting world, as Mrs. Adolph Toepperwein according to the popular press. It appears the press only was hung up by the formality of the day, because they had no restrictions in reporting her ability, though that, too, took time. She was listed in the results as a 39th-place finisher in the otherwise all-men's field at the 1905 Texas State Shoot in Waco. No other mention was made.[24] Just three months later, when she finished second in events on consecutive days at the Reunion Shoot near Mexia, Texas, against some familiar foes from the Texas State Shoot, she made the headline: "Mrs. Toepperwein's Great Shooting":

> The main feature was in the daily exhibition, of Mr. and Mrs. Toepperwein, of the finest rifle shooting in the world. Mr. Toepperwein had trouble in getting the enormous crowds back in order to give his exhibitions. Mrs. Toepperwein is unquestionably the greatest lady shot with a shotgun.[25]

Winchester started taking the first steps to accepting her. She completed a tour of the South firing as a Winchester exhibition team with her husband and accomplished trapshooter J. Mowell Hawkins in the fall of 1906. As the calendar flipped to 1907 and a Winchester tour hit twenty-eight towns in thirty-eight days during February and March, Lizzie was credited with hitting 2,529 out of 2,645 targets from the traps, a .956 percentage, during that tour.[26] She did that on the same days she performed with Adolph, and it was a grueling schedule. When she later in the year finished third in the Lock Haven, Pennsylvania, Gun Club Target Tournament behind Hawkins at 347 hit from 380, a reporter remarked, "[s]he has had a strenuous trip through the East and traveled all night to get to the shoot, and her presence was highly appreciated."[27]

Winchester, through its subsidiary American Powder Mills, placed an ad in the May 1907 issue of *Outdoor Life*, stating: "Mrs. Ad Topperwein, who is considered the greatest woman shot in the world, uses Dead Shot exclusively, for the maximum results it always gives."[28]

The couple that San Antonio knew as Mr. and Mrs. Toepperwein was on a historic threshold. Starting right around 1901, rifle companies were stepping up efforts to get their guns in the hands of someone talented enough to use them and make the guns look good. Frank Butler, the husband-manager of Annie Oakley, had been hired by Union Metallic Cartridge Company to travel with a team of other shooters and demonstrate the ammunition. It was product placement, and the Winchester product was being placed by The Wonderful Topperweins. Lapel buttons with both of the performers—Winchester was referring to him as Ad and her as Mrs. Topperwein—were produced and handed out at their shooting demonstrations. Posters were hung at stops on the tour in the days leading up to their appearances.

The trip to see the exhibition shooter was a chance to arrest and impress the senses—to have feel, sight, audio, smell, and taste, even, forcibly impressed upon. Its match would only come years later in the way of IMAX, Pixar, and the likes of high-tech movies. The squeeze of the ignition process in the gun indeed triggered a flood through the senses. There wasn't just the sound of the gunpowder at work; there was the feel of the blast clapping against the skin. There was the sight of the target exploding, the sound of a slug's force wave through it, the smell of a navel orange after it exploded at the point of a fired bullet.

This was one of those rare, and maybe the only, times in the entertainment of the day when an organic process was at work: And often came a message, and from Ad Toepperwein it was a simple one. "You don't need custom-built ammunition or firearms to accomplish the same sort of feats. All you have to do is go to any country store, buy what they have, and go practice."

Empowered by the success with his wife, Ad turned to his sister Clara and taught her to shoot. Clara showed up to compete at the Texas State Shoot in July 1908 overlooking the banks of the Colorado River at the Austin Gun Club.[29] Each competitor was to shoot at more than one hundred and fifty targets a day with the shotgun. Lizzie had a strong second day in the competition, missing only seven of the one hundred and seventy-five targets presented, including eighty-six straight when the handicap slid back to twenty yards. At the end of the three-day shoot, it was reported that "For the first time in the history of this state the highest championship honors fell to a woman, when Mrs. Ad. Topperwein of San Antonio, Texas, the famous Dead Shot expert, won the high professional average for the three days with 461 out of 490. The remarkable score gave Mrs. Topperwein the greatest score of the tournament as well, regardless of class."[30]

The thirst for shooting competition in Texas warmed up more with the creation of the Sunny South Handicap at Houston in February 1909. It was a demanding competition, and when Forest McNeir (an eventual member of the US shooting team at the 1920 Olympics) fired at two hundred targets each of the first four days, "My gun was kicking me so bad the last day I shot that when I got home I had to get in the bath tub to soak off my bloody undershirt," McNeir said. "I didn't shoot the last two days." A man couldn't, but Plinky did. In the final, she hit ninety-six from her one hundred to win.[31]

The men were appreciative enough that they adorned Plinky with some of their own adornment—gold, brass, diamond medals, rings, and stick pins. And when she made it to the Prince Theater to pick up her official prize—$100 in gold that was made into five $20 pieces attached to black silk—the men started laughing.

"She looks like a walking jewelry store," McNeir said, before noticing that Plinky was feeling a bit out of place. When she gave a hard look at Ad, McNeir listened in. "She told Top if he didn't quit laughing at her she would split his mustache with the toe of her boot."[32]

The recognition had her beaming at ensuing exhibition shoots. When she and Adolph appeared for Winchester at the summer resort area of White Fish Bay on Michigan's Upper Peninsula along Lake Superior in 1909, she was referred to by some as "Plinky." People thought she was about twenty-four years of age (she was twenty-six). It was an incredible setting, for they were perched at the end of a steep bank overlooking the shore, which made the glass waters of Superior as the backdrop for their targets.

Plinky's slow pace to start gained speed as the show progressed. She slipped a .32 Smith & Wesson revolver into her palm and started shooting at clay pigeons attached to a pole. It first came in a normal position, then she pulled out the mirror and shot from over her shoulder. Ad grabbed sticks that had potatoes jabbed onto them. She clipped those with a .22 repeater. Ad grabbed a clay disk, and Plinky started chipping away at it until she fired one final shot that crumbled the disk out of Ad's hands. So Ad pulled out a deck of cards and held a card by the corner and stretched it out at arm's length. She cut a series of heart spots out of the card with her bullets. He flicked the thin edge toward her, and Plinky hit it. Then he picked another couple of cards and somehow struck them together at right angles, forming a cross. She laid a bullet in there where the cards met. This all was done between ten and fifteen paces.

Both went to firing at aerial targets, hitting some of them multiple times before they hit the ground. Plinky put her .22 caliber automatic on the ground and stepped back about eight paces. Ad fired eggs into the air just about as high as he could throw from fifteen paces, and Plinky raced over to pull the gun up and fire off shots to hit them all—two at first, then three, four—before they hit the ground. By this time the action got so fast-paced spectators weren't sure how many Plinky got off. "If I am not mistaken," one observer noted after leaving the show, "she scored five eggs in total—a sensational score."

Spectators were allowed to inspect—even touch—the arms and ammo that were displayed on a table, but to dispel any doubts Plinky put the stuff to the real test. Ad tossed a little tin can up into the air, and Plinky made it ring out with rifle shot between six to ten times before it crimpled down to the ground. She did it with repeating rifles bored from .22 upward.

It was an exhibition with stunts "so varied I can hardly remember all of them," one onlooker said. "Mr. Topperwein seemed to have fired with more refined accuracy, if I may say so." His use of the lever action "was, in the proper sense of the word, wonderful." He put a piece of brick onto his gun butt and sent the brick skyward. He quickly got the gun into shooting position and rattled the lever action before he fired a direct hit onto the brick and turned the fragments into powder. He clutched a piece of coal with his left hand and suspended a rifle on the index finger of his right. He started spinning the gun and fired the coal upward with his hand. He grabbed the spinning weapon and cocked it with the lever before hitting the falling chunk into two pieces, and those pieces into two more pieces each, clacking the lever between shots. Each stunt was repeated several times, so the people left commenting as to the integrity of the shots: "There is no doubt."

It didn't all come off without a flaw. It took him four tries to shoot the bullet out of a cartridge that he had thrown into the air. He made sure of the next target when he switched to a .35 caliber to fire upon a tomato can he threw into the air. The bullet tore the can right open and spilled a red gush against that blue canvas of distant, deep Great Lakes water.[33]

At Baltimore, a writer dedicated his write-up almost entirely to Ad. First, Ad took a Russian model .44 revolver and measured off a dozen paces, turned his back, looked between his legs, and shot a clay target that was sitting on a stake. J. Mowell Hawkins held him by the legs so Ad could stay balanced on his own head. Looking through a mirror he shot another stationary target. He sat between two targets that were forty feet apart, crossed his arms and hit both targets on each stake while firing simultaneously. Almost as quickly as Hawkins got other targets airborne, Ad clipped them. He hit two-inch targets so early in their ascent that he could strike them three times before they hit the ground. Ad threw two walnuts into the air, and the reporter wrote Ad "cracked them with bullets faster than they could be cracked with nut crackers or hammers." A boy's small baseball bat was thrown high into the air, and Ad hit it four times, "sending it bobbing in the air each time he struck it." Then someone from the audience was asked to hold a potato while Ad put a few shots into it, so J.H. Moxley of the Prospect Shooting Association volunteered. Ad laid on his stomach in a position facing away from the potato—and the man holding it—then shot away at the potato while aiming with the looking glass. Ad complimented Mr. Moxley, who responded, "Why I'd let that man shave me with a pistol." A sheet of tin was placed against a board. The tin was unmarked, until Ad walked back fifteen paces and started firing with a .22 automatic. "Bullet holes about a quarter of an inch apart appeared rapidly in the tin, and faster and more accurately than most men on the ground could have drawn it with a pencil, the head of an Indian was depicted, feather, plumes and all." He switched over to a pump shotgun and ejected a shell, pumped another one into the chamber and used it to fire the ejected shell out of the sky. He threw an egg into the air, ran fifteen feet to pick up a gun and fired it to break the egg in the air. "In action," the reporter wrote, "he was quick and physically wiry, but was never nervous."[34]

The Wonderful Topperweins act quickly took on the status of standout. The pundits could find no reason to believe they were being hoodwinked.

"The Topperwein couple did not use any shooting tricks," one European historian noted. "Theirs was legitimate shooting art."[35]

It was what Ad had wanted to hear. He wanted to hit more targets than anyone else, and he wanted to do it in a way that no one could doubt. And what more could he ask than to have his wife stand beside him and become as respected as he was, to prove that good shooting could be taught to anyone?

The first trapshooting club for women was established in 1913 by Harriett D. Hammond in Wilmington, Delaware. It was a women's group that had access one afternoon a week to the range used by the Du Pont Trapshooting Club.[36] Jeannie P. Hurst was one of a number of women quoted in a pamphlet published by E.I. Du Pont de Nemours Powder Company, and what she had to say clearly indicates that women were following the career of Plinky: "The quality of Mrs. Topperwein (the champion woman shot of the world), that captivated and charmed us all was not so much her wonderful shooting as her wholesome and unaffected womanliness."[37]

Well, sometimes. Pranks from the "boys club" that always surrounded her at shooting competitions could get old. One of her fellow trapshooters said he wanted to take a picture of her sitting between two other men competitors. Blinded by the sun, Plinky could not see that the camera instead was a box spring-loaded with a toy snake. Instead of opening a shutter, the click of the button sent all nine feet of the fake reptile into Plinky's lap. She fell backwards and tumbled down an embankment. "You never did see so many skirts upside down," trapshooter Forest McNeir said. "When she got up it looked like a half-peeled banana. Everybody enjoyed it except for Mrs. Top. What she said . . . wouldn't do to print."[38]

Winchester guns were selling at great levels, from about 75,000 annually in 1890 to 275,000 and heading upward by 1906. And the office back in New Haven responded by pushing the promotion of its prized shooting team even more with those buttons and posters. People saw them and talked about them:

"The button is an inch across and bears a photograph of the two," a collector noted. "She is a bluff and bulky-looking individual in a white shirt and a black tie. She has a large mouth and dark hair. He is standing next to her, in a dark suit. He has a thick mustache, and looks to be the passive one of the pair. Both wear large-brimmed hats, his blocked in the "trooper" fashion. The button reads 'The Wonderful Topperweins. Who always shoot WINCHESTER guns and cartridges.'"[39]

CHAPTER THIRTEEN

The Man with the Plastic Gun

It's the Weapon of Choice for Tom

Gary Cooper looked at the new gun with a raised eyebrow. Nylon 66. Wasn't that what women were wearing on their legs? This gun was made almost completely of structural nylon, Zytel, Tom Frye could tell him. It was the same material that was being used on military missiles.

Cooper, known for playing the no-bull lawman from the movies like his Oscar-winning role in *High Noon* from seven years earlier, was giving the Nylon 66 a good once over while Tom held it in his hands as they stood inside a lamp-lit exhibit hall. While others interested in the exchange looked on, Cooper stuck out his right hand and grabbed the receiver of the rifle, right where Remington covered the man-made, phony wood, with a steel plate situated above the plastic trigger guard. Tom wore the Remington shooting jacket and had the short hair, but wavy locks, of his youth. He stood in a classic pose of a firearms demonstrator and held the rifle at chest level with his left arm and explained the finer points of this .22 caliber. With his right hand he playfully tossed the long-rifle bullet slightly into the air. Cooper seemed intently interested. With one hand already on the gun, a catalog and designer eye-frames bunched in the other, he looked, glaringly almost, at the trigger apparatus. Dark-haired, neatly combed, and tanned, he was fashionable and definitely had the means and taste to dress appealingly. Tom the firearms demonstrator could share the wares according to the company line and from the intimate knowledge he possessed from years of experience

In the summer of 1958, Tom Frye appeared on the set of *Gunsmoke* where he gave hands-on instruction to James Arness (left) and Dennis Weaver. Another picture including Frye and Arness appeared on the December 1958 cover of *Trap & Field* magazine. Collection of Dean Dunlap and Luke Dunlap.

handling weapons, but Cooper had the look of someone who would only be satisfied if he figured out the display himself. He wore a button-down short-sleeve sport shirt with a dominant white background vertically lined with thick stripes of a darker color. A belt wrapped his thin waist, and below stretched fine light-colored slacks. An expensive-looking watch adorned his left wrist.[1]

Cooper put a grim look to this gun because that's what it required from any traditionalist in 1959. When the hunter saw a buddy with it and standing maybe twenty paces off to the side, the gun did not quite have the brilliant wood-finish gleam of a brand-new gun, like this one supposedly was. Yet, draw closer, and it didn't have either that warm dull appearance of a trusted gun that had been out afield countless times with the hunter and brought home cherished stories along with the kill. Made to resemble wood grain, it just had a strange, different look to it. It was curious, racked up there with the hunter's other arms. A reach for it to lift it away and sight it was irresistible, but the resultant grab brought another rush of sensations totally unexpected to the warm feel of shooting. It hardly weighed anything compared to the other arms logged in the gun cabinet.

Most of those guns came crafted from the workbench. But the one in Gary Cooper's hands right now came from a lab. This was the advance of business and applied science, the progression of a French immigrant family from ammunition maker to chemical-manufacturing goliath. This was Du Pont, and guns got in the way when the corporation bought controlling interest (a fifty-six percent stake) in Remington Arms Company in 1934.[2]

There were some obvious synergies between the companies, but others needed to be investigated. That meant Remington would have to push into the goings-on of Purity Hall, a Du Pont lab where a team of industrial chemists had a history of cooking up some inventive polymers. Clearly, even before Remington was acquired, Du Pont management had an eye for diversification.

Purity Hall was becoming a legendary place.[3] It was the company's research lab, and the chemicals and groundbreaking substances oozing from it memorably were mentioned in pop culture. It came, comically and succinctly, in the 1967 motion picture *The Graduate* when Dustin Hoffman's youthful character named Benjamin Braddock was given advice for his future: "Plastics."

This industry found great commercial impact upon the first formations of nylon. Du Pont had to construct two new plants to keep up with the demand when nylon was crafted into women's stockings. The company found other uses for the stuff during World War II, notably parachutes, but when the post war boom came, the door opened further for the uses of nylon.

Over time, the executives at Remington were ready to step into the breach. They inquired of Purity Hall (by now known as Du Pont Polychemicals Department) to produce a gun body—the stock, receiver and forearm—that could be made with a substance with improved durability and strength over the traditional wooden models. Yet all this newfangling could not warp from the basics of the gun: it had to be dependable and accurate. The work of transforming plastic into a firearm was easy enough when it started with the low-kick .22 caliber. Four months after Du Pont's lab received the specs for the gun, the lead firearm designers Wayne Leek and Charles Morse were presented with a substance called Zytel Nylon 101. It was a bar of not-yet-meshed nylon, and Leek and Morse had it hollowed and sculpted and fashioned with the normal steel barrel and plates. A company memo dated in

July 1955 claimed it was a successful prototype firearm. It fired almost flawlessly (a .005 malfunction rate from 75,000 test shots, or 375 jams or other problems), and over the next two years the fabricators found a way to bond together two molded pieces into one gun rather than continue to use the shaved nylon bar.

In January 1958, Tom Frye received two models of this gun in a shipment from Remington. All the company's field reps got a pair of guns and instructions to test them. The rifles were odd, right from the start. First, one of the guns was green. The other had a walnut color, but it sure didn't feel like wood. It was about a pound lighter than any .22 Tom had cradled in those long arms of his—a four-and-a-half-pound rifle.[4]

Once they got over the shock of seeing a gun built in this manner, they read the instructions from the company: Fire at least one thousand rounds through each gun, find a way to put the guns under some strain, then compile the results with comments and ship the guns back for further examination at the home office in thirty days. The commentary by a field rep named Delbert Conner was outstanding, tremendously in depth. His report to designer Leek was dated February 23, 1958, and ran four pages. "My first impression of these guns," the report commenced, "was that they were just toys—or maybe air rifles for Buck Rogers. I doubt that the color or material will make much difference on the first showings. The public will refer to them as plastic."[5]

But Conner didn't blow off these guns as gimmicks. He did as the company instructed and got in his two thousand shots, sometimes using different makes of ammunition. Among those were about one hundred shots that came after he piloted his boat to the middle of a lake and weighed anchor with the fully loaded rifle, a string attached to the plastic trigger guard. He pulled it back in, drained it, and fired away. He gave the guns a totally different sensation one day when a cold front blew through and allowed him to fire into the blowing sand. If the trip toward the bottom of the lake wasn't enough, Conner ran over it with his station wagon. Finally, he tossed it from some ways up over the ground, imparting a crash landing onto a concrete sidewalk. That finally put a crack in the stock, but it kept firing every time he pulled the trigger, just as well as it did when he first pulled the new rifles from the box. Conner was sold. "Looks like a plastic toy—performance and accuracy unbelievable," Conner reported.

When it was time to return his rifles and his report to Ilion, New York,

Conner added a validating addendum for Leek and his designers: "I would surely like to have one back—charged to my sample account—if and when available."

Oh, they would be available, all right, and Conner wouldn't have to wait long. Less than a year later, Remington was assembling 4,450 rifles under the model name Nylon 66. Conner would be charged less than $50 to his account for one of those rifles by the time they hit the market in January 1959.

But the first impression Conner wrestled with haunted other gun buyers. "I haven't fired the thing," stated an outdoors writer for a Reno newspaper, "and I don't know whether I want to or not. This is made of the same stuff as lingerie and hosiery—nylon. After all, it comes in 'Mohawk Brown' and 'Seneca Green,' and it's doubtful if I could explain why I spent a day cheek-to-cheek to 'Seneca Green' nylon."[6]

Remington did its best to tie its efforts in with a military, man's world line of thinking. In several daily newspapers, this ad began appearing:

"This new 22 autoloader is years ahead of all other 22 rifles in the world. The same structural-nylon used in missiles and industrial machine parts has been used to create a beautiful, super-strong stock that reduces the gun's weight to four pounds. And because structural-nylon won't warp, the same barrel-bedding principle used on the world's most expensive target rifles is yours. The result is a rifle that hits targets with tremendous accuracy."

This gun would take some proving, something beyond Delbert Conner throwing it into a mudhole and fishing it back out and still firing off a few hundred rounds. It was so unconventional, breaking so much on the side of being Space Age, that it sure could use some gun expert to come along and stamp its legitimacy. Yes, there was the ease of use that Remington was pitching. To that point, the engineers at Remington found that with the self-lubricating properties found in the synthetic material, the Nylon 66 required little maintenance, even in the coldest of climates. But Remington could talk about "ordnance steel" all it wanted, and it still couldn't change what this gun really was. Plastic! It was a plastic gun. What a contradiction in terms.

Remington kept the advertising machine humming, seemingly confident the worth of the Nylon 66 would come out. Delbert Conner seemed to have proved its durability. And when people like Jack Heath got their hands on it, and Heath one day would work as a field rep for Remington, they found it to be entirely accurate. "The gun worked," Heath immediately noticed of a gun that initially struck him as unconventional. "And it's very accurate, even though I prefer the Remington 550 because it had a barrel that was screwed in, and the 66 had the barrel pinned and clamped to the stock."[7]

A sharpshooter in the league of Tom Frye could discern a gun that was off in its sighting. But the fact that it was so light lit up Tom's world with possibilities. He looked at the Nylon 66, which got its color from the swirling of pigments in the Zytel. Good things were swirling in Tom's life in the summer of '59. His back appeared to be repaired, his exhibitions in Bakersfield, where Col. Newt Crumley and friends kept tabs on shooting competitions, serving as proof of his health and fitness. He successfully shot with prominent movie stars and, like Gary Cooper, they were interested when he talked about guns. He had a girlfriend who said "yes" to his marriage proposal, and she was from a family of shooters and sporting guns enthusiasts.

Tom didn't file the sort of report with Remington on the Nylon 66 that Delbert Conner supplied. As wild and through the roof as that one was, it wasn't maverick like Tom Frye. From some corner of his mind Tom contemplated the unthinkable. Not since the days of the Winchester exhibition shooter Ad Toepperwein, more than fifty years earlier, had anyone seriously tried marathon endurance shooting events. But Tom pitched the idea. He could use the Nylon 66, which checked in about a pound lighter than Winchester's Model 1903, a gun of traditional walnut stock weighing five and three-quarter pounds that Mr. Toepperwein used. Dick Baldwin, a trapshooter of accomplished note himself, was an advertising executive at Remington's headquarters. He heard that Tom "pleaded with Remington to let him try to break the shooting and endurance record of Winchester's Ad Toepperwein." Baldwin knew full well Remington was conservatively content on "promoting sales through other methods."[8]

Tom was willing to push this one. He just needed to talk with someone who believed in it as much as he did.

Part Three

San Antonio, Texas, December 1907

Adolph Toepperwein's idol Doc Carver fired aerial targets while shooting a gun from horseback. Annie Oakley tried similar stunts while riding a bicycle. Adolph Toepperwein lived during the advent of the horseless carriage, so he shot targets from a moving automobile while his brother Fred drove.
Collection of Kenneth Toepperwein.

CHAPTER FOURTEEN

Captain of the Exceedingly Monotonous Spectacle

Ad Builds Up to His Monumental Endurance Shoot

He was Ad Toepperwein. He was thirty-eight years old, and already he had found what some people needed years more to accomplish—if ever. He was getting paid every day to do something he had loved and desired all his life, and he was doing it all next to the woman he loved. With the help of the Toepperweins shooting tour, firearms at Winchester Repeating Arms Company in 1907 were coming up on a three hundred percent increase in sales from fifteen years earlier. He was stamped, his acceptance signified every time someone pinned on one of those buttons proclaiming that his shooting, and the shooting he taught to his wife, was "wonderful."

So why would he pursue that line of shooting that went beyond a show, something that required as much endurance as accuracy? He probably would not gain much more in the way of money from Winchester if he broke the record. If baseball players were any judge, pay for performance on the sporting field was not that great. The gambling scandal of 1887 in baseball involved players who were believed to be underpaid by the owner of the Louisville Grays, and tightwad owners who were believed to shortchange their players still were creating the same underlying tension in baseball into the 1900s. And while Ad technically was endorsing a product, such contracts like the one Honus Wagner had in baseball during the 1890s to promote Hillerich & Bradsby "Louisville Slugger" baseball bats were taking time to proliferate into high-dollar deals.[1]

The costs for the endurance shooter, however, were great. Captain Adam Bogardus started the concept during his January 1878 shoot when he fired at enough glass balls to record five thousand hits in five hundred minutes at Gilmore's Gardens in New York. He stood to promote his glass target balls and spring-loaded traps, yet he barely made it through the ordeal. First off, he was firing shotguns of 10-gauge and 12-gauge. Before he got through his third set of one thousand, his right arm began to cramp and he took extra time to rub it down with a mixture of arnica and brandy. Past shot No. 4,000 the pain worsened, particularly in the hand around his trigger finger. But the crowd gathered around him and urged him on when he struggled; he sat in a chair to fire off the final three hundred hits. The reporter for the *New York Times* credited Bogardus for an effort that "brought into play both phenomenal skill and marvelous endurance; and although, as a spectacle, it was exceedingly monotonous, it was yet interesting enough to keep together a very considerable attendance in Gilmore's Gardens the eight hours it lasted."[2]

That was it. People were interested in it. Doc Carver knew. When he broke Bogardus's record about six months later in 1878 by firing his rifle at 6,208 targets and hitting 5,500 in ten minutes less than Bogardus did, he didn't shoot for a month after soothing his eyes with applications of ice. He made it back out on the road, and people asked him when he would try to beat the record.

"Did you ever stop to think what a task that is?" Doc responded.[3]

Ad was as captivated by the thought of endurance shooting as everyone else seemed to be. And when he was asked about the record, he thought big.

"Man has always attempted the seemingly impossible. In all fields," Ad said, ". . . man has striven to overcome what appeared to be insurmountable obstacles. Without this spark, this drive, man would still be nothing but a clod."[4]

Endurance was the rule of the day, even in other sports. Old Hoss Radbourne, in 1885, was a pitcher for the Providence Grays, and he was one of six pitchers in baseball's National League who had each won back-to-back complete nine-inning games—in both ends of a doubleheader. "Tired out, tossing a little five-ounce baseball for two hours?" he asked. "I used to be a butcher. From four in the morning until eight at night I knocked down steers with a 25-pound sledge."[5] Boxers fought until submission prior to the 1860s. There was a 276-round fight between Jack Jones and Patsy Tunney at Cheshire, England, in 1825.

But for Doc Carver, the pure thought of etching his name into the sports records books wasn't the spark that led him to push endurance shooting to an incredible new standard, well, well beyond his Bogardus-passing 6,200-target shoot in 1878. With Doc, there was always a flip side, always a motive underlying. He had a "whale" in his corner, and Doc was making bets and accepting whale-sized action. As early as January 1878 there were reports that an unnamed "rich English sportsman" was betting that Doc would complete his endurance shoots and splitting the proceeds with Doc. A one-day trial of five thousand hits on the targets was spectacular when it broke Bogardus's record, but it no longer whet the appetites of gamblers. An outrageous figure might bring them back, and an endurance event of 60,000 shots over six days planned for New Haven, Connecticut, was said to bring $50,000 worth of action to Doc's English backer.[6]

There was no way Doc could be flippant about the sanctioning of the event, if he expected gamblers to pay up when he hit the mark stipulated for the bets. So when the 60,000-target shoot got under way on January, 12, 1885, at Lincoln Rink near Doc's home at New Haven, Doc brought in titled people to say the event was fair and square. He had five people listed as judges, including two generals, a colonel, a commodore, and the mayor. His referee was a professor, a lieutenant was counted among the five scorers, and he fired at wooden blocks.[7]

Doc claimed his guns weighed about ten pounds, and there certainly were enough rifles on the market matching that description. So it didn't even take until noon that first day before Doc started complaining, saying his right wrist was bothering him. Yet he performed until 10:40 p.m., and fired off 13,017 shots. His miss rate was relatively high, 11,089 hits with 1,928 misses for eighty-five percent on the mark. He'd have to focus in, because those bets would require that he hit 60,000 in six days before they were paid his way. At the halfway point of the shoot, he was ahead of pace by hitting 31,180 total targets while his miss rate continued to drop. By midnight of the fourth day, one of the New Haven newspapers reported that a table next to Doc "was covered with all sorts of liniments." He became nauseated the fifth day, yet Doc would not take the medicine prescribed by a doctor that was on hand. Instead he bettered his success rate again by missing only 487 of the 10,500 shots (better than ninety-five percent hit) that day. Despite the sickness, the pain in the left arm and right wrist, Doc was clearly in a rhythm on the sixth day and didn't even need to reach 9,000 more targets to put this one in his back pocket. He finished before 10 at night, all together needing 64,881 attempts to hit 60,016 targets.[8]

There was wide acclaim for Doc. Three years later, Doc was encountered taking a break during his travels at an Iowa hotel, and he was asked, "Have you done any fancy shooting of late?"

"I shot 500 balls at Kansas City in fourteen minutes, beating all my former records. Since then I have not done much shooting."

"You have never endeavored to beat your record of six days shooting of 10,000 balls a day, have you?"

"No, although at Kansas City they wanted me to do so, and sometime when I am feeling well and able for it I will try a 70,000-ball shoot in seven days."[9]

Doc certainly let it be known he believed he could do better than his New Haven performance in terms of accuracy, so another endurance shoot was planned for Minneapolis. He reminded everyone how difficult things had been in New Haven.

"I lifted in that exhibition a ten-pound gun 10,000 times a day, or each day I lifted 100,000 pounds," Doc said. "Follow that up with six days and you see that 600,000 pounds have been lifted. That of itself is hard work, to say nothing of the fatigue that comes from the recoiling of the gun and the pulling of the trigger, and the loading, etc."[10]

On December 24, 1887, at Minneapolis's Washington Rink, Doc got started with a half dozen .38 Winchesters ready to go.[11] Doc offered prizes to anyone who could lift the ten-pound rifle into a shooting position for five straight minutes. The sideshow injected some badly needed relief into the feature of someone shooting targets thrown into the air for hours on end. Reporters who were covering the event started having a go at the rifles, according to the *St. Paul Globe* on December 28. Most of them offered a few last words before the challenge died in their arms. "Is one minute up yet?" said one. Another, through several pants of air: "Say—boys. This—confounded—gun—weighs—about—900—pounds." Just being able to breathe through it apparently was a challenge, according to the next: "It's all right—but I prefer to quit now, before I have a conniption fit."[12]

Doc claimed to be having trouble as well. He let on to one of his friends that he accepted morphine injections from a Dr. Towers of St. Paul to quiet the pain in his arms as early as Day Two.[13] Doc still managed a long run of 771 without a miss. Then word went out on Day Five that this Dr. Towers told Doc that if he kept at it his arm would need to be amputated. Still, Doc was closing in on the record, and this time much more accurately than New Haven. At the end of six days Doc needed 60,674 to hit 60,000 on the money—almost ninety-nine percent accuracy (he reached ninety-two percent in New Haven). This, and Doc's friends contended the scales showed he had lost twenty pounds.[14]

So, Ad heard about the way these endurance shoots literally hammered the body. Cramps. Pain. Nausea. Weight loss. Agitation. Liniments. Conniption fits. Morphine. Amputation. Well, that's a heck of a list, right there. And that doesn't even mention the pressure from gambling; Ad wasn't one to speak of getting into the action with his own money, but he'd sure hate to let down any friends who might be willing to throw down a buck or two.

Doc did have some encouragement for anyone who might want to follow him. He said shooters had a reserve they could draw on that others couldn't.

"The strongest man that I know of cannot bring up his left arm for five minutes at a time with a ten-pound gun without tiring him out," Doc said. "John L. Sullivan, strong as he is, could not do it. How can I do so much of this lifting? A certain set of muscles is brought into play and these have been trained since I was a boy. I can do nothing of any account with dumb bells. It takes another development of muscles to do that, so you see this laborious feat, and it is one, comes mainly by long practice."[15]

If Ad wasn't connected to the gambling world and wasn't seeking a coup as Doc did, he had other motivation. He had always boasted, particularly with his cousin Rudy, he would be a shooter and he would do it better than Doc. Competition sparked Ad, and a few years after Doc's record at Minneapolis, Ad was stoked to defend the work of his idol.[16] As monumental a feat as Doc's 60,000-target record sounded, someone was able to beat it. It was Captain B. A. Bartlett, who had been passed off by the shooting mainstream as a little-known performer.

Like Ad, one of the gigs for Captain Bartlett was the circus. He was touted as the "champion rifle shot," and his name was associated with the Roger's Great Inter-State Circus.[17] While it was true that his name at trapshooting competitions lagged behind the best shooter of the day, Rolla "Pop" Heikes,[18] the fancy shooting Bartlett was reported as having done in the 1880s and '90s sounded a lot like the program Ad would be doing starting with the following decade. Indeed, Captain Bartlett was an exhibition shooter, the sort of ground a lot of people believed Ad was pioneering when he signed with Winchester. Captain Bartlett shot for Burgess Gun Company, and his show in the 1880s was "a very clever and interesting exhibition of fancy and rapid shooting, performing many difficult and startling feats," according to copy that was circulating among newspapers in the Midwest upon Bartlett's return from a tour of California. To be more precise, he used his repeating shotgun to hit six objects that had been thrown into the air all at once, picking them off before they hit the ground. He would turn handsprings, pick up his gun, and hit two or more targets, and while standing on his head he could hit double targets. With his rifle, the same news copy credited Captain Bartlett with breaking 64,000 glass balls in sixty hours, 1,000 in thirty minutes, and 500 in fourteen minutes without mentioning where or when he did such astounding feats.[19] He toured through the West, namely Kansas City, as early as 1896 "for some time in the interest of the Winchester Company."[20] Bartlett and Heikes were a feature in the *Lima* (Ohio) *Gazette* in a November 18 report, noting that Bartlett was representing Winchester Repeating Arms Company. [21] Appearing again with Heikes at Logansport, Indiana, the next month, Bartlett tossed his gun into the air, threw two clay pigeons skyward, caught his gun, and shot both the targets. A tin can was placed twenty feet from the duo, and one of them, the reporter claimed, shot the ground in order to get the can into the air. One fired under the can, the report went on, and another repeated fire until the can went upward with every shot and finally it was shot to pieces.

Reports of his breaking the Carver record were thin and sketchy. They had him doing it at some point in 1889 at Buffalo, one of three New York cities Bartlett at various points claimed as hometown (Lakewood and Rochester being the others). Though that canned copy circulating in the Midwest newspapers cited a 64,000-glass ball performance, others reported Captain Bartlett shot at 60,000 and quit. From the 60,000, chroniclers had him missing 280.[22]

Doc was not heard to quibble about it. In fact, Doc was promulgating a set of standards for endurance shooting, and he entitled them the "Carver-Bartlett Rules." He wasn't losing sleep over it, probably because he wasn't losing money over it. Where once shooting was his bread and butter, Doc was coming up with another idea to entertain people. His daughters were getting into the business, and Doc pointed them to the idea of jumping horses off platforms down into a pool. He came up with the idea, he told his girls, when he remembered his days in North Platte, Nebraska, and he was being chased by outlaws. To evade capture, Doc claimed, he rode his horse out onto a wooden bridge where loose planks split and he and his mount broke through and splashed below into the Platte River. "A few years later my father was in Europe giving marksmanship exhibitions for the crowned heads of Europe," Lorena Carver said. "He saw some high divers for the first time in his life. He remembered the horse going through the bridge, and he put two and two together."[23]

Participation in sports shooting was growing in 1907. There were seventy-four people competing at the Grand American Handicap of 1900, and the number of entries increased wildly—more than six fold to 495 people—less than a decade later in 1907.[24] Though successful participants spent days shooting at hundreds of targets flying through the air, it appears none of them stepped up to stage an individual endurance shoot. To do so would be to place oneself at the cutting edge of the sport. But the long, successful walk would gain entry into the hall of legends, if not make a few bucks in the process.

Ad had a pretty good idea what he was getting into, for as early as his mid-twenties in 1894—some seven years after Doc Carver's final run at the record and about five years following the record-breaking performance of Captain Bartlett—newspapers were taking down the shooting records of the young Adolph Toepperwein. When Ad shot his .22 and recorded a straight run of 214 clay birds or saucers on December 13, 1898, it was reported to have broken a record; Doc hit 183 straight.[25] Reporters noticed that Ad was loading his own gun and that he was shooting targets thrown twenty feet from him. By the time he started using the Winchester Model 1903 he was able to use loading tubes that slid the maximum ten cartridges into the magazine contained through the butt stock of the rifle. It was his idea to load the gun himself.

"[The tubes] saved time in loading," Ad said. "All I had to do was open the magazine and reload the rifle with ten cartridges. This operation only took five or six seconds."[26]

On some shots during The Wonderful Topperweins tours, he had multiple guns already loaded while firing at a long run of objects thrown into the air from an unconventional platform. While Doc Carver and Annie Oakley shot at aerial targets from horseback (and Annie also shot at them while pedaling a bicycle), the advent of the automobile meant the platform for a few tricks by Ad. It proved to be a ride with a few bumps in it; his shooting absorbed the shocks of the chug-holed road. He had a driver accelerate to full speed, and Ad turned the gun from out of the car's cockpit and shot at one hundred blocks tossed up above the car. He hit eighty-five of the 2 ½-inch cubed blocks.[27]

It obviously was done for entertainment, not competition. There was some of the latter out there. It came from Captain A.H. Hardy, who had his own exhibition shooting act that sounded a lot like The Wonderful Topperweins. When a newspaper in Kansas reported on the Hardy show, it listed nine stunts or variations of the stunts—including portrait shooting of an Indian head's profile—similar to Ad and Plinky's work.[28] Another newspaper reported that in 1905 Captain Hardy broke 5,152 wooden balls measuring 2 ½ inches without a miss on Christmas 1905 at Lincoln, Nebraska.[29] He was presented as a representative of the Peters Ammunition Company,[30] and Ad thrilled at the idea of competition from someone he respected like Captain Hardy.

"For a good many years, no one tackled this kind of job, until my friend Captain Hardy, shooting for Peters, and myself, commenced to stir up the old scores," Ad said. ". . . [W]e were competitors, we would shoot a score, and one of us would try to beat it. We had a good number of runs."[31]

When Ad was promoting a shooting event for Scheuermeyer's Park in San Antonio, he claimed he would fire at enough targets to consume between 20,000 and 25,000 rounds of ammunition. This would effectively double the amount of targets from any of his previous endurance shoots.[32] He started shooting on September 17, 1907.[33]

The hot Texas weather of summertime greeted him, yet his first day was stellar. He rifled through all 7,500 flying targets presented to him—2 ¼-inch wooden cubes thrown straight up from thirty feet—and didn't miss any. He came back the next morning, and in the first hour of shooting he missed his first block. Much later in the day, after he stopped the session and he headed home, he wrote of his performance: "Make me run of 8,840," he scribbled of his new mark for consecutive shots without a miss.[34] That would break Hardy's mark of 5,152. While Ad was perfect through his opening 8,840, he missed ten of his next 11,160 to finish the four-day shoot. Considering his first day of perfect shooting, to miss ten sounds like a lot. But from 11,160 targets—he was hitting 2 ¼-inch cubes thrown by inconsistent human releases from thirty feet away and about thirty feet in the air—at a .9991 percentage. His total that went into the books was 19,990 hits of 20,000 targets.

"This marvelous record will stand for a long while," a reporter wrote, "unless he himself breaks it."[35]

Break it himself? Good idea. The next one would be the biggie, where he would attempt to put the record for accurate shooting upon 60,000 aerial targets next to his name.

"I figure it's only a matter, then, of picking the right time and place," he said.[36]

As for a place, Ad looked two miles south of downtown San Antonio to a place known as the International Fair Grounds. It had plenty of room to accommodate a big crowd, safely, for a shooting event. Less than ten years earlier, US Army Lt. Col. Theodore Roosevelt camped there with his volunteer bunch known as the Rough Riders. There, 1,250 men and their horses drilled before they headed off ultimately for San Juan Hill in Cuba during the Spanish-American War.[37] It had access. A road was scraped and pressed into shape so streetcars could deliver fairgoers. And when automobile traffic got cranked up, it wasn't long before the first drag races were conducted along the strip. On one Sunday in 1904 there were at least seven speeding citations written, not to mention a few crashes that needed to be cleaned up.[38] A main building had been built of wood frame. Lacking any mason work, it looked impressive nonetheless. There were cupolas and turrets mounted along the roofs, and from the fourth floor sprouted a two-story central tower.

He'd need to get 60,000 targets of some sort hauled down there. One of Ad's friends, and a good shooter in his own right, was Albert Steves. He owned the Steves Lumber Yard, so it was the place where Ad turned to get wooden blocks as targets for his shoots.[39] The sawing off of wood into 2 ¼-inch cubes was no big deal. Kids used them, once they were appropriately finished, as alphabet blocks. But Albert didn't take to the idea. He got in an argument with Ad. He told Ad he was crazy. The order would be more than double the 20,000 blocks he fired upon about two months earlier at Scheuermeyer's Park.[40] In his mind, Ad didn't understand why he was being called crazy by a good friend like Albert Steves.

"I was sure then [after the Scheuermeyer's Park shoot] that I had finally developed the endurance to break Carver's and Bartlett's great records," Ad said.[41] "Nobody knew better than I what a job it would be."[42]

And through his prep shoots, particularly in September at Scheuermeyer's Park, Ad knew he had a firearm he could trust. The Model 1903 produced a number of "firsts" for Winchester. It was the first rifle with a hammerless firing apparatus and the first to load a line of cartridges once the magazine was supplied; self-loading, it was pitched.[43] It all meant Ad would not have to "cock" the lever underneath the gun near the trigger guard, a massive advantage compared to the models Carver and Bartlett were plodding along with in their era. That doesn't even mention that, at five and three-quarter pounds, it was almost half the weight of their guns.[44]

Ad preferred to shoot rifles like this. "When you get control of a small-calibre [*sic*] gun you will use it in the field in preference to a shotgun," he said. "It is cleaner, cheaper, lighter and when a bird is hit that is the end of it."[45]

The white pine blocks were being sawed and stacked in wagons ready to be pulled by horse to the fairgrounds, and Ad had the arrangements in order.

"I also hired three husky young boys to toss my targets for me," he said. "I arranged to have a scorekeeper, judge, and referee on hand to keep official count of each shot."

He knew he had to do that. Another endurance shoot, this one again by Captain Hardy at Lincoln, Nebraska, was reported just weeks earlier in November 1907. Captain Hardy first fired at 1,000 marbles and hit 992 (breaking Ad's record of just less than 970).[46] Then he stepped up the record, passing the 8,840 consecutive that Ad recorded in September. He had gone past 13,000. It sounded legit, having come in front of "three reputable judges, who later gave their affidavit as to the correctness of the record."[47] It sounded like the sort of shooting Doc Carver would advise. Doc wrote down for Ad the instructions, requirements really, that he thought governed endurance shooting. Doc dated it 1897, and handed Ad the sheet:

"I advise you to follow this exactly if you want any marks you make to be recognized as official."[48]

Ad kept the list of five rules in a safe place. For this shoot, he'd done everything that Doc did, except boast. And now it was time. On the morning of December 13, 1907, seven wagon-loads of blocks,[49] pulled by horses from crotchety Albert Steves's lumberyard, were in place. The blocks were pushed out of the wagons into what Ad could only verbalize as a huge mound. It was a jagged stack of blocks, becoming several feet tall as they were dumped and collected, white pine sides shining here the best they could under the cloudy sky, yellowed edges falling into little crevasses, and in some spots black shadows swallowed light in between. When they'd tumble they'd do so lifelessly, uncaring, really.

"I will admit," Ad thought, looking at it all, "I [have] some misgivings. Would I be able to go through with it?"

There was reason to wonder because his rival endurance shooter had met with some degree of calamity. There was a report that Captain Hardy had set his consecutive-hit record of 13,066 up in Lincoln, but then he stopped. "A judge," a newspaper reported, "had to leave, and this stopped the shoot."[50] Couldn't anyone in a town the size of Lincoln be found to replace the judge? Sounded suspicious. What really brought the shoot to a stop? Ad wondered.

"Captain Hardy broke 13,066 before he missed," Ad had been told, "and he let it go at that."[51] Ad, meanwhile, already let on that he hadn't been sleeping well.[52]

But this morning had a chill about it that would carry the already flowing adrenaline. The blocks, scooped out by shovels of the Hispanic laborers, were tumbling about next to the young, husky throwers set up near the oval where the International Fair conducted horse races. People lined up behind Ad. If they were looking for sporting events to follow, the local boy's shooting was one of their few options. Professional baseball arrived in San Antonio sixteen years earlier, yet the 1907 season was just the seventh time a team played there. December marked the offseason. College sports—football teams at the University of Texas up in Austin had not joined a major conference and basketball had just started the previous year—were nascent at best. Leagues or associations for pro sports were nonexistent.

Adolph Toepperwein was a familiar name in the sports pages, and the man San Antonio came to see tried to keep himself occupied. He wiped oil from the barrels of his gun one last time. He slid .22 cartridges, the Winchester ammunition made specially for this Model 1903 auto-loader, into the tubular magazine on the butt of his gun. He reached down, then lifted coffee to his lips for a drink, making sure to wipe it off his lips with the back of his hand. He looked at the hazy sky, blocking brilliant shine but not the red from the sun behind it. The weather looked iffy, but not the support from Ad's employer. Winchester sent a public relations official down from New Haven, and he busily covered a table with white cloth centered with a big red W. The ammunition that Winchester provided could be stuffed into the loading tubes there.

Plinky loaded ammo when she wasn't starring during her own ample portions of the Wonderful Topperweins show. On some of her shots, she'd walk over to Ad, holding a target for her to shoot from his fingers, or mouth, and she'd step up and kiss him. But she had no shots planned for today, or the next ten days. This was Ad's daring trick. But she did it anyway. Plinky, Lizzie, pulled her husband's head down toward hers, and she gave his cheek a kiss.

"For luck, honey."[53]

CHAPTER FIFTEEN

Boil a Big Pot of Water

Ad and His Total Focus

"Throw!"

It's the only thing Ad had to say to start his day at the firing line. Once he got through the first few blocks, when he simply would not shoot at the few cubes that went wayward while the tossers got acclimated, he quickly got in a rhythm with the husky boys throwing those blocks into the air some thirty feet. To those watching, when they were able to keep their attention on the proceedings, it seemed that as a block reached its apex and was shot by the marksman, another block was in the air even before the echo from his .22 had finished bouncing off the exhibit hall and the other buildings on the International Fair Grounds. He'd shoot through his ten-round magazine and pause, taking his five or six seconds to reload.[1]

Ad's shooting kept the scorekeeper busy scratching his tabulated sheets with marks on the "Hit" line. At the end of the third day the scorer had enough marks there to signify twenty-two thousand hits. He had one mark—one—in the "Miss" column. Plenty of people thought it had come earlier, but in a show that one of Ad's keenest tools as a shooter was his eyesight, he looked toward the referee's table when he failed to hear someone over there keep up the almost automatic comments:

"Hit.

"Hit.

"Hit.

A spot near the staging table would show a spectator at The Wonderful Topperweins shooting demonstration that, indeed, a woman named Elizabeth Toepperwein could fire guns expertly right along with her husband Ad. Collection of Kenneth Toepperwein.

"Hit. . . ."

Pause. No hit?

"I think I was on it, boys," Ad suggested to them. "Check the block." The kid who threw the chunk into the air saw it had not splintered as so many had before. But when he picked it up, he saw the fine .22 caliber groove grazed along one side. He showed it to the referee, who seemed satisfied he made a mistake and was ready to correct himself.[2]

Ad wanted all his shooting to be pure, but he often seemed to draw a heckler in the crowds gathering at his and Plinky's exhibitions. This included a stop in New Mexico when Ad believed the table that would display his guns and ammunition had been moved by pranksters next to an obscured bumblebee nest before the start of a show. When one of the bees buzzed through the performing area, Ad heard hecklers chant, "Shoot the bumblebee! Shoot the bumblebee!" "For a while," Ad said, "I endured their

A wider view during their shooting exhibitions showed Ad and Plinky Toepperwein to be a popular entertainment draw. Ad takes his turn to shoot, with Plinky watching, during a 1920 show at Lighthouse Point in New Haven, CT. Collection of Kenneth Toepperwein.

disturbance, knowing full well that a bumblebee is a very poor target while buzzing around erratically." Finally, Ad had enough of the loudmouths and their buzzing bumblebee. "So, at the peak of his circle I shot him. And that angry bumblebee just vanished from our sight. Those troublemakers tucked tail and left the tent."[3]

In order to keep those episodes at a minimum so he could keep about his business in a timely manner during a demanding endurance shoot, Ad's instructions were to have any block in question tossed up to the crowd. "[That] would at once dispel any doubt whether or not it was hit," he said.[4]

Seeing everyone pleased, the referee was back at it, and so was Ad.

"Hit."

The monotony of this, the dumb and lifeless line of blocks tossed into the air and rifle shots knocking a few splinters out of each one, over and over and over, dulled beyond conception the outstanding fact of Ad's shooting.

It was unprecedented through these three opening days, for even if the visual observations were sidetracked by boredom, the mathematics painted the command Ad had of his rifle. His one miss from twenty-two thousand targets—just one miss—brought calculations figuring an astounding .99995 percentage of targets hit. Plus, he was doing it at a pace that was pleasingly ahead of schedule. His announced intentions had him shooting at five thousand blocks per day. He was more than forty-five percent ahead of his aimed-for three-day total of fifteen thousand.

But signs of wear and tear, if one looked closely enough, were beginning to creep in as the days went on. Despite the cool weather that started temperatures in the 40s when the firing commenced at 9 a.m., and wouldn't creep past 70, if that, in the afternoon, Ad slipped out of the coat he'd been wearing before he completed the day at 5 p.m. When he did, his shirt was lined here and there with perspiration. After shooting through the hours in the mornings, he would take an hour for lunch and rest. At times for his break he'd slump down to the ground. "How do you feel, Top?" he was asked. "That little rifle is beginning to get a mite heavy," he answered, grinning and putting a stretch through his arms. "But I think I can make it."[5]

He obviously stuck with the fundamentals. He'd preached it all before to any shooter who would listen, remembering on these flying targets to "get your aim just as they have risen to their fullest height and then begin to return to earth. Always hold under them and take a full sight. . . . Never follow an object you want to hit. Let it come to you in all cases."[6]

Plinky and the couple's friends would gather round him and engage him in conversation, but Ad looked to his gun to keep him otherwise occupied during breaks. This included the minutest details. "The first thing to keep in mind is the fact that one cannot give his gun too much attention," he'd say. "Above all things, clean it after emptying the magazine or it will get foul, contract a leaded barrel, and might as well be thrown away. . . . Keep your gun clean and it will never fail you."[7]

Just as he would with the boys throwing the targets, Ad was rotating his pair of .22 caliber M/03s at the same frequency as he was with the boys, every five hundred shots. "The barrels would be pretty hot," he said after laying one gun down and picking up the other one. When asked how the guns were operating, Ad replied, "I have no trouble whatsoever. . . . They work beautifully."[8]

Wet weather stayed in the forecast the first few days, and clouds dropped drizzle during the fourth day. The mist painted a dreary landscape, and the temperature barely rose above 56 degrees.[9] "The weather [is] very bad, cloudy and chilly," Ad said. "[It does] not help matters much."[10]

On the fourth day, December 16, Ad fired at seven thousand targets to bring his totals to twenty-nine thousand attempted and three misses. Three? After days when he either missed none or just one, he missed two on the 16th. When he was done for the day at the Fair Grounds, his hot meal awaited him. So did an alcohol rubdown. It wouldn't take away all the soreness. Something was up.

This all started so well. If he was nervous about shooting at more than fifty-thousand wood blocks, if he was like the boxer fearful of being hit until that bell rang at ringside and called him out for the first round, no one could tell when he cleared his throat with those first words on Day One of the shoot.

"Let's get going, boys," he called out to the young men standing among those little pale cubes yet to be pocked by the rifle fire. He toed the line next to the white stake where he was standing, to mark up to thirty feet from the spot the boys would toss the targets. "Throw those blocks as though you're trying to hit the top of the flagpole, and keep 'em going until I have to reload."[11]

It was the call that could bring a Texas whoop and a holler.

But it had faded. Things were fading. It was 7 o'clock, and in the shorter winter days the night had drawn in. He was gone from the fairgrounds. He was in bed.

Cubes flew into the air. Hit-Hit-Hit. . . . Cracks from his rifle were heard right from under his ear. Hit. The butt of the rifle would move ever so, kicking backward on the clothes covering his shoulder, close to where the sound came. Hit. The referee's voice did not divert his attention. Hit.

Dreams can be funny. And, what a thought, that Ad could be dreaming about shooting blocks at night? But it was happening, he told his friends.[12] It was a classic dream pattern, when repetitive tasks performed over long cycles during the day creep out of the subconscious while in deep sleep. Such as the misbehaving child at school who dreams of writing "I will not talk aloud in class" one hundred times. Or the homemaker who licks envelopes, stuffs them with holiday greetings at Christmastime. Maybe even Plinky, years ago, had dreamed of seeing that cartridge upon cartridge upon cartridge was loaded properly on that assembly line in the Winchester factory at New Haven in those days before she and Ad exchanged glances and started courting. After four days of shooting and hitting all but three of those twenty-nine thousand wooden blocks monotonously thrown into a monotonously grey sky, they formed an eerie, subconscious loop, and blocks were returning to him during his sleep at night.

The next day would start, as usual at the Fair Grounds, with first shot at 9 a.m., not long after he had a rubdown to get the day started in counterpart with breakfast and coffee. Ad kept his face toward his business, firing away at the blocks quickly as they kept getting tossed into the air. Today, somehow, seemed to be going at a quicker pace. People could try to make out his face in between that hunched-up left shoulder and arm running toward the barrel and the hat that covered his increasingly greasy hair. Plinky tried to help her husband to keep himself clean, but she was losing the battle. She had swabbed his face at night in an effort to remove the residue that collected between his whiskers and attracted ample dust from the Fair Grounds. Only when Ad turned from his shooting for a break could anyone really notice how this was wearing on him. Above that five-o'clock shadow were eyes that appeared to have sank below the beginnings of the circles bordering his sockets. Those eyes could be made out, only because they were red, shot with blood.[13]

He managed to shoot, and Day Five was a remarkable one, a clean run through eight thousand targets. It was his best one-day performance of the event, and now time to get his warm meal, his rubdown, and by 7, he was out.

But the cubes flew into the air. Hit-Hit-Hit . . . The rifle cracked. Hit. It recoiled. Hit. The referee went on. Hit. If this was ever funny, it was losing its novelty pretty quickly. Plinky had no idea. She was washing his face, and Ad popped out of sleep. He looked at her wild-eyed, in a way no one knew the pleasantly mannered Ad to look. Suddenly, he had the energy to get up from bed.

What was this?

"I was dreaming, I guess." His tone was quiet, and he dropped back down to relax again. "Kept seein' thousands of blocks flying through the air, and I couldn't keep my sights on them." Soon, he was back in a deep sleep.[14]

Day Six arrived. The temperature at the shooting line wasn't even 40 degrees, and the winds at more than 10 mph made it feel worse. It just aggravated a feeling that hit him on Day Four and—like those damn nightmares—wasn't going away.

". . . [I've] had very little good sleep," Ad complained. "I [am] in constant physical misery. My arms and shoulders ache, my neck muscles [are] painful. My whole body aches, as if somebody had pounded me all over." His right hand and wrist cramped, and Ad was saying that this caused him a great deal of pain.[15]

From the beginning, the Ad who smiled at the Winchester shooting exhibitions, the man who openly delighted in the shooting done by his wife, Plinky, the man who did not hesitate to shake a hand, was a different person as the first shot went into the air a few days ago. It was cold, and it was purposeful. He had roped off an area for spectators and had given strict orders to his assistants to not let anyone through the ropes hoping to start off some chitter-chatter. Why the change of his stage personality? ". . . [D]id not feel like talking," Ad bluntly stated. "I [have] no desire to speak to anyone. . . . [A]ll of my attention [is] centered on the job that's before me. In order to do this job well, I [have] to concentrate on each and every shot."[16]

The only reason he put this shooting on display was to confirm to as many eyes as possible that he indeed did this. After going through this excruciating ordeal, if he could indeed keep it up, he wanted no one to have avenue to ride up and say his endurance shoot was one big lie he had tried to conceal. That he was able to shoot and have the crowds managed gave him peace. He was able to fight through all the pain, or at least keep it sequestered while he had the gun in the air. This was a strange world, a world that had become one in the same with the time at night when his eyes were closed.

"This concentration plays havoc with the subconscious mind to such an extent that all you know and see is the thing that you are about to do," he thought. "I seemed to be in a world all by myself, and the only things I saw, or seemed to see, was a block in the air and the fellow who was throwing it."[17]

Ad was oblivious to how many people came out to watch. He only knew when he turned from his shooting at the end of the day and walked off—without speaking to any of them. As the light rain drizzled on, he noticed that the people that had come out had taken cover underneath awnings of buildings, popped open umbrellas, stayed below the roof over at the pavilion. But the boys helping him did not. One even offered him his raincoat.

". . . [A]fraid that it would hamper my shooting," Mr. Toepperwein told the boy.[18]

Another of the target throwers thought of starting a fire. He placed a kettle over it and heated up some water. Ad obliged. He dipped his hand in it—frequently. Then he readied to shoot, and he looked over at the boys who came out in this weather and devoted themselves to the task. He paused. "I'm not the only one that [is] uncomfortable," he thought. "My boys . . . were also suffering from stiff necks and pains in the arms. However, they [don't] complain and [are] on the job every minute."[19]

As bad as Day Six was, as much pain that would shoot right back at him once he stopped firing long enough to think about it, there were sources of inspiration. Certainly, Ad was all over those blocks with his marksmanship. Again, he knocked down a mark no one had conceived. The consecutive-hit run of his 8,840 in September was blown to smithereens. Now in his record was a straight run of 14,540.[20] He had beaten Captain Hardy's mark.

The boys headed home, and so the blocks were down for the rest of this day. Or were they?

CHAPTER SIXTEEN

I Would Have Run Up 75,000

Blocks, Blocks, Blocks—and Nightmares—Float through Ad's Mind

There were ten thousand more shots to fire off, and Ad would have to do it while his trigger finger and wrist were cramping into debilitation. His shoulder was swollen in the spot where he had to brace the butt of the recoiling firearm. Every flex of his arms he used to hold that rifle and lift it into position caused cramps to knot up the biceps. There was one way to deliverance. He had to rely on the basics to get him through this ordeal. It was Day Seven, and Ad had shot at fifty-one thousand of those wooden blocks and had missed four. The seventh day, Thursday, December 19, saw him miss none of the seven thousand blocks that had been thrown into the air. And this all came despite starting his day in temperatures of about 39 degrees and winds that had been blowing steadily at 12 mph just an hour before he was to shoot.

He'd preached the basics time and again at his exhibitions, and he'd live by them when he shot. They came as naturally and mindlessly as putting one foot in front of the other.

"[Judge] accurately and instantly the distance and the speed at which your target is traveling," he would advise, "and most importantly of all, the angle. Your moving target does not accommodatingly stop in mid-air, to wait for your bullet, at the instant you press the trigger of your rifle. It is on its way and it keeps going! And while the firing mechanism of your rifle is operating, and the bullet is getting out of the barrel and to the neighborhood of that sailing target, the target has been making a get-away."[1]

With the grandstands of the International Fair Grounds at San Antonio, Texas, in the background, Ad Toepperwein sits atop a stack of the 60,000 wooden blocks he shot during the 1907 endurance shoot. In order for Toepperwein to extend the record number, more than 10,000 blocks were re-used or cut from lumber on site. Courtesy of John L. Stein collection.

No dawdling. Get the shot off and go to the next one when the cubes flew into the air. All of this kept registering into his mind, without him thinking hard—or hardly at all. There were sounds to accompany him, yet they played like a heartbeat, vital, and hardly noticed. There was the rifle shot echoing off the exhibition building at the Fair Grounds. The referee's voice. Hit. More cracks of the rifle. Hit-Hit. Even the muted sound of the bullet piercing the block. Hit. Hit. Hit. It happened over, and over. The blocks kept going up.

He was keeping at it, employing the basics to "all the time keeping your sights lined up. At the turning point of the [target] . . . where it stops going up and is going to start down . . . hold a little below the [target] and squeeze your trigger to let go the shot."[2]

He was done with Day Seven of the shoot, yet he had the urge to squeeze that trigger, the thoughts somewhere in his brain, his body, that the blocks had to be shot. He could not miss. It was like the weight of all those blocks laid down on him, and they would not let him up. He could offer no resistance, put up no fight, when he slipped off to that "world all by myself, and the only things I saw, or seemed to see, was a block in the air and the fellow who was throwing it."

So a block was in the air, and this time there was no noise. No crack of the rifle? The judge silent? Nothing? Why isn't the bullet coming out from that barrel? He told everyone that his guns were performing, as he put it, marvelously. Now they were going to make a liar out of him by jamming? He saw to it that the guns were cleaned every night. The blocks are going up, but the bullet is just not firing.[3] Out of frustration he could really put the grip to that trigger, tighten it, but the basics don't allow it.

"Never pull or jerk the trigger," was Ad's pointer. "Learn to apply squeeze all the time you are following your object, and to let the shot go by tightening your squeeze at the correct time. Pulling or jerking spoils shots, squeezing gets hits."[4]

The gun started working again, so what else could be gnawing at his mind to make him think such thoughts?

"I advise you to follow this exactly if you want any marks you make to be recognized as official."

The rules. He kept a copy of the rules, that piece of paper where Doc Carver wrote everything down for anyone wanting to beat his record, and the Captain Bartlett record:

The shooter could use any kind of rifle shooting a solid bullet. Check.

The targets were to be standard-sized (2 ¼-inch) composition ball or wooden block. Check.

The assistants tossing the targets were to stand between 25 and 30 feet in front of the shooter. Check.

The targets were to be thrown in the air at a height of 25 to 30 feet. Check. And if they weren't, Ad wouldn't shoot at them.

There must be a duly appointed set of officials present at all matches: a judge, a referee, and a scorer.[5] Check.

He had it all covered. He certainly got a reminder every second he shot that the judge, referee, and scorer were there.

Hit. Hit. Hit. Hit. . . .

And the distance? The distance? Look! The blocks are going up a mile away from the Fair Grounds![6] Even though he recommended that a zone of about one mile always be kept clear for safety ("these .22s go a long way when there's nothing to stop them," he said[7]), trying to shoot a block from a mile away was crazy.

The only way this could be explained was by way, again, of Doc. He noted that the strain on the eyes was one of the worst things a shooter had to get over following an endurance-shooting event.[8] But, as cold and damp as the weather was, didn't his eyes get a break in some way because of it, even though they had become two days earlier red and inflamed?[9]

". . . [I]t's very uncomfortable, [but] I feel that it's to my advantage, because I could always shoot better on a sunless day than when the sun was shining brightly," he said.[10]

No matter how he could assure himself, Ad's mind would not stop playing tricks. "These blocks [are] so impressed in my memory," he said.[11] Look now, the blocks are just hanging there, floating all around him. A block that would just hang there could at least make the job easier, if it wasn't for the gun again. Wasn't Ad, and Ad alone, supposed to be the one reloading this thing? He was, and he reloaded it through the portal to the magazine through the butt stock of the gun. Problem was, that's where the bullets were firing right now, backwards, away from the blocks.[12]

"I advise you to follow this exactly if you want any marks you make to be recognized as official."

Hit . . .

My whole body aches.

Hit . . .

. . . the only things I saw, or seemed to see, was a block in the air . . .

Hit. Hit.

I seemed to be in a world all by myself.

Hit. Hit.

I am in constant physical misery.

Hit. Hit. Hit.

"I advise you to follow this exactly if you want any marks you make to be recognized as official."

Doc Carver couldn't hit these things! Capt'n Bartlett neither. There's not a man alive who could!

Ad finally cried out! He wasn't out at the Fair Grounds. He'd just crept out of his own mind after another dream—a nightmare, ". . . one solid nightmare," Ad griped.[13]

Actually, it was a good problem to have. If Ad was going to go beyond Doc Carver's endurance shoots, if he was going to without question beat Captain Bartlett's world record, he would have to find more targets. Yes, it seemed Ad was making an eleventh-hour contemplation of the pulverization of the records. But there were not enough wooden blocks to fire upon the more than sixty thousand needed. He knew his shooting well enough to know that there were some blocks grazed or hit in such a way that those blocks had not lost their form. There were others that, in Ad's words, were "not mutilated too much" and he still felt comfortable shooting at them in their smaller sizes and broken-off edges to make the score.[14] He was going to break that record.

With Plinky's help he would. She was getting Ad dressed and undressed each day. She had hired a barber to come in and shave Ad's face while he got the last few winks of sleep each morning. She knew that once Ad slowly raised his arms above his waist he could not lower them back down without tremendous writhes of pain. But how far would she be willing to allow her husband, her "daddy," to push himself when she became uneasy while hearing Ad clear the question about re-using the blocks with the judges?

"Fact is," he admitted, "I'm in pretty sorry shape."[15]

"You're nearly there, Top," came a voice from among the officials. "Can you keep it up?"

"Hell," he answered, his voice going the way of his body. "I've just caught my second wind. Get me some more cartridges and another load of blocks."[16]

Somehow, the bravado he showed that first day when he told the boys to "Throw those blocks as though you're trying to hit the top of the flagpole" was back. So everyone got busy. His boys were so dependable throwing the blocks, and they didn't let him down now. They dug through the pile and looked for the blocks that came closest to the original 2 ¼-inch cube. That was a job as painstaking as throwing the blocks, for the pile of wood was turning into a hillock. By this time it was more than four feet high, could have been twenty feet wide and stretched perhaps more than fifty feet in length. They would need more than ten thousand blocks. To be sure, a search went up for anything resembling a block. There was, leftover from who knows what, a stack of basswood slabs, perhaps cedar, that were almost like a wood plate. Men who claimed to be carpenters thought they could fashion targets close enough in size, and a cacophony of saws cutting through wood had risen with the comeback of Ad and his rifle cracks.[17]

Despite his four misses on Day Eight, the 20th of December, he was at fifty-eight thousand shots with eight misses and closing in on the magical sixty thousand targets that Doc Carver fired upon. Unless he succumbed to the torture of it all, he'd break Captain Bartlett's record on Day Nine.

Some other things might succumb. Ammunition. Not only did he need more, he probably would need more of the right brand. With the Model 1903 at Winchester, gun designer Thomas ("Tommy") Crossly Johnson was able to craft an auto-loading gun through a "blowback" method. In other words, at the trigger squeeze a cartridge would fire away from the breech, and the gases released from the ignition of the powder would "blow back" the breech bolt and leave space for a new cartridge to enter the chamber "automatically" from the magazine through the loading mechanism. To get the right balance for the bullet to first leave the barrel and then the breech bolt to be pushed rearward, Tommy found it necessary to formulate a new cartridge. It was the 22 Winchester Automatic Rim Fire Smokeless.[18]

Word traveled through the place that Ad's assistants were out and about buying up every cartridge that could be found. As some of them returned on December 21, a loud cheer was heard. It wasn't for them.

Ad had done it. He broke through the Bartlett record. They were counting 60,000, and Ad did it in far less than Bartlett's credited two hundred and eighty misses.

Ad could read the report the next day at the top of page 6 from the "The Sporting World" section in the *San Antonio Light* and chuckle, if he had the energy left—and if someone could hold the newspaper up for him to read. "He is not even yet satisfied. . . ." Really?

The people had been coming out and forming nice crowds, and Ad would be letting them down by not continuing after what was printed in the morning paper: "[He] will continue to shoot in exhibition at the fairgrounds today, whither a crowd of enthusiasts will journey to see the greatest small caliber marksman in the world go after still more records. He expects to pass the 70,000 mark today which in itself is a record mark for continual shooting. Today will be the tenth of steady firing. The public is welcome to attend the closing hours of this event, which is the greatest in the annals of marksmanship."[19]

Well, looks like the only way to end this is to take one last squeeze of the trigger, one last irritating peer into the brightness past that steady dark barrel and those trusty iron sights, and finish off one last block at some nice round number that everyone could remember. Just say it's done, and everyone would go home. And rest.

Plinky, as supportive as she had been, was having none of it. His friends came by and piled on the pressure to stop. Even the spectators, who cheered wildly when he broke the record, urged him to quit. But he kept his back straight and looked through those sights, and the boys tossing the targets were convinced to keep it up. Looks like he ain't quittin'.[20]

So it all sat off in the background, some out-of-focus image off behind him, the level of surprise in the crowd maybe only made out by hands slapping against pants legs or fingers pointed toward the blocks. If they kept begging him to stop, they got their only answer when the man looked down a barrel and kept squeezing the trigger. He had broken a record, but what is that if not making your own mark? Not to skim by, but to write what you think is a conclusive sentence and savor the feeling gained from pressing pen to paper for that final dot. Period. Exclamation mark.

"I just can't stop now," Ad said. "And I feel fresher now than I did three days ago. I'm going to keep shooting till I drop or as long as there's a cartridge for this rifle in San Antone."[21]

Plinky kept protesting. Ad admitted everything that happened on that ninth day was "pretty much a blur to me." He wasn't eating much. That body that took him to the shoot more than a week ago was limber, fit, and lanky. But the one he wanted to take out there for a tenth day was cramped and damaged, and he lost so much weight that he knew if he slapped on a pair of overalls and had straw sticking out of his clothes that someone would mistake him for a scarecrow.[22]

They could even show him the copy of the morning's paper, if he was thinking his record would one day be caught. "The Sporting World" reporter from the *San Antonio Light* wrote that Ad had "peppered at 66,000 and missed eight, three runs of 13,000 without a miss," and had "continued to peg away until he has now raised the record above any chance of successful competition."[23]

Finally, he allowed a line to be drawn. "Ten days," he said in response to Plinky's demand to stop. "Ten days should be enough."[24]

December 22, 1907, was the tenth day. Every day, up at seven. Then a soaking bath and rubdown. Plinky dressed him, and they were out to the Fair Grounds. Ad could barely make it. It was just about nine o'clock. The boys greeted him and they had to almost carry him out to the firing line.

Ad made out a voice coming from the officials, asking him if he was able to continue.

"Sure."

Almost as soon as he said it, the blocks were in the air, and Ad was shooting.[25]

"Hit."

Somehow he managed to keep sniping away almost flawlessly, and he caught glimpse of that pile of blocks. Maybe it was like the marathon runner who passed that final hill, entered the stadium, and from across the oval of the track afforded himself a snap look at the finish line while still trying to keep his tired legs between the running lane. It wouldn't take much longer. Still loading his own weapon, Ad managed to line up another loading tube and pour ten cartridges through the port, even when his fingers felt the cramp through his wrist and hand. This could be the last line of cartridges. He fired through it.

"Hit. Hit. Hit. Hit. Hit. Hit. Hit. Hit. Hit. Hit."

Someone's watch said 3:20.[26] Ad knew it was late in the afternoon, that's all. The sky, from what he could tell, was darkening. His gun was empty. So was his body. It was grabbed by friends, and the boys who were throwing the blocks now were carrying him. That last block one of them threw was shot all to hell. The people at the officials' table reported that 6,500 had been thrown so far that day—the fewest from any day of the Ad Toepperwein endurance shoot—and, still, a hit percentage of .9998 would go in the books. He'd just missed one the entire day.

It was almost inconceivable. The total would be hard to grasp. Ad, however, wasn't having a hard time grasping something. As they carried him over to a covered pavilion, the gun stayed in his hand that was too cramped to relax its clamp.[27]

With Plinky there grabbing him now, Ad asked, pushing out the words, "Wha'sa final score?"[28]

"The damndest score made by anyone, Top," a voice came out from the pack. "Out of 72,500 shots, you missed just nine."[29]

People remembered that Ad had to be "carted off to bed; he was completely done in."[30] But he had enough energy to make one prediction.

"That record," he said, "should stand a while."[31]

The next day, just the first of many that his young target tossers would spend fighting stiff necks,[32] Ad could open a newspaper and gather in the breathless report.

He possessed "three records that bid fair to stand as long as the present style of firearms are [*sic*] in use," the reported spouted: 72,500 shot over ten days, nine misses, and a long run of 14,540 hits in a row. "He effected [*sic*] a performance that has never even been approached in the history of marksmanship." He did it on that final day "in the presence of a large crowd, hitting 6,500 with one miss in the face of a strong wind that caused the small block targets to fly off their course," and that was "probably the most remarkable of the entire affair." The paper reported the targets were 2 ½-inch blocks of wood, and "the pile of fragments alone bears mute testimony to the multitude of the shots fired." It was made high by consecutive runs to include 14,540, 13,599, 13,292, 13,219, and 10,393 from this shoot.[33]

Ad made sure his own report went out. He wrote a lengthy detail to Winchester, making plain his efforts to make sure future shooters recognized this as an official event, although it was sanctioned by no official governing body. He mentioned everything, and one regret:

> While I was, of course, glad when I got through with the big job, I would have liked very much to have been able to continue a little while longer, in order to be able to shoot at 75,000 targets. I was still shooting good [*sic*] toward the last, and although the day was drawing to an end, I believe that I could have accomplished it with maybe a couple of more misses. I was very tired and the day was very dark, so I had to let well enough alone.[34]

The itchy fingers in the Winchester advertising office, promoters like the company's advertising manager William Clark who would be ruled off from playing up President Theodore Roosevelt's hunting trips with the Winchester rifles, had in Ad Toepperwein a shooter they could embrace. They answered Ad's report with a fancy display advertisement. With a youthful mug shot of the tie-and-vest-adorned Ad Toepperwein, Winchester announced the record in the tone of a smart-aleck on another page of *Sporting Life*: "These record-breaking, history-making scores, were made, without the aid of a notary public, before large crowds of people in a public park—not in a far-away back lot, or down on the farm out behind the barn."[35]

Plinky had tried to talk him out of it by the end. Now, if he could only get her to stop from trying these sorts of crazy things with her gun.

Part Four

Dayton, Nevada, October 1959

Newt Crumley served as a Nevada state senator from Elko, and he promoted efforts of the American Cancer Society here with Gov. Grant Sawyer, who began a first term in 1959. Courtesy of the Nevada State Library, Archives and Public Records.

CHAPTER SEVENTEEN

100,000!

Newt Convinces Tom to Give It a Shot

"Newt Crumley and I were talking about Ad Toepperwein," Tom Frye let on, ". . . just talking."[1]

The forty-three-year-old Tom knew a few things about Ad Toepperwein, and he had ever since growing up among all those nationally attended shooting competitions in Ohio. It had been fifty-two years since the Winchester Repeating Arms Company exhibition shooter Ad Toepperwein shot at 72,500 wooden blocks thrown into the air, missing nine, way back in San Antonio. In the summer of 1959, it was thought of along the lines of Lou Gehrig. It was the record of an Iron Horse, and it may never be broken.

"Nobody would try to beat that record, let alone beat it," Tom told Newt.[2]

Yet Newt Crumley was willing to talk about it. Not only did he talk about it with Tom, he actually wondered about someone breaking it. In business and pleasure, Newt had a stunningly lengthy list of examples where he pushed the edge. If Tom had any doubts that Newt could help him do something special in the shooting world—perhaps take a run at the Toepperwein record—all he had to do was talk to the people in the sport-shooting community around Bakersfield, California, where both men had contacts.

Ronald "Torque" Landis made a pass through Bakersfield as well. Landis, who gained a reputation as a barnstormer around the mid-Atlantic states, was doing duty in World War II by flying cargo and transport missions on the C-54 aircraft. He flew into Minter Field near Bakersfield in 1945 and approached the offices of the airbase when he saw something that struck him as familiar. A bulletin board had the name of Col. Newton H. Crumley posted to it. "Torque" saw a sergeant walking through the base hallway and asked:

"Who's Colonel Crumley?"

"He's the base commander," the sergeant replied, "and he's standing next to you."

"Torque" turned and saw someone whose face he immediately remembered.

"Have you burned up any P-12s lately?" "Torque" rather boldly inquired of a base commander. Yet Colonel Crumley had to smile, for "Torque" was one of the people on location at Mexico Farms airfield in Maryland when Newt, then a lieutenant, landed for a refueling and his P-12E pursuit plane burst into flames. This was eleven years earlier, and the incident was caused when a careless WPA worker flicked a cigarette toward the gassing area. "Torque" and Newt escaped injury that day, and now in Bakersfield they repaired to the Crumley home for dinner.[3]

Perhaps they could trade stories: "Torque's" barnstorming stunts along the East Coast, and Newt with another of his close calls just a few weeks before his pursuit plane burned in front of "Torque." This one was in 1934 when Newt was called to fly US Mail in a twin-engine bomber between Cleveland and New York City. Not even halfway into the flight something was amiss. "The right motor is giving us a little trouble," Newt's crewman Lt. Don Baxter said. It got worse. "It quit cold." With a plane loaded with mail, there was no keeping her up. At two thousand feet of altitude, Newt, Baxter, and the final crewman, Private William Le Tart, bailed out over the Susquehanna Valley near the township of Winfield, Pennsylvania. The flares they fired off—and the burning wreckage up along the hillside—were spotted, and the local people found them and took them to the village of Sunbury. No one was injured, and Newt was ready to be cleared for his next mission.[4]

So, what to do in the meantime? The aspiring officers, Newt and Baxter, met up with Herman Reich, a US attorney for the middle district of Pennsylvania. He and his wife, Kathryn, invited the airmen along for a night on the town. It was a Thursday night, and two other women (Rebecca Mellott and Mrs. Paul Bateman) joined up. They were four miles east of Sunbury when, in the up and down and winding terrain, Reich missed a curve and his vehicle ran down fifty feet worth of embankment. The car stopped when it hit a tree. Reich's nose and lower jaw were fractured. Baxter was cut up pretty badly, but he would survive. So would Newt, who thought his right leg was banged up enough that he probably broke it. Miss Mellott and Mrs. Bateman had minor injuries. Reich's wife, Kathryn, was critically hurt. Her skull was fractured, her chest crushed, and she sustained fractures of both an arm and leg.[5] Newt got out of the wreck with fifteen days rest in the hospital.[6]

Newt's honorable discharge came later in 1934. He took an office at the Commercial Hotel, yet behind the desk he would keep flying on his mind with company letterhead designed with airplanes in flight past city scenes of Elko. He purchased a private plane, and he cranked it up when civic duty called. It did around Christmastime of that year when Thomas Stinton and his family laid to rest their seventeen-year-old child, Jule, after a funeral in Elko. The family was to be flown home after the service, and the traveling party was split between the small planes of Newt and fellow pilot Floyd DeLong. Newt carried the parents in his plane, and the children—sister and brother June Stinton (sixteen years old) and Donald Stinton and friend Ruth Womack (both thirteen)—climbed into DeLong's single-engine biplane. The route was to take the planes about fifty miles northward to Mountain City. Fog banks were intermittent, and when Newt arrived with Mr. and Mrs. Stinton at Mountain City, DeLong's plane was gone. On Christmas Eve, a search party entered the steep-faced Owyhee Canyon and trudged along with heavy boots and snow shoes through mists that were turning to freezing precipitation. The plane, unburned but obviously flattened by head-on impact with the canyon wall, was found with the four bodies pushed to the front of the fuselage.[7]

Two years later, in early spring of 1936, DeLong's brother felt no hesitation to fly along with Newt. Irvin DeLong (he was a truck-line operator) and Harry Elliott (manager of the Elks Club in Elko) hopped into Newt's plane for a trip to Reno, and they saw clear skies when the plane started its return trip. But worry soon set over the Elko community when it heard the plane had not shown up for its scheduled landing. In fact, a local writer sent out wire copy that exclaimed Newt and his companions were "beloved victims of a plane disaster." The search was to go out to the Ruby Mountains near Elko, where a rancher could hear a plane engine through the bad weather that had blown in. It stayed bad, and a rescue was delayed. In the meantime, Elko area ranchers, hearing that their neighbor from the Crumley family was in trouble, lit large contained fires just in case Newt was still up there somewhere and he could see the blaze well enough to try to come down.[8]

The weather worsened. Twelve miles west of Elko, a dozen vehicles were stranded on a highway. The day began to clear, and late in the afternoon Ed Chapin saw someone walking through his Tremewan Ranch about fifty miles north of Elko. It was DeLong, who said his two friends were back somewhere toward where the plane crashed ten miles away. Chapin sent out a sleigh, and an exhausted Newt and Elliott were picked up and immediately sent to safety with DeLong. They told of the night before, when the weather became so severe it killed the radio on Newt's plane. Before long, the engine sputtered, then the stick went dead and the gliding started. Newt was able to manage to find a rough but level ridge up on Badger Mountain. He put it down and landed, not having trouble until one of those rough spots tore away the right landing gear and wing and provided for an immediate stop. A fire next to the plane allowed the three men to keep warm during a brutal blizzard. They got moving at about seven in the morning,[9] but they had a difficult time getting through the heavy snow on the ground. Newt would sink into a snow bank, and his body would trick him into feeling it was such a warm, peaceful place. But his mind and will rallied. He told himself he had to climb out of there and keep moving. Finally, they all got out.[10]

When his second tour of duty was done after World War II, and his country's Legion of Merit medal pinned to him in 1946,[11] Newt returned to life in Elko. But he took his command abilities with him. Though Newt and his family thinned their ranching interests with the sale of some of their land to Bing Crosby, Newt knew the importance of the Herefords out on the ranges of Elko County. A *LIFE* magazine article in 1949 cited an $8 million income to the county because the rest of the nation was paying cattlemen "fabulous prices" for beef.[12] And when a severe winter was hammering northeastern Nevada in 1952 and Gov. Charles Russell said the state could lose $10 million from damage to the herd, President Harry Truman declared a disaster.

Newt took action. He was listed as an emergency director for an effort between Air Force cargo planes and Army bulldozers trying to get feed to 600,000 head of livestock. Cargo planes from Hamilton Field in San Francisco were to fly to the Elko airport where bales of hay, and ranch owners to guide pilots, were waiting. This was "Operation Haylift." Newt, the expert pilot, called for the haylift when he flew over northern Elko County and saw cattle "so weak they couldn't shake off flocks of magpies." The drop would duplicate a similar effort using C-124 and C-82 aircraft in 1949, which saved "thousands of marooned livestock."[13]

Newt made time for family vacations. Even there, however, his uncanny ability to see adventure spill over to danger came along. The young family had a bumpy ride when reports surfaced that "A prominent Nevada family, shipwrecked in the Bahama islands, was rescued and flown to Miami today none the worse for a perilous passage ashore."[14]

Newt, his wife, Frances, and three of their daughters got away from Elko in the winter of 1953 for someplace balmy. They were a part of a sailing party aboard an eighty-three foot yacht named the *Catita II* owned by Lawrence J. Holland of Reno that was cruising through the Berry Island group. They chose a spot off Frazer's Hog Cay, and the five crewmen onboard anchored the vessel for the night some thirty miles northwest of Nassau. But winds picked up and grew increasingly fierce. Newt estimated the winds at 50 knots (about 57 mph). He got onto the radio and was able to hail the US Coast Guard out of Norfolk, Virginia.

"We're taking quite a beating," he relayed, "and might have to abandon ship." Help arrived, and by the morning they were on firm ground, but not until after the Crumleys were recovered from their damaged vessel.

". . . [T]he anchor slipped and the yacht went aground with a hard crunching sound," Newt told a reporter. "[We're] exhausted and looked a mess but we're all very happy to be alive."[15]

Back on the firmest of ground, Newt was a steady hand in the community. He was on the board of regents at the Reno campus of his alma mater at University of Nevada. He was elected to the state senate and certainly kept his Elko interests in mind when he was regarded to have taken the lead in the legislative debates in 1955 and '57 that led to the creation of the State Gaming Control Board. He chaired the Senate Taxation Committee. He also chaired the Fish and Game Committee and was credited for being "a strong believer in allowing local sportsmen a voice."[16]

His term in the senate took him from his regents' seat at University of Nevada, but he was thinking about getting back to Reno full time. His father had passed away, and by 1955 Newt announced he was selling the Commercial Hotel and the sixty-eight-room Ranchinn Motor Hotel he had developed at Elko in 1946. He was being mentioned as a gubernatorial candidate.[17] His acclaim locally was noticed on the national level when *LIFE* magazine included mention and a photo of Newt in an edition from 1949. It referred to Newt as "Elko's No. 1 businessmen and impresario . . . [a] husky, blond, native Nevadan, former college boxer, colonel in the Air Force . . . he looks exactly like a magazine-cover version of a rich and successful Westerner."[18]

Whether it was hospitality or politics, Newt would be a force in it. "He [has] an almost fanatical desire to see people well-served, not only in his hotels, which [is] his business, but by their public servants as well," his wife, Frances, said.[19]

The sale of the Elko properties opened the door in 1958 for Newt to negotiate a deal with a group headed by Norman Biltz to buy managing control of the new Holiday Hotel in downtown Reno next to the Truckee River. It cost Newt and his investors $5 million.[20] There was no gambling on the property, yet Newt quickly had a casino fashioned. The Holiday, which was said to be close to $300,000 in debt and usually having about five percent of its rooms occupied a year after it had opened, soon saw its occupancy rise to 95 percent.[21]

Newt was back on the board of regents at UNR, and the image he struck on campus at Morrill Hall was immediate. Sitting across from him during meetings often times was a young man by the name of Bob Laxalt. This was the younger brother of a Nevada county district attorney named Paul Laxalt, a budding politician among Republicans who that decade made his first step into politics when he unseated a Carson City incumbent. Bob directed the university's information and publications and was a journalism instructor. He had enough in common with Newt—both spent some of their days at the university on the school's boxing team—that he drew close to him. And when Bob looked up at that panel every month and saw Regent Crumley, he hardly saw a loafing, dozing bureaucrat satisfied with a crony appointment.

"Death [is] no mystery to him," Bob wrote. "He [has] touched hands with it too many times before. And he damned well [isn't] afraid of it, because he always seemed to be daring it a little."[22]

What was it that made Tom Frye, a man who was half of a calendar removed from back surgery, want to get cozy with the idea of breaking a marathon shooting record that would have him on his feet for more than ten days firing away at wooden blocks with a rifle? Even if he would be using the Nylon 66, no matter how much it was advertised by Remington as a lightweight marvel, it still weighed a little more than four pounds and, theoretically, he would be lifting more than 300,000 pounds if he raised that gun in place enough times to pop the record. That's about one hundred and fifty tons.

Was the desire to go after the record borne of his own ambition? Because of his bad back, Tom hadn't won any awards the past two years at the Grand American Handicap at Vandalia, Ohio, and perhaps his longing to get back into competition had him flashing back to scenes of the time when he shook Mr. Toepperwein's hand.

"My hometown, Findlay, wasn't far from there," Tom said, "and I went once with my dad as a kid to see him shoot—I never dreamed that one day I'd break his record."[23]

Perhaps he was falling under the sway of Newt, who appeared to be able to grasp a concept that had fallen out of, or never entered, people's minds and place it into a plan that could work. Bob Laxalt could see that trait existed in Newt during the regents meetings at University of Nevada.

> "I used to think that Newt was born out of his time, that he didn't fit in this age of too much talking and too little doing," Bob wrote. "To me, he never really did look comfortable making small talk. There was always a little tenseness about him, a sort of caged thing that told you he would rather be doing than talking. He was a straight-talking man, the kind Nevada used to have a lot of when we were growing up. If he had something to say to you, he said it to your face. He could say things in a hard way, but you didn't mind because it was what he believed, and there wasn't any meanness behind it, and you respected that."[24]

As Newt and Tom conversed about shooting, no one had come close to Joe DiMaggio's hitting-streak record in baseball. Weren't some things insurmountable? As the summer of '59 progressed, Tom saw Newt didn't think that way, didn't live that way. Newt's vigor often switched the safety to red—he was ready to fire—when it came to his love of the gun sports. In Elko, Newt had established the Ranchinn Skeet and Trap Club and was able to attract prominent shooters such as the actors Robert Stack and Andy Devine and the outstanding skeet shooter and outdoor goods retailer Alex Kerr. Newt and Mr. Kerr were competitors, Newt winning a 410 national championship and finishing second to Kerr in the 20 gauge, and Newt even got the mention of outdoors writer Jimmy Robinson as a member of the All America Skeet Team chosen by *Sports Afield* in 1954.[25]

Newt proved often that he clearly was proficient with guns. The National Skeet Tournament was conducted in Reno, and on July 29, 1953, Newt of Elko won the sub-small .410 championship on opening day of the event, hitting ninety-eight of one hundred. But Newt was disqualified in the two-man division even though the winning score of 194 shot with William Venters of Culver City, California, topped the closest competitor (Kerr and T.H. Mettler of Bakersfield) by four. Crumley and Venters were DQ'ed because they were not from the same state, which was a tourney requirement.[26]

Newt's aim with the gun opened his eyes to how good a shot Tom was. And as adroit at drawing attention as Newt was, Tom didn't lack for magnetism himself. In his not-too-distant days at the Grand American, people would follow Tom while he walked the shooting line. The line of traps was about a mile long, and once Tom would step down and continue his walk toward the building Remington had on premises and used to sell and service guns, Tom was surrounded by people who wanted to know what it took to bust targets like he did.[27]

Newt was quite impressed by the shooting Tom performed at his exhibitions. Like Ad Toepperwein had done years before him, Tom was proficient while drawing images into metal using .22 bullets from about twenty feet. It took Tom seven minutes to shoot his Indian head drawing. And, like Toepperwein, the artistic flair seemed to be dominant in the gene pool.

"You can't erase this lead," Tom said. "I got it from my family. My father was a draftsman, and I have two sisters who are illustrators."[28]

Shooting the profile of the Indian head was a static trick: however brilliantly it turned out, he stood there and fired for this one. But the rest of Tom's show arrested and impressed the senses just as The Wonderful Topperweins had a generation earlier. Fruit as big as watermelons would be thrown where they would meet destruction from Tom's gunpowder-fired metal volley. They were transformed into a glucose vapor, drawing an every-sense curtain—an entertainment experience that played with feel, sight, audio, smell, and taste even—in front of a crowd that always grew into the hundreds. People were impressed by watching the solid forms they saw every day turned into nothingness at seemingly the same instant as the sound of the powerful gun. It was a shocking elemental change developed at inconceivable speed.

If Tom was going to contemplate a run at the Toepperwein record, he'd need to get back in shooting shape. If he did his research, he'd know that Ad Toepperwein conducted a 20,000-target prep shoot two months before he went about the record-breaking shoot. But, with more than fifty years passed, it looked like some details were so foggy to have been totally missed. Tom's only listed prep came out in the form of a recollection of a joking comment he once told to his old brother-in-law Fred Waldock back in Ohio, that skeet shooters were "broken down trapshooters." There was no questioning that Tom was broken down, since he just in the winter of '59 was in the hospital recovering from the surgery to fuse and mend his four vertebrae. He could use a skeet competition to keep his shooting practiced without having to worry about the quicker movements trap required to lead and hit targets. In August 1959, Tom entered the prestigious Western Grand Skeet Championship at Harolds Trap and Skeet Club in Reno. And the results he saw had to please him. He won the professional honors in 20 gauge, 28 gauge, and 410 gauge divisions.[29]

Tom was just about convinced to give this thing a go. While he was thinking it over in his head, Newt and the Holiday Hotel were sending forty-five boys from the Reno Babe Ruth Baseball League to San Francisco via plane to see the 1959 Giants' home opener against the Chicago Cubs at Seals Stadium. They also toured the under-construction Candlestick Park and a maintenance building for United Airlines, which was typical of the pilot Newt.[30]

That trip, noticeably reported in the daily newspapers, struck right at the heart of what Tom needed to know from Newt. This thing, having Tom shoot at the Toepperwein record with Newt's Holiday Hotel involved, sure did look like a publicity stunt. Newt admitted as much: "The event would help publicize [the] Holiday," Newt told Tom. But Tom thought about it some more: ". . . [H]e sure wouldn't want me messing around making the hotel look ridiculous. This gave me a certain confidence."[31]

He was well on his way to becoming convinced. Others were not.

If Dick Baldwin sat in his Remington advertising department office and wondered what sort of copy he could generate over one of the company's shooters fabulously breaking the fifty-two-year-old Toepperwein record with the "Space Age" gun being marketed as the Nylon 66, he soon saw it would not become reality. He heard what company executives were telling Tom Frye about his marathon shooting idea.

"Don't try and break Toepperwein's record," Baldwin said, relating to friends the conversation he knew was going on between Remington and its upstart field rep. "If you do, we'll be right back where we were 50 years ago—one [firearms company] trying to outdo the other with spectacular shooting performances."[32]

That made it sound like Remington was afraid of Winchester Repeating Arms Company, for whom Ad Toepperwein worked when he broke the endurance-shooting record in 1907. Indeed, there was a suspicion in the sports-shooting community that the firearms companies were cutting back on sponsoring or employing someone who could promote the merchandise with a traveling show of skill. Ad and Plinky Toepperwein had traveled the country. Herb Parsons, Mr. Toepperwein's successor at Winchester, had been doing it until his death in July 1959. Frye was limited to shows on the West Coast for Remington.

And perhaps this is what triggered it. Somewhere inside Tom, covered by an outward personality of reserve and matter-of-factness, was an ego that sometimes was hard to see. But it could, as Tom's fellow reps at Remington knew, emerge to be as big as the great outdoors.[33] It was wired, spring-loaded, inside him. Yet when sprung it didn't bounce around through the room with words. It was action.

The admonition Tom heard from Remington?

"Tom listened to this with only one ear, and being a shooter he couldn't hear too well with that one," Dick Baldwin told people. "He decided if Remington didn't want him to do it on their time, he'd take vacation and do it on his own time."[34]

What had gotten into him? He was snubbing his nose at his own employer. He had to have some sort of backup plan if this thing fell apart. Was it Newt? Was it his fiancée, Carolyn Kerr, from the wealthy family of sporting goods retailer Alex Kerr?

Just three years earlier, noted firearms pundit Col. Charles Askins wrote an article appearing in a 1956 edition of *Guns Digest* that reminded everyone of Ad Toepperwein's record. "So discouragingly lethal was the performance of this amazing marksman," Col. Askins wrote, "that no one to this day to the best of my knowledge has had the temerity to even tackle his record. It will unquestionably stand for all time."

A few days after Tom and Newt were "just talking" about no one breaking the Toepperwein record, when Newt told Tom, "I think you could . . . you shoot blocks in your shows and never miss . . . why don't you just keep going?" Newt pulled the line and set the hook, and he caught Tom. Newt once battled a 286-pound marlin for five hours and forty minutes in the Sea of Cortez. His friends said it was a world record,[35] and Newt wanted nothing less now that he landed 6-foot-2, 210-pound Tom Frye. "Newt mentioned,"

Tom started telling others, "that he had scouted up a lumberman who estimated that 100,000 blocks . . . would come to eight truckloads and cost about $3,600."

Eight truckloads of wooden blocks? It would cost $3,600? One hundred thousand blocks—100,000!

"Just to keep it in round figures," Newt said.

Such a number, kindly kept in round figures by Newt, would absolutely shatter a record that supposedly never would be broken. Tom's mind couldn't turn off the thought: Newt really thinks I can shoot.[36]

CHAPTER EIGHTEEN

Pack 'Em Up, Move 'Em Out

Clint Eastwood Follows Tom and Newt to Nevada

With every shot, it was almost like a faint black mark, a smudge, could be noticed upon the material's surface. The squash court had been built right there next to the kitchen in the Crumley house in Elko. There was a gallery, a sort of landing, where people could watch the games being played below, that little black ball being hurtled into the high wall with those long racquets. This was how passionately Newt Crumley took on his sports. He had a gym in the house, his belief in fitness spurred from his college days when participation in boxing finally began to beef up that skinny body of his.[1]

The squash games continued to show Newt's flair for getting things organized, often with sporting events, for the ultimate presentation that would serve to promote his business endeavors. He had formed the Elko Squash Racquet Club, the only club west of the Mississippi to be affiliated with the national organization. He'd get teams from air bases in California to fly in for matches.[2]

It was a complement to his work, where Newt's family knew he tended to twice daily. His first trip to the office came during normal business hours. But he went back at it after having dinner at home. His children thought it was normal for a man to shave twice every day.[3]

"From the time he took over the Holiday . . . he introduced a type of personalized service which is difficult to obtain in this day and age," said Robert Dill, who was public relations and sports director for the Holiday. "He made

Among the actors who attended the 1959 shooting event outside Dayton, Nevada, was Clint Eastwood, standing closest to Tom Frye. Eastwood was enjoying a breakout role in the CBS-TV show *Rawhide*. Remington Society of America.

it literally a 'Home away from home.'" Eddie Gersich was a bartender at the Comstock Bar in the hotel when the place opened in December 1956, and he said, "I've been out hunting with him and Mrs. Crumley. I knew his dad before I came to the Holiday. He's a great all-around guy."[4]

And so it was with the marathon shoot he planned for Tom Frye. Newt did everything he could to see that it would go off orderly, and that his guy would have every chance to succeed. There was the $3,600 Newt shelled out for eight truckloads of wooden blocks, which appeared to be cut to a size of 2 ½ inches to 2 ⅝ inches.[5] Throw in the $1,600 worth of .22 cartridges from the Remington-owned Peters ammo group. There was also the group of seven local men who would alternate to assist Tom at the shoot—the equivalent of the "husky boys" who were so helpful to Ad Toepperwein. They would register the score, toss blocks into the air, and load the weapons for Tom and keep them coming, grabbing one gun from Tom when the magazine was emptied and handing a loaded one back to him to keep him firing as quickly as possible. They were Charles Bewley, Leslie Downs, Glenn Mackie, Alvin Nelson, Dave Poole, Bill Williams, and Fred Willis. They believed Mr. Crumley made it clear what he expected from them. "I have a lot of confidence in Tom Frye," he told them. "It will be up to you fellows to record each shot that is fired and to afterward sign every score sheet. I want it accurate. Understand?" Everyone nodded.[6]

The Holiday Hotel would be the base of operations. Tom would be put up in a room there. He would be driven to the Holiday Game Ranch, about an hour away from the hotel and located below Dayton, Nevada. The ranch was advertised as a place for gamblers who chose to get away from their high-stakes action at the tables to partake in hunts of four-legged critters and fowl. Pheasant hunts were particularly boosted. It was stark countryside—right at the edge of the Sierra Nevada Mountains and the Nevada desert—with low-lying foothills and distant mountains and plenty of scrub and brush. There was plenty of room to shoot guns, and have the Holiday name attached to a world record, at the game ranch—in the middle of nowhere.

Tom's roaring appetite would be fed like a high-roller's at the Holiday's dining rooms when he ate nightly with his fiancée, Carolyn. Everything else would be taken care of, too. Tom didn't need a reporter's question the night before the event to ask him if he was ready.

"I'm well aware of the physical grind I am facing," he responded.[7]

Again, Newt was more than on top of it. He maintained a family doctor between both cities when the Crumleys split time between Elko and Reno. Dr. Louis Lombardi—Newt referred to his fellow University of Nevada regent as Louie—was the family doctor in Reno.[8] He was the team physician for the athletic teams for the Wolfpack. He would check Tom daily. There would be rubdowns, mornings before the shoot and at night following.

Tom would be taken care of. The shooting was up to him.

The score sheets were laid out across the rectangular table that was covered by the Remington green cloth that Tom Frye always took with him and spread out for everyone to see at his exhibitions. Even without their blessing, the Remington brand was sewn onto that familiar jacket Tom wore at all his shoots. So much for Tom being forced to back down from something. Dick Baldwin, the ad rep, had news for them. "Newt Crumley . . . provided . . . the money to do it," he would say. "Four men were assigned to work in pairs, throwing the targets into the air. [He's] using two Nylon 66 autoloading rifles. Tom settled down to work."[9]

If Remington couldn't stop Tom from shooting, they could make sure he got back to work when he was scheduled. Tom had the standard two-week vacation. The first day leading into his vacation would be the weekend, Saturday, and it was hand-printed as October 3, 1959, at the top of that scoresheet. These were the same scorepads with the Remington and Peters brand names at the top that Tom provided for trapshoots throughout his territory in Southern California. There was a blank next to the word "City," and into this was written: Reno. There were twenty-five little squares lined off across the sheets, and six lines worth of squares. But there was only one person looking at that right now, for about ten feet away a pair of long arms lifted a four-pound rifle, butt stock against shoulder, a finger from the right hand squeezing a trigger just ever so when the shooter's two open eyes glared past the gun's sight and watched a cube of pine tossed into the dry Nevada air.

Crack. The sound went out into almost nothingness, diffusing through sagebrush, only to carom off those foothills before ever reaching those distant mountains.

A diagonal line from right down to left was marked through one of the tiny squares printed on that sheet. It looked like whoever was doing the scorekeeping would have to go through quite a few of those sheets before a zero was marked into any square.[10]

Tom told everyone he intended to keep that scorekeeper busy, and he was said to make some boastful comments as the shoot had begun. One writer reported, "Tom vowed he'd not only clobber 100,000 targets, but miss fewer in 100,000 than had Ad in 72,500."[11] But the only actual quote in this regard from Tom the writer used for the story was, "If I beat the 72,500 mark," Tom said, "I want to beat it good."[12]

If he shot for fifteen days straight, using eight-hour days, Tom would have to average more than 6,500 each day. Ad Toepperwein had shot at an average of a little more than 1,000 blocks per hour, so Tom would get a break there. He wouldn't have to quite reach 900 per hour to make it to 100,000, if that was really a break. But it was. Toepperwein used ten days to shoot 72,500 blocks. That's 7,250 a day. Maybe Tom could get his 100,000 out of the way with days to spare, but he had fifteen open dates on his calendar that he could use. If he elected to use them all, it would mean his work load would average less than 6,750 a day. Whatever; shooting 3,000 the first day was putting him behind woefully from the start. But Tom knew the pace of his shooting was not totally in his control; Newt was the guy who took him in when Remington would not, so he had to march to the drummer. When the reporters and autograph seekers were out on Day One, people could see and hear that Tom was accommodating everyone.[13]

He had to pick up the pace, not even into his second day. And, not even into his second day, he started getting an idea what Mr. Toepperwein had gone through. Tom looked at his trigger finger. His skin had been rubbed through. Those shots might not have bounced off far-away mountain walls, but they were bouncing around somewhere. He lay down in his bed at the Holiday that night following Day One, having not even shot 3,500 rounds, and yet he could hear those shots echoing through his head. Thank goodness for Dr. Louie. Tom grabbed a sleeping pill, swallowed it, and had little complaint after that. He was up at 6:30 for his shower, his breakfast, a rubdown, and then an application onto his finger of "liquid skin" that Dr. Lombardi had taken out of the football team's medicine kit. He drank up the coffee—four cups was nothing—and turned that caffeine into commands.

He wanted three men from the crew throwing the blocks on the second day to start sending them up in rapid succession. Three of them stood there and sent them skyward one right after another. He blitzed through the fourteen shots contained in his autoloader, grabbed the other reloaded one that was handed to him by another assistant. In twenty minutes, Tom fired with a sore trigger finger and hit 1,700 blocks without a miss—eighty-five per minute and obviously better than one per second after the more than 120 handoffs of the rifle from an assistant.

"From a distance," someone in the crowd said through a chuckle, "you'd have thought some Joe was triggering a machine gun."[14]

Tom had another fifty-minute session without rest where he hit 2,000. That was more than twice the amount he needed to average each hour. If Newt wanted Tom to rub elbows with celebrities that he might bring out, press the flesh with kids and anyone else who wanted an autograph or to shake his hand, Tom was in. He'd proven he could make up for lost time, and his accuracy wasn't suffering on account. Finally, through all those sheets from the scorepad, there was one "0" written while David Poole was keeping score on Day Two. A miss.[15]

After a couple of days not reporting on the event, apparently swamped by college and pro football scores and the World Series going on between the

Dodgers—newly moved to L.A. where they played in front of an unprecedented crowd of more than 92,000 in the Los Angeles Coliseum—and the "Go-Go Sox" from Chicago, the *Nevada State Journal* from Reno reported that after four days Tom Frye had shot at 20,300 targets thrown into desert air that could be as cool as 28 degrees in the morning yet warm under brilliant sunshine to readings in the 70s by the afternoon. Although the "weary, sunburned rifleman," the paper reported, "headed for Reno for a rubdown, medical checkup, hearty dinner and sound sleep," by late the next day he was at 27,310. The report after six days, Tom "firing continuously every day since Saturday," was that he shot at 35,250 blocks and missed two.[16]

No one at the newspaper did the math, or reported it. But the results were ridiculous. His shooting percentage was .99994 at that point. How could a man do that?

The splinters from 43,723 wooden blocks were strewn in front of the scoring and staging table covered with the green cloth and the white TOM FRYE REMINGTON GUNS lettering sewn into it. Beyond, a landscape of desert sage rising to the horizon of dry, sand-colored mountains framed the work of the rifleman and his assistants. This wood-chipped mess made by Tom's shooting was blending right in with the rough countryside.

This also was a scene of efficiency, of momentum, and Newt Crumley wasn't going to let it blend in with anything. Not when his own banner—Newt Crumley's HOLIDAY in Reno—was unfurled on the growing pile of blocks Tom had shot through. It was emboldening, for Tom's shooting really had put more than 40,000 chunks of wood over there—bullet holes in all but two of them to prove it. After a week of shooting, Newt had seen that Tom and his Nylon 66 rifles had pierced the wooden targets at a rate of more than 6,200 a day. He wasn't at Toepperwein's pace of 50,750 through seven days of the shoot more than fifty years ago, but he was on pace to break the record with twelve days of shooting. And his pace picked up on Friday; he actually shot at 6,475 that day.[17] If he surged past the record on Day Twelve, it would give him three more to reach 100,000, if he was up to it as he boasted at the shoot's startup.

But the shooting would have to take a backseat. Promotion was on Newt's mind. On Saturday, what would be the eighth day of the shoot, Newt's budget had convinced two of America's rising stars on the emergent medium of television to come and look good with a guy shooting a mind-numbing amount of blocks over and over again out in the middle of nowhere. The Gil Favor–Rowdy Yates duo from the new television series *Rawhide*—Eric Fleming and Clint Eastwood—was packed up and moving out to Dayton. The University of Nevada ROTC rifle team was to attend. Newt, the man who was an only child growing up, had buses of orphaned and disadvantaged kids brought to the shooting site from the Nevada State Children's Home in Carson City, also known as Sunny Acres. Tom's hand was getting a break from the gun, but it stayed busy when the boys asked him for autographs of the wooden blocks he had shot holes through. And to catch it all, NBC-affiliate KRON-TV was sending cameraman Charles Stanyan from San Francisco, a significant market for the gambling in Reno, to be on hand with plans to shoot footage for a national airing.[18]

They found Fleming and Eastwood to be in fashionable, if not businesslike, dress. Eastwood was in a short-sleeved dark shirt with dark slacks, and Fleming rolled the sleeves on his white-cloth buttoned-down shirt midway up his forearms and left his collar loosely unbuttoned. His hair was slicked back, and the dress shoes looked awkward as Fleming scaled the wooden-block heap with Tom wearing work boots.[19]

Each smiled in photos. Eastwood was enjoying a breakthrough year. By the time 1959 rolled around he had appeared in almost a dozen movies. Executives at CBS were attracted to Eastwood's height, 6-foot-4, and he was sent to Arizona for the shooting of *Rawhide* with the aim of appearing in the fall season of 1958. When CBS inserted the show as a mid-season replacement in January 1959, fan mail for Eastwood's Rowdy Yates character soon outstacked that of main man Gil Favor, played by Fleming. Eastwood, who could make $750 for a movie, was making $600 a week at the beginning of *Rawhide*. By the time he showed up at Dayton, that salary was doubled.[20]

The day finished and the stars were to eat dinner with Tom and his fiancée. Carolyn was not impressed with Eastwood. His air rubbed Carolyn the wrong way. "Now," Tom warned her, "Mr. Crumley paid good money to bring these people in to help promote the shoot."[21]

It might have made the society pages, but the sports pages of the *Nevada State Journal* and the *Reno Evening Gazette* were practically blank when it came to the shoot. It was a football weekend. The sports section didn't mix in anything from the shoot site until October 14, a Wednesday, reporting on activity from eleven days after the event started. Some of the reports stated that Tom had started firing on Saturday, October 3, and that he "has devoted the biggest part of each day since to firing," and that he was confident that he could reach 100,000 blocks before he finished his vacation and was due back at Remington.[22] Because Tom "lost time Saturday and Sunday [October 10–11] due to numerous visitors and interruptions," he played the catchup game again and fired at 10,500 blocks with one miss. He had reached his 65,500th block.[23] Another day like that, with no stars or hardly anyone else there that he was obligated to pose alongside, and the Toepperwein record would go.

CHAPTER NINETEEN
Killing Crows
Tom, His Record Chase, and the End of His Vacation

Tom Frye took pills to silence the bullets ricocheting through his mind at night. He could dab "liquid skin" onto his raw trigger finger. He was seen as the "weary, sunburned rifleman," who shuffled off to Reno after his first few days of firing. He slept some, but groaned a lot.[1] And this was just the first week of his two-week vacation.

He shot. He shot. He shot. He shot. He shot. He shot. He shot. He shot. He shot. He shot. He shot. He shot. He shot. He shot. He handed off an empty gun to an assistant. He accepted a return of another Nylon 66 loaded with fourteen cartridges ready to go, he carried the four-pound gun into an aiming position. Blocks went up.

And he shot. . . .

As Tom had finished up at the event site for the day, he placed a call for his fiancée, Carolyn. "How'd you do today?" she asked. "Oh, about seven thousand. Didn't miss any." She didn't hear him complain, or at least not bellyache over the pain he was feeling. She knew what she had in Tom. "He's tough," she thought.[2]

Pain wasn't the problem, at least not to this point. Yet what was bothering Tom the most was so obvious, and it was persistent beyond belief.

"Boredom became a problem," Tom reluctantly admitted.[3]

Yet he shot, and he shot, and. . . .

It's over. Tom Frye gets his picture atop 100,000 wooden blocks at the completion of his October 1959 endurance shooting event on property owned by Newt Crumley's Holiday Hotel and Casino outside Dayton, Nevada. Remington Society of America.

Such was the degree of monotony, of flat-out dull periods with nothing else to do. The Reno newspapers even stayed away. It was almost like a blackout had been imposed over the numbing goings-on at the Holiday Game Ranch. There was in the Reno sports scene, but the newspapers were catching it over at Pyramid Lake where the Reno Regatta was being conducted. There, hydroplane speedboats skipped along the water and rumbled forth an exhilarating lion's roar compared to the pipsqueak .22 caliber.

That changed with the appearance of the TV stars. He may not have shot much that weekend—the dailies did not report a count—but Tom kept busy with autographs and obliging the media. He was on his feet, and he shot in the neighborhood of one thousand targets for all the visitors so they actually could see what he was up to.

It, the "interruptions including stints for television cameras and autographing targets, [has] slackened his pace," a reporter wrote upon finally returning to the shooting site for the tenth day of the event. With likely fewer than fifteen hundred shots fired over the weekend, it put him behind his pace again. But, perhaps, it was worth it. It had broken the boredom. It had lifted his outlook. The reporter heard Tom say that "he has experienced little of the physical beating he had anticipated." The writer put the credit on the lighter rifles. Certainly, Tom had a lighter load.

A photo that appeared in the October 13 edition of the *Nevada State Journal*, two days following the Eric Fleming–Clint Eastwood visit, captured the shooting machine known as the Tom Frye world-record marathon. The image captured Tom shooting very closely to the stack of blocks that was grabbed at by one assistant, subtracted piece by piece, and handed to the assistant who was throwing the blocks in the air at the time. He had one in midair that Tom aimed upon, another one was in the grasp of his right hand, right next to Tom, and his left hand about to be restocked by his fellow assistant with another block.[4]

This was the stance Tom and company would have to take from here on out. He was behind. When Ad Toepperwein set his record in 1907, he used the ten days to shoot at 72,500 with the nine missed. Through his ten days, Tom shot at 55,000 and missed just two. He had five more days to go. Looks like he could get the Toepperwein record, and perhaps keep it under the nine misses that was his goal to start. But Newt paid for 100,000 blocks. Almost half of them were still sitting over there. To get through them would mean he'd have to use that damaged trigger finger to pop a stunning 9,000 a day. Could he maintain such strain for five straight days?

He'd start it off with breakfast. It was what could only be called a "slab" of ham that was the foundation for four whole eggs. He made it sink to his insides with three cups of coffee.[5] His visits with Dr. Lombardi meant more care for his trigger finger, more bandaging and wraps to cover bandages already covering the liquid skin. After he hopped out of the chauffeur-driven car to Dayton he'd drink more coffee. At 8 o'clock he shot. And shot. He'd empty one gun and start in on the other. Two of the Nylon 66s were used, though two more also got into the rotation at times. As many as three people would reload them at the table and have them ready to hand off to Tom. Every hour he and the crew took a five-minute break. Reporters now were assigned by editors to keep showing up to record it.[6]

The crowd picked up on the morning of Wednesday, October 14, the twelfth day of the shoot. At midday, it was clear why they were there. About one hundred people rimmed the staging table. There was the obvious crack of the .22, but other than that only an intermittent sound here and there could be made out by those drawing close. Tension, and long-awaited expectation, seemed to finally draw out details from the mundane proceedings.

These rifle cracks were answered only by a stroke onto the Remington Peters trapshooting scoresheets from a worn-down pencil tip at the hand of the scorekeeper. He rechecked his tallies, just to make sure before he announced the count on the upcoming block to be thrown into the air: "72,499." Someone else knew their math and whispered, "Three more to go." A block went airborne and Tom stuck it with a bullet. The same for block 72,500. He'd tied Ad Toepperwein's record, and no more than a couple of seconds later—"One more to go, and he'll have it," came another hushed sentence from the gathering—No. 72,501 was in the palm and fingers of another tired assistant. A casino boss, who came to watch the shoot while off from his shift, scratched a match across the black strip on his matchbook, his waiting cigarette drooped from between his lips while the flame ignited. Just as haltingly, a woman eased a soft-drink bottle down to her side. It was labeled in white cursive on the side, making its brand clear in an instant. The graphite tip tallied a mark on the scorepad there next to Tom. Then off, way off, perhaps from those foothills, an annoying noise. It was a caw of a bird.[7] It traveled through the air and mixed up there with the tossed wooden block—and shooting history. This was target 72,501. Tom's racket was much more penetrating than the bird's.

He shot. And . . . it was hit.

"He's done it," somebody said through their desert-air raspy voice. "Done it!"[8]

It was about time someone spoke above a whisper, for how could any talk really bother a guy whose mind was mushed by a number of shots that was approaching the population count of Reno's 84,000?[9] Even though he topped Toepperwein's record number, Tom appeared to go about everything unsentimentally. His hands retained their grip around the rifle, only releasing to flip on some sunshades there underneath the hard bill of his shooting helmet. He got that helmet back in place and said something to the assistants grabbing and throwing the blocks right at his side: "Keep 'em coming. We're headed to 100,000."[10]

That's how adrenaline speaks. Tom felt the rush of the record, even if he didn't show it.[11] Maybe it took him a day and a half longer than Mr. Toepperwein to reach 72,500, but Tom beat the record and missed five fewer in the process. And he was back to work. He was working through a nine-hour day. He could rein down another 2,750 bullet-pierced blocks before it was quitting time. Newt had shown up to the shoot, his face bronze but showing the signs of coming age with a crease here and there along with the squints and the smiles underneath that fedora he was wearing. A vest, too, and a flannel shirt that made it look like he just pulled a rod away from his favorite trout brook. He brought out Rex Bell, the actor-turned-politician and sitting lieutenant governor of Nevada, wearing a pressed straw cowboy hat. He wasn't out there to pressure Tom to keep going. But it was clear what Tom needed to do: Reach 100,000, and he still was right around 25,000 away with three more days of shooting before it was time to go back and fill sales orders for Remington's customers in Southern California. He was extending the run for his record. Ad Toepperwein did, too, cruising well past the Carver-Bartlett record of 60,000. But, for Tom, was this extending a record, or meeting a quota?

The rocks and sand of western Nevada still crunched under his boots. The metal tubes that would slide even more cartridges into the magazine of the Nylon 66 angled and crisscrossed as Pixie sticks from out of a bucket sitting on top of the staging table. And blocks would not stop rising into the air, spinning first with the English imparted by the assistant who threw it, and changing that rotation into a sort of flip once the slug that Tom had fired made its connection. Sometimes, rarely, a toss would not get the block high enough, and Tom would pass up a shot like Ad Toepperwein did on occasion. Tom felt he could still get a good pass at it, but such a shot would bring into play some purebred beef on the hoof grazing not too far off. As much as the assistant could try to make a consistent toss so as not to break

Tom's rhythm, those efforts couldn't pull Tom away from the state of mind he was experiencing.

"Because of the repetitiousness," Tom explained, "you are shooting in a dream state. The rhythm helps, but nothing can take away the cramps which develop in your forearm and shoulder. This hurts so much that the fact that the skin has peeled off your trigger finger isn't as alarming as it otherwise would be."[12]

That finger looked a mite grisly. Not only had it become painful on every shot, it was sore just to touch it. Even when Tom wrapped his right hand around the grip to slip a finger through the trigger guard, it was easy to see that his hand was swollen through to the trigger finger and thumb. He couldn't even pull the arm on the slot machines back at the Holiday's casino. But he wanted to keep shooting, to get it over, so he began balking at the idea of the five-minute break everyone else wanted to take each hour. But the assistants sat him down and gently stretched the fingers and worked Tom's shooting hand. Someone else would get him more coffee and stoke it with sugar. He was up to a gallon of java a day.[13]

Yet the firing continued hardly without pause not counting the short breaks, until one of those blocks kept its spin through the air and fell to the ground without a flight-altering tip-over. He missed. Were they sure? That was the call from the staging table. A few of the assistants went over to double check as Tom waited. The only thing neat about those wooden blocks at this point in the tiring shoot was the short line of blocks that had not been hit. And this block went into that line. It became the fifth without a hole in it.[14]

Although, as Friday, October 16 went on and it looked like he would shoot past nine thousand targets for the fourth day in a row, not even the thought of having about five thousand more to shoot on his final scheduled day on Saturday could relieve the tension that was appearing in Tom's face and body. Even though he was wearing tinted shooting glasses, the process of picking out the pale-colored targets from an almost constant sunny sky was bothering his eyes. He said, in fact, that they were burning, and the redness was proof. His arms, quite understandably, were growing very sore. His legs were cramping.[15] Usually a very upright fellow, Tom began stooping ever so slightly as he edged past the ninety-hour point of the shoot. Even the pills, the muscle-relaxers, Tom thought, weren't quite pulling their prescribed load anymore.[16]

If the pills no longer registered their full kick with Tom, he found a more natural way to put a little flair into the proceedings. He didn't mind the five-minute breaks anymore. When they came, Tom got away from the blocks. He grinned. He pointed off some ways where a crow was gliding not too far off the ground. He'd creep along, perhaps fifty yards, not worry about the pain involved in moving his rifle into the aim position, and fire off a round that would eliminate the crow.[17]

"If I hadn't seen it," a spectator rattled off, "I'd never had believed it. The guy finishes triggering 1,000 shots in 60 minutes . . . then bird-stalks, for just one more shot."

"Why not?" Tom answered back. "It's as good a way to relax as any."[18]

He could relax that final day. He had a little more than five thousand shots to squeeze with that worn-out finger. A casino executive who joined the crowd for that final day figured it was rubber-stamped. "He'll bust 100,000 today, sure."[19]

He took it at a leisurely pace, not finishing the thing until sunset was near. Because he continued on through the Toepperwein record, he now chose to afford himself with a piece of history. The shot he fired on block No. 100,000 darn near went through the center of one face of the cube. Tom laid down a Nylon 66 that had done its job well, without a misfire or malfunction, one among the four he used. He walked out to the spot where the block had fallen and tumbled. He looked down, reached, and picked it up. That one went in his pocket, and he turned back to the staging table with a smile turning up one edge of his mouth. "Guess we've got one for the books," he said softly, "one that'll stick around for a while."[20]

But Tom took up arms again. He had his assistants grab more blocks, and he put them under fire. He stamped out ten more. The extra shooting allowed him to say he definitely not only shot at 100,000 blocks, he hit 100,000. It was a unique signature to put at the bottom of his statement to the shooting world.[21]

The stats from the shoot, then, were utterly remarkable. He'd hit 100,004 of the 100,010 that were tossed into the air by the assistants who had been standing right next to him. Missing six, that's a .99994 clip. Not only had the Ad Toepperwein record of 72,500 been well surpassed, the consecutive run of targets hit was pulverized. Mr. Toepperwein's best was 14,540 in a row. Tom had one stretch of 32,860 consecutive hits. There were other lengthy runs: 14,322 and 13,017, according to the score sheet.[22]

The telegrams offering congratulations would wire in soon enough. Tom

As the careers of Ad and Plinky Toepperwein winded down during the World War II era, their tours for Winchester Repeating Arms Company became more limited mostly due to wartime rationing. Targets like tomatoes, which painted a vivid red burst through the air when shot with a .22-caliber bullet, were replaced by the go-to wooden blocks the Toepperweins had used for years.
Collection of Kenneth Toepperwein.

had the first one of those in his hands even before reaching 100,000. But at the bottom he read that he had to, the day after he was done, arrive at a Boy Scouts' encampment in another western state to get ready for a show. Tom laughed. It was from his old friend Lee Braun, who also was his immediate supervisor at Remington. "I [have] to go," Tom said.[23] But not before he climbed that mountain of blocks, 100,000 of them. He propped a Nylon 66 onto his thigh, looked out from underneath that shooting helmet, and smiled.

So this was it. One of the headlines told the story the next day: "Frye Satisfied, Hits 100,000th Target, Then Quits." He was credited with the "world marathon shooting record." He'd worked through the soreness in his wrist, arm, and shoulder and did something, he told reporters, he had wanted to do since he started shooting guns. He shot past the record of Ad Toepperwein.

But word only trickled out in some places. Remington, in fact, didn't get around to sending out a release acknowledging the record of its own man until December—about seven weeks later. At that point newspapers all over the country picked it up and told the story.

And maybe that's what brought about this next note to Tom. It was a letter that would make the heart stop. It was typed and addressed simply to the Remington Fire Arms Co., Bridgeport, Connecticut, and dated December 19, 1959:

> Dear Mr. Frye,
>
> I have been informed of your wonderful record which you made recently and hereby offer you my congratulations for your wonderful preformance [*sic*].
>
> While I do not know exactly under what conditions and rules you shot this score, it is certainly a very wonderful performance. It calls for wonderful endurance and accuracy. Your score is so wonderful that you probably could not have done better if you had put them on a fence post. I know that you must have been very tired and I hope you will have no ill effects of your great undertaking and continue your good shooting for a long while to come. Don't let your trigger finger get rusty and keep your powder dry. Good luck and my best wishes for your continued success.
>
> Sincerely yours,
> Ad Topperwein[24]

Part Five

The Spent Casings

Sitting down on the job. It took more than 200 shots for Ad Toepperwein to complete one of his "bullet drawings," this one of Uncle Sam, while Plinky was ready with more ammo. Collection of Kenneth Toepperwein.

CHAPTER TWENTY

Broken Hearts at Creve Coeur

Triumph and Tragedy Visit Ad and Plinky

It didn't take Ad Toepperwein long to come up with the thought. In fact, he answered almost instantly when asked what his considerations were as to the sort of livelihood he wanted to pursue.

"I would rather be a good shot, be able to pass the idea of straight rifle-pointing along to our coming generations, than to be President of the United States. Both Mrs. Top and I like our work—or, I should say, love it. We never get through or get tired of shooting. I rock myself to sleep at night thinking and planning the next day's shooting and trying to figure out how to improve and why I missed those shots today."[1]

Judging by the sales generated at Winchester Repeating Arms Company as The Wonderful Topperweins began to tour together as exhibition shooters, there were plenty of people who caught on to Ad and Plinky's enthusiasm. The fancy shooters' employment coincided with a sharp upswing in sales at Winchester. Business out of the New Haven plant boomed as America peacefully enjoyed the years of triumph after the war with Spain. From 1890 to 1914 firearm production increased a factor of five; employment was up a factor of four.[2]

As they had tried with Clara, Ad's sister, Ad and Plinky believed the idea of passing straight rifle-pointing to the coming generations started at home. Indeed, they taught marksmanship and gun safety to their only child, Lawrence, by the time he was a teenager. Ad began shooting when he was six. He had wanted to do it.

Ad Toepperwein often looked in a hand mirror and shot objects behind him. The man holding the target is identified by family members as likely Lawrence Toepperwein. Collection of Kenneth Toepperwein.

Just seven months following Ad's record endurance shoot in San Antonio, Plinky lined up for what was going to be her most ambitious performance with a gun. Topping her five hundred target shoot when she hit four hundred eighty-five clays from sixteen yards in two hours and twenty-five minutes in June 1906,[3] this time she would shoot at one thousand targets sprung from regulation traps. Only two people—both men—had ever been known to have tried this before in a regulation setting. One writer warned her it was "no child's play."[4] Plinky knew, and she fired two sessions on July 18, 1908, between two hours, fifteen minutes and two-and-a-half hours each at Scheuermeyer's Park, the site in San Antonio the previous summer of Ad's 20,000-wooden-block shoot. One writer estimated that she was taking twenty-seven pounds of recoil from her seven-and-half-pound shotgun on every shot. Blisters formed on her hand from the vibration and the heat from the barrel (she would dip the barrel regularly into water to cool it off). The sun was in her eyes in the morning, yet she fought through it to post only fifteen misses from her first five hundred. She was on pace to break John W. Garrett's record of nine hundred sixty-five from one thousand targets, set four years earlier at Colorado Springs in 1904.[5]

But she couldn't hold on. Even though she broke her last hundred with two misses in sixteen minutes, and at one point had a consecutive run of one hundred and eleven, she finished with nine hundred and sixty-one—four short of the record.[6]

She continued shooting in various competitions and matches against men. Plinky had won the Indiana State Shoot hitting three hundred and eighty-eight out of a possible four hundred in heavy winds. Later in 1914 at the Grand American Handicap at Dayton, Ohio, she was the only woman in a field of more than five hundred and fifty. She broke ninety-nine of one-hundred the final day.[7] In a preliminary round of the 1916 Grand Southern Handicap at Memphis, Tennessee, she broke all one hundred targets. She beat about sixty other gunners, all men, in the program. The best of them hit ninety-eight.[8]

The Wonderful Topperweins tour with the Winchester Shooting Team was completing a run through the South. The break came in November 1916 after performing in fifteen states. The cool temperatures of fall were coming, and in Montgomery, Alabama, Plinky told the newspapers she could spend a day shooting at one thousand—or more—targets sprung from the trap of the local club. "The announcement . . . created quite a stir among the local shooting fraternity," came one report.[9]

What could follow at the trap field of the Montgomery Country Club would be akin to the action that could be had in the galleries below the ring at boxing matches. Who could prevail? Who would score the knockout? What were the odds? A crowd would show up to watch the shooter and sit for hours to see if he—or she—could prevail over himself. Here was the thirty-two-year-old Plinky ready to lift her almost eight-pound Winchester Model 97 pump-action trapgun in 12-gauge.[10] And she talked about going past one thousand blasts? No woman had done that with regulation traps. The betting was open.

From a distance measured and marked at sixteen yards, Plinky stood and fired. She got through her first line on the shooting grid of twenty-five squares with one 0 signifying a sole miss. Her fourth line went through without a blemish, giving her an initial one hundred with four misses. Again, she was after Garrett's mark.[11]

But there was a complication. The trap that hurled the clay target malfunctioned right around the three hundredth pull, and Plinky had her worst set of one hundred after that. She missed five. She recovered nicely through the next race of one hundred to miss but two. It gave her an opening five hundred with four hundred and eighty-four hit. That was a .968 percentage, and that clip would see her breaking the Garrett mark—by three—if she kept it up through the second five hundred.

But something familiar, something she experienced eight years ago when she did this, was happening. It was incredibly inopportune, for she had shot through ten-consecutive perfect events of twenty-five targets hit, had completed a marvelous consecutive run of two hundred and eighty broken targets, when in the final dozens before she reached one thousand she was working a blister onto her left hand.

Plinky had done it. She already had broken the Garrett record by ten. Did she really have anything left to prove? A doctor began examining the hand and applied a bandage. Plinky got back up to the line, and the trap was pulled. The second one thousand was on the way.[12]

But like a blockbuster heavyweight match, this was becoming difficult for the faint of heart to watch. Just six shots into the second one thousand, Plinky pulled off the bandage: "It's bothering me," she told Ad. The hand became raw. It bled. She missed four from that first set of one hundred. But then came a perfect one hundred. The next couple of hundred still managed ninety-six or better. Then came a pair of ninety-nines. She had knocked down consecutive runs of one hundred and thirty-nine, one hundred and eleven, and one hundred and six. She needed ninety-seven from her final one hundred to surpass the percentage from her first thousand. She was perfect through her first fifty pulls. She failed to bring down two in the next-to-last event of twenty-five. Still, she had one miss allowed in that final twenty-five for her to beat the first thousand—when her hand wasn't raw and bleeding like it was now. She didn't need the cushion. She was perfect. She was done. And she was in the record books: 1,952 hits from the 2,000 in five hours, twenty minutes.[13] The only chagrin she could produce among men now was that she made some of them who had bet against her dig into their pockets and pay up. Everyone else was heartily impressed and readily included the woman into realms sequestered to men. One journalist wrote to claim Mrs. Ad. Toepperwein "broke the world's record for continuous shooting."[14] The *Sporting Life* described it as "one of the most remarkable exhibitions of trap shooting ever seen," and that the "large number of local sportsmen" who were in attendance "were not disappointed, the score below will show, as they witnessed an exhibition of skill, pluck, nerve, and endurance never before seen at a shooting exhibition."

The local boys weren't the only ones left to wonder. News of the record went out over national wires. The *Washington Post* was among the large papers to pick it up, and some ran the headline with a picture of the smiling, sturdy Plinky in the striped blouse with the matching hat: WOMAN HOLDS MARK FOR WORK AT TRAPS. Mrs. Topperwein Demolishes 1,852 [*sic*] Out of 2,000 Targets. Record Endurance Feat.[15]

When Lawrence was thirteen, five years from coming of legal age, Winchester was interested in taking The Wonderful Topperweins exhibition to the military during the World War's spring of 1917. Henry Brewer, now vice president at Winchester, wrote to US Army Signal Corps Major Leonard A. Horner to see if the Toepperweins could teach trapshooting, firing at aerial targets, to aviators. "We have especially in mind Mr. and Mrs. Topperwein, who have a nation-wide reputation as marksmen with the shotgun as well with the rifle," Brewer's letter read. He broached—mindful of a society suspicious of "Huns"—the Topperwein surname, and this was after the company shortened it a few years earlier from Toepperwein. Brewer claimed their man was "of German origin but he is certainly not of German sentiment. He is a husky Texan and his wife is a New Haven girl. Both of them are keenly patriotic Americans." There were other things to consider. "I hesitate to suggest Mrs. Topperwein," Brewer allowed, "for the reason that her position in military camps would perhaps be rather embarrassing for her. On the other hand, she is a very charming ladylike woman and a first-class shotgun and rifle instructor."[16] Horner wrote back in the affirmative on the idea, with a condition: ". . . it would seem desirable to have Mr. Topperwein in the service and Mrs. Topperwein used for training men who would later assist in the schools."[17]

Ad appeared by himself at the School of Military Aeronautics in Austin for more instructing in August 1918 (he had spent some time there months earlier). They used a tower to both release the targets and station aviator trainees for fire upon the gliding targets as one of the ways to simulate the attack on the German's Boch aircraft. Mrs. Toepperwein was reported as a "close second" to her husband's ability and was expected in a few days to "assist Mr. Toepperwein in his work."[18]

With the end of hostilities, they could come back and keep Lawrence active in shooting sports. Just a few days after his fifteenth birthday, Lawrence competed in shooting matches near the Toepperwein home. In a pistol competition, Lawrence had a score of ninety-one of one hundred while shooting at a five-inch bull's-eye from twenty yards at the Municipal Range in San Antonio against a field that included majors, captains, lieutenants, and other officers.[19]

Lawrence could be joined on the firing line by his famous parents. In an event that resembled greatly Ad's instruction with the aviators headed to the World War, an eighteen-year-old Lawrence climbed atop a tower to shoot targets at San Antonio's Municipal Traps in a type of event said to be rapidly growing in popularity. Lawrence thrilled with a clean slate of fifty hits, winning by two. His parents competed on the ground in the traditional trap shoot, and Plinky won with ninety-four out of one hundred compared to Ad's ninety-two.[20]

It was a rare occasion that Ad had appeared in a competitive shoot. "So far as I know and I believe," Ad's close friend Frost Woodhull told others, "Toepperwein never shot in a [competition] in all his career. That simply isn't in his line."[21] He was an exhibition shooter, and it did him no good to risk his luster at a spot where he could lose. But he could make an exception, and he did when he accompanied his family into competition.

Lawrence had a top finish in front of his parents. He held targets for them in practice. But he seemed to drift away from competitive shooting. Just a few weeks prior to the success over traps on the tower, Lawrence was following his father's early professional successes, but those from the art department of his old employee at the *San Antonio News* building.[22]

He continued his education and work, and his parents departed again and again as The Wonderful Topperweins tour seemed unstoppable. Their activity away from home—and Lawrence—came with an incredible pace. A 1924 tour hit Florida: Pensacola, Ocala, Quincy, and Lake City. More than five hundred people were reported to have shown up in Quincy. Winchester's count had the average attendance at four hundred people. "Top answered questions on the field and at the Winchester dealer in each town. In many places he organized gun clubs," company newsletters reported. In '24 he and Plinky gave exhibitions in 130 cities in nine states and fired at least five hundred shots per stop—about 65,000 total during the tour. They went 16,000 miles and were credited for shooting in front of 130,000 people, the Winchester publicity machine claiming crowds as big as 7,500 people came to see the free show. After the next year's spring and summer swing, Winchester circulated photos of a stop at Fairview, Oklahoma, that showed a crowd with people stacked about eight deep, so thick that some had to find ways to boost themselves where they could see. And this sign appeared at the storefront of the Smith Hardware Co., in Clinton, Oklahoma: HEADQUARTERS, Ad Topperwein, WORLD'S CHAMPION SHOT, Thursday, May 21 At Stock Pavilion.[23] This was 22,000 miles of travel between March 1 and July 22, and a matching amount was expected by year's end. The window displays at hardware stores continued to announce upcoming exhibitions, and the dealers would write Winchester thanking them for sending Toepperwein. They claimed that business picked up after the appearance.[24]

In the middle of a busy 1925, smack dab in the fast swing of the Roaring 20s, The Wonderful Topperweins tour performed in a rare setting. Ad and Plinky were scheduled to perform at the Rexall Convention of druggists at Pemberton, Massachusetts, on July 22, 1925, with President Calvin Coolidge and the First Lady to be the guests of honor.[25] It was organized through the efforts of Louis K. Liggett, who Ad knew as a major shareholder of Winchester Repeating Arms Company stock. Liggett also was founder of the Rexall chain of drug stores and a political contributor to the president. About 3,500 people awaited the presidential party's arrival aboard a yacht named the *Mayflower*, and when the dignitaries finally arrived, Ad and Plinky were allowed to perform for the president for about twenty minutes. They went for a high-powered finish, a stunt they called "scrambling eggs" because Ad would toss as many as a half carton of eggs into the air, pick up his gun, and blow the things out of the air before any could be cracked upon impact with the ground. The First Lady, a bubbly, effervescent companion to "Silent Cal," clearly was thrilled. While she joined right in with ready applause, it looked like the president remained under the rocking effect of the ocean even on dry land. Ad and Plinky thought he was sleeping. He finally was rousted when the eggs were scrambled in the air. Mrs. Coolidge came over and warmly thanked the Toepperweins, telling them she thought their talent was about the most wonderful thing she'd seen. The president followed, his words a trademark few: "That was a very splendid exhibition of skill in shooting," President Coolidge uttered, "but it was a shameful waste of eggs."[26]

Plinky and Ad had a ten-week run of two exhibitions a day on Young's

Million Dollar Pier on the Atlantic City Boardwalk. Above her dark dress and blouse, and her standard two-inch heels, Plinky wore a simple bonnet and smiled widely while holding her gun between two sales displays, including one for an emerging market. It was for the Winchester Junior Rifle Club for kids.[27]

But childhood, for Lawrence, was gone. And he drifted further from guns. His eye was caught by the striking looks of Lydia Pagel, who a few years earlier had been voted "Most Beautiful" at Gonzales High School in 1924 and 1926.[28] Lawrence Toepperwein was impressed, and he reacted with his own natural talents. He took a broad-tipped pencil and committed her glamorous face and brilliant, wide curling hair to stencil pad. In his cartoons published in the San Antonio newspaper, Lawrence liked to portray women in flimsy dress that was accepted for the day. This was the day of the young woman as a "flapper," and Lydia boasted of being one. Her brothers would complain to their mother, asking her why she allowed Lydia to dress in such a provocative way.[29]

It didn't bother Lawrence, whom—the Pagel family could see—wasn't one to refuse a drink. When he was about twenty-eight, five years older than Lydia, they were married in 1932. And Lawrence soon opted out of his work as a cartoonist. He turned to crime reporting.[30] His stories, including the blow-by-blow descriptions of the manhunt for suspected murderer and robber Lawrence Rea as told by San Antonio chief of police Owen W. Kilday, appeared in crime magazines such as *True Detective Mysteries*.[31]

Yet as Lawrence poked around in this world of cops and robbers, it appeared he never left the long shadow cast by his famous parents. He would take his policemen friends out to the land near Leon Springs where the family had a large area to practice shooting, and they wanted to practice with Lawrence's famous father.[32] Lawrence was having trouble coping with life. In one scary incident, a fishing trip Lawrence took near Leon Springs, for some reason, almost turned tragic. Four years following his marriage with Lydia, Lawrence wandered near a Hill Country bluff. He took a bad step, lost his footing, and tumbled thirty feet down the cliff. He was taken to a San Antonio hospital and was treated for a deep gash to his head and bruising.[33]

Rumors circulated about Lawrence. People had believed Lawrence had lost a thumb, for reasons not everyone knew. Frost Woodhull, a family friend, touched on it: "Mr. Toepperwein's son is a superlative shot, although one of his hands was permanently injured and he has never regained full use thereof."[34]

Lawrence, with Lydia, continued living with his parents. There, hanging on walls or stuffed away in drawers, were the ribbons that Lydia, taught by the Toepperweins of course, had won in shooting events.[35] And there, as his parents were out on the road, Lawrence could not kick his drinking problem. As 1940 arrived, people noticed Lawrence was battling sickness. "He'd been ailing for some time," people who knew him from the newspaper said. On Friday, October 20, 1943, Lawrence became seriously ill. His doctor prescribed rest, and Lawrence seemed to improve. But his conditioned worsened quickly either late Saturday or early Sunday. He could not recover. And that fast, Lawrence Toepperwein died in the family house at Brackenridge Park. Clara, the aunt who helped raise Lawrence while his parents were out on tour, was at his side. That much was noted on his death certificate. So was the cause of death, stated bluntly before a more standard reason was proffered for his demise: Alcoholism. Cirrhosis. He was thirty-nine.

His father was seventy-four, and perhaps Ad on that October day would turn his barrel rolls onto the ground, pick up his gun, and shoot the eggs that had been thrown into the air. It was the sort of thing the crowd, which had gathered in its usual number into the thousands, would want to see when The Wonderful Topperweins would perform there at the Creve Coeur Shooting Club at St. Louis. The show would start in just moments. But not today. Their son, their only child, was dead. They heard the news about midday on that Sunday, the day of his death. They were back in San Antonio by 4:30 the following afternoon. Creve Coeur? Translated from the French, it means "broken heart."

Nothing seemed to be the same from those days in the Twenties. Winchester had fallen apart and went into receivership as the Depression worsened. There was no telling what would happen to the historic Winchester line if Remington Arms Company would follow through with its negotiations to buy Winchester, which were ongoing at some point prior to September 1931. But those talks were distracted when October came and Du Pont made its first investment in Remington.[36] On December 22, 1931, ammunition maker Western Cartridge Company of Alton, Illinois, stepped up and bought Winchester and, under the seemingly benevolent oversight of Western chairman John Olin, continued to operate as Winchester Repeating Arms Company.[37] Old hands like Henry Brewer, who from his days as a foreman over cartridge assembly at the New Haven plant had a relationship with Ad Toepperwein, stayed on under new ownership. So did Ad and Plinky, but there was a deep sense of loss.

"We still have a home in San Antonio and we are now alone as our son Lawrence passed away . . . ," Ad wrote to Brewer. "He was a newspaper reporter and artist and was [nearing] 40 years old. His mother has never gotten over the shock. We were about to begin a shoot at St. Louis, over 2,500 people waiting for us to begin when we got the telegram. Of course, all this happens to all of us sometime, but we poor mortals simply cannot understand WHY."[38]

Thoughts of neglected children jumped into the minds of the American public after the 1941 release of the motion picture *Blossoms in the Dust*. Greer Garson played the lead role, which was based on Edna Gladney and her extensive work as a child-welfare advocate. Gladney lived in Fort Worth,[39] and her appearance in San Antonio just a few months after *Blossoms in the Dust* appeared on the screens was cause for quite a gathering. The high-end, San Antonio–based Frost Bros. department stores sponsored a "Style Show" with Mrs. Gladney as the featured guest at the upscale and high-balconied Anacacho Room inside the St. Anthony Hotel downtown.

Mrs. Gladney was treated to a head table that was laid with green cloth elegantly decorated with irises and jonquils—white or yellow flowers with long, narrow, rush-like leaves. Matrons at other tables instructed the help to decorate with sweet peas and narcissuses. And there was the collection of tables that would seat forty-eight guests invited by the lady listed as Mrs. Adolph Toepperwein. When Plinky got a hold of the plans for the table, it was to heck with the flowers. Huge rifle targets protruded as a centerpiece. Gun holsters were placed at intervals along the table. Plinky, the smoker, had cigarettes placed in miniature targets with names written on them for use as place cards.[40]

Life was not all guns and smokes around Plinky. When trips returned home to San Antonio, she relished in the large, extended Toepperwein family. Plinky could come home with attractive bits of turquoise, and she'd give these to the young girls of the family. In front of family, she looked much more feminine than the old woman who could be seen grabbing and pointing guns in pictures the newspapers often seemed to print.[41] Those were images the girls of the family had a difficult time comprehending. One of the girls, Collette, attended archery lessons at Brackenridge Park. As she was becoming proficient at getting her arrows closer to the bull's-eye, she heard a deep, older voice from behind. "Good shot." Collette turned and saw her Uncle Adolph looking at her, stopping during the three-mile walks he now was making every day from his house not far away. He couldn't resist: "Why don't you ask your parents about letting me give you some shooting lessons?" Ad asked her. When everything was discussed with her parents, Collette decided against it. She just couldn't get those images of Plinky out of her head, those pictures with the guns that just seemed to her young mind to be out of place for a woman.[42]

As The Wonderful Topperweins tour rolled on, it passed through Portsmouth, New Hampshire where Annie Oakley and her husband, Frank Butler, were spending summers in the days after Buffalo Bill's Wild West around 1915. Annie was fifty-five and Frank sixty-five. Annie was conducting shooting clinics for women, which gave her interest in seeing Plinky shoot.

"I take my hat off to you, Mrs. Top," Annie was said to have exclaimed. "You're the greatest shot I've ever seen." Later, they were approached by two women. One asked Plinky, "What makes you such a good shot?" "Practice. Practice. Practice," Plinky replied.[43] Indeed, Annie echoed her thoughts to anyone who would listen, that she regarded Plinky as the greatest of all women trapshooters.[44] As for who would win a competition between Annie and Plinky, Ad would not hesitate to bet.

"I'll tell you this," Ad said when asked of Plinky's shooting, "she could shoot smoke-rings around Annie Oakley or any other woman marksman who ever lived."[45]

At the completion of one shooting competition, a photo showed four arms stretched their entire length and pointed with dead aim, a pistol gripped in the hand of each, toward a target twenty-five yards away. This line was staggered, allowing the person viewing from the side to take in the swath of the finest woven and tailored business suits, wide-lapel jackets, and pleated slacks, until the bare ankles of one in the line showed. That's just about where her skirt fell, not far above the two-inch heels she seemed to always wear in competition. A neat blouse covered by a long-sleeved sweater draped off her firing arm. But it wasn't a bother, nor was her black, wavy hair that was clipped back so she could clearly see the bull's-eye she rarely missed. This member of the Liberty Pistol and Rifle Club from Wetmore Road in San Antonio was listed as Mrs. Adolph Toepperwein, and her team had won the 1933 national 25-yard championship with the pistol over ninety-six teams. Their final match was a twenty-point victory over the Frankfort Arsenal from Germantown, Pennsylvania.[46]

"Mrs. Toepperwein's skill is phenomenal, her reputation and experience great," the family friend and gun-collecting jurist Frost Woodhull said. "[She] is, I believe, the best woman shot in the world."[47]

At the outbreak of World War II, The Wonderful Topperweins toured army training camps and instructed aerial gunners, which was a repeat from their involvement in the Great War leading up to 1920. "Since Pearl Harbor they have been shooting in Army camps across the country, nearly 200, as of Aug. 1944," a Winchester company newsletter claimed.[48]

But, like everyone in the face of the war effort, they had to make sacrifices. Many of the props they often used, tomato cans that would spread violently like red paint when struck by a hollow-tip slug, were being shipped to troops overseas.[49] In another one of his recurrent letters to Henry Brewer in the Winchester front office, Ad hardly sounded a complaining note that the tour was kept to areas around San Antonio and Austin:

"While we would rather be busy as usual I guess we can stand a little rest . . . [because] the summer is pretty hard and both of us have been somewhat under the weather; not as young as we used to be. Mrs. T is holding up remarkably well and is shooting better than ever if that is possible. I was at New Haven last May and there are mighty few of the old boys you and I knew left, and it won't be long when they will probably all be gone. I am just finishing my 44th year and am very proud of my association with the company and the boys. We hope you part company with doctors and nurses."[50]

Ad was seventy-four, and Plinky sixty-two, when he still allowed his wife to fire a .22 at empty shotgun shells placed on the ends of his fingers. "Never lost as much as a fingernail, Ad said."[51] Yet, when family members made it out on the weekends to the couple's shooting grounds up at Leon Springs, they could see Plinky was not herself; she was fighting through the coming of her old age.

After they watched the still-nimble Ad shoot right through one of his rifle drawings, this one of Buffalo Bill, Plinky wanted to join the action. Her hands trembled, and she tried to control the shakes the best she could. Finally, her uneven hand reached over and grabbed a pistol. She looked at Ad and had him put a cigarette in his mouth. He did, and Plinky's hands still showed shakiness as she lifted the pistol away from her. Ad had often commented to people that the pistols, like the one Plinky was about to shoot by his face, were "I believe . . . the most difficult . . . to master. It keeps you guessing all the time. It just won't behave all the time."[52] Anyway, Plinky inched it up to her firing position, and suddenly her hands quieted and were as still as a rock in a field. Bang. The sound went pow off the side of the hill that formed the backdrop of the shooting range at the shack. Ad turned. Plinky's bullet had just blown it clear off. The cigarette, it was gone, shot right out of his mouth.[53]

Suspicions of her failing health were confirmed in October 1944 when she had a heart attack. She had told friends that the last tour she and Ad completed a year earlier was pleasurable. But she admitted it had exhausted her.[54] Ad could tell as it was happening. He carried along small notebooks, perhaps three inches by five, and made equally small notations about what was going on in their professional life. He flipped to a page marked January 27, 1945. He scribbled one word in his cursive handwriting. He circled it. Plinky. She was dead.[55]

Ad was her "Daddy," for he brought Elizabeth Servaty into the world of accurate, fast, and fancy shooting. And, sitting by her side at their home at Brackenridge Park, he saw Plinky leave it. The company newsletter at Winchester Repeating Arms Company listed her records as so many other tersely worded obituaries would in newspapers across the country where The Wonderful Topperweins performed. The corporate office, which now was located in Alton, Illinois, knew Plinky's personality just as well as her brothers and sisters who grew up with her close to the old Winchester plant in New Haven—Lawrence, John, Jacob, Anna, and Rose:

"But not a living soul who knew 'Plinky' will ever forget her great warm heart, which she wore openly on her sleeve in adoration of her accomplished husband," the Winchester newsletter informed. "And nobody would forget her ready wit, her firm handclasp, her cheerful voice, and the way her eyes crinkled in the ever recurring smile."[56]

In the span of fifteen months, Ad lost Lawrence, his boy, his only child, and then Plinky, his lady. He had, for all those years on the tour with her as The Wonderful Topperweins, called her his "first wife."[57] He wasn't looking for another one.

"How'd the two of you meet?" he was asked after her death.

"Well, sir, to make a short story shorter, we hit it off right away. A lot of folks think we met in the plant, but that isn't true," Ad said with a smile. "She did work for Winchester assembling cartridges. But I first met her . . . in New Haven [Green]. Right romantic place; all green grass and trees. I spotted this bright-looking redhead right away, and she seemed to notice me, too. You know Texans—when we notice something special we go for it hard. Sure, I was scared all right, but I got up the nerve to tell her my name and ask her for hers. Elizabeth Servaty it was, and it sounded like music to me. We were married a few weeks later. It sure pleased me when she took an interest in my shooting. Most women are scared of guns."[58]

Ad scribbled again in his small notebooks with few words. On pages in April, May, and June he wrote another name: The Linds. Dot and Ernie Lind of Springfield, Massachusetts, were sent down to "The Shack" by Winchester to be trained for a shooting act by Ad. Later, he would sit at his desk and look over at another photo he placed in a frame. This one showed the Linds, holding guns in their hands, smiling. He pulled out the three-by-four-foot metal sheet he had shot a rifle-bullet drawing into: Buffalo Bill. He shined it cleanly. Other things around that house, however, were forgotten if they didn't have anything to do with guns. Dust started to collect on the tops of the handles of the drawer on that desk.[59] Ad came in from his mailbox, into his empty house, and read a letter. This letter was from Winchester executive Ed Pugsley thanking him for ". . . your experience with the Linds, and I am glad to hear they are coming along so nicely."

"I know how badly you must miss Mrs. Topperwein after a lifetime of companionship."[60]

CHAPTER TWENTY-ONE

I Might Be Moving to Montana Soon

Tom Leaves the Bright Lights of L.A.

Few people would really know the depths he would miss her. She was gone. And the big changes he would make in his life, changes that no one could figure out why he made them, could be traced back to the time she left him.

Anyone who left a home in Los Angeles, and the chance to mingle with movie stars, for life in Montana qualified as someone making a big change. Yet that's what Tom Frye was doing. And a woman was involved? The word got out when Tom made his usual popular stop as the exhibition shooter at the Kern County Fish and Game Protective Association BBQ at Bakersfield's Hart Memorial Park. When he did on April 24, 1960, as a crowd of 10,200 people attended and attempted to eat through the 5,100 pounds of the beef that was being served, Tom found time to let association president Walter Muller know: This would be his last appearance in California. He was getting a transfer from Remington to go to Billings, Montana.[1]

Billings? Well, it would be a great location for working through a territory that included Montana, Wyoming, and a part of Idaho. Having proven that his back could handle the constant recoil of a firearm, he was shooting competitively again. But he was leaving more behind than he appeared to be letting on.

Rumors were out there. Yes, a woman was at the center of some of the talk. "He was involved with Alex Kerr, who ran the gun shop to the stars, Kerr Sports Shop," fellow Remington field rep Jack Heath said he had heard.

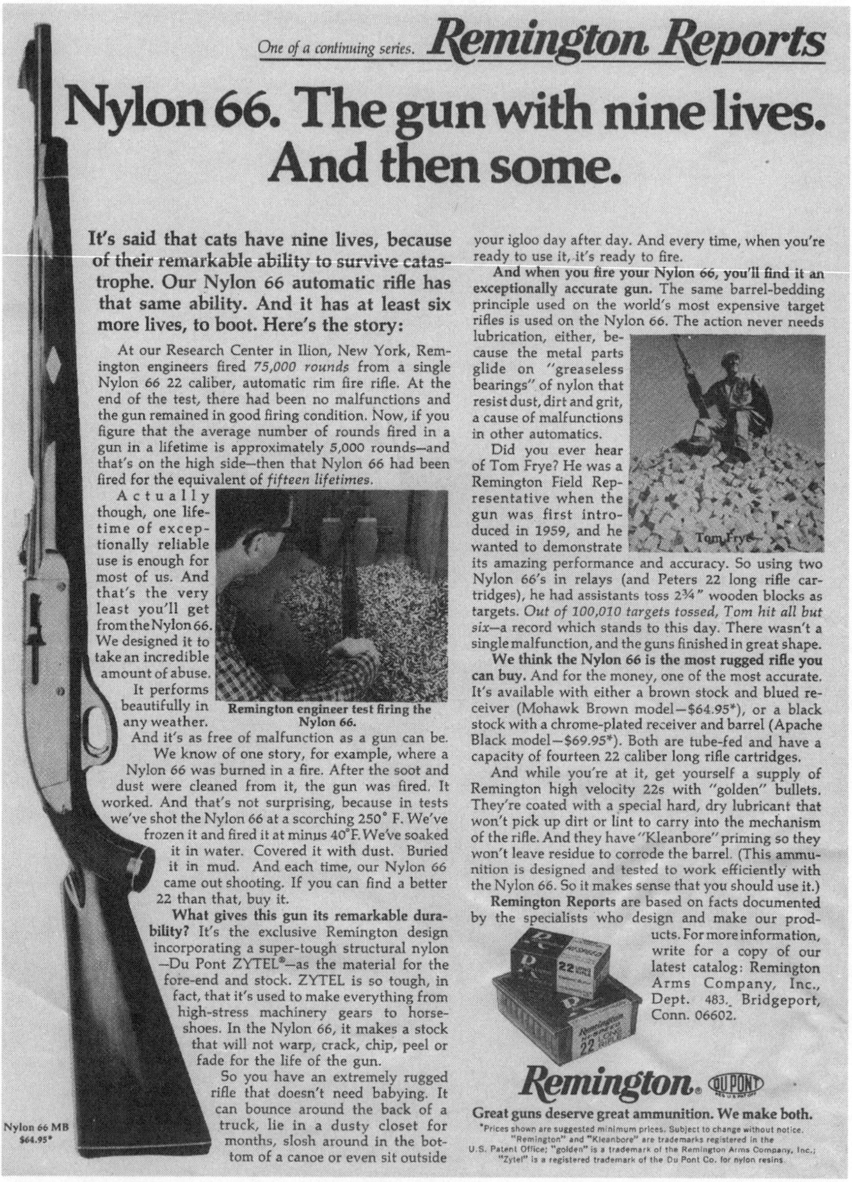

One of a continuing series. **Remington Reports**

Nylon 66. The gun with nine lives. And then some.

It's said that cats have nine lives, because of their remarkable ability to survive catastrophe. Our Nylon 66 automatic rifle has that same ability. And it has at least six more lives, to boot. Here's the story:

At our Research Center in Ilion, New York, Remington engineers fired *75,000 rounds* from a single Nylon 66 22 caliber, automatic rim fire rifle. At the end of the test, there had been no malfunctions and the gun remained in good firing condition. Now, if you figure that the average number of rounds fired in a gun in a lifetime is approximately 5,000 rounds—and that's on the high side—then that Nylon 66 had been fired for the equivalent of *fifteen lifetimes.*

Actually though, one lifetime of exceptionally reliable use is enough for most of us. And that's the very least you'll get from the Nylon 66. We designed it to take an incredible amount of abuse.

It performs beautifully in any weather.

Remington engineer test firing the Nylon 66.

And it's as free of malfunction as a gun can be.

We know of one story, for example, where a Nylon 66 was burned in a fire. After the soot and dust were cleaned from it, the gun was fired. It worked. And that's not surprising, because in tests we've shot the Nylon 66 at a scorching 250° F. We've frozen it and fired it at minus 40°F. We've soaked it in water. Covered it with dust. Buried it in mud. And each time, our Nylon 66 came out shooting. If you can find a better 22 than that, buy it.

What gives this gun its remarkable durability? It's the exclusive Remington design incorporating a super-tough structural nylon —Du Pont ZYTEL®—as the material for the fore-end and stock. ZYTEL is so tough, in fact, that it's used to make everything from high-stress machinery gears to horseshoes. In the Nylon 66, it makes a stock that will not warp, crack, chip, peel or fade for the life of the gun.

So you have an extremely rugged rifle that doesn't need babying. It can bounce around the back of a truck, lie in a dusty closet for months, slosh around in the bottom of a canoe or even sit outside your igloo day after day. And every time, when you're ready to use it, it's ready to fire.

And when you fire your Nylon 66, you'll find it an exceptionally accurate gun. The same barrel-bedding principle used on the world's most expensive target rifles is used on the Nylon 66. The action never needs lubrication, either, because the metal parts glide on "greaseless bearings" of nylon that resist dust, dirt and grit, a cause of malfunctions in other automatics.

Tom Frye

Did you ever hear of Tom Frye? He was a Remington Field Representative when the gun was first introduced in 1959, and he wanted to demonstrate its amazing performance and accuracy. So using two Nylon 66's in relays (and Peters 22 long rifle cartridges), he had assistants toss 2¾" wooden blocks as targets. *Out of 100,010 targets tossed, Tom hit all but six*—a record which stands to this day. There wasn't a single malfunction, and the guns finished in great shape.

We think the Nylon 66 is the most rugged rifle you can buy. And for the money, one of the most accurate. It's available with either a brown stock and blued receiver (Mohawk Brown model—$64.95*), or a black stock with a chrome-plated receiver and barrel (Apache Black model—$69.95*). Both are tube-fed and have a capacity of fourteen 22 caliber long rifle cartridges.

And while you're at it, get yourself a supply of Remington high velocity 22s with "golden" bullets. They're coated with a special hard, dry lubricant that won't pick up dirt or lint to carry into the mechanism of the rifle. And they have "Kleanbore" priming so they won't leave residue to corrode the barrel. (This ammunition is designed and tested to work efficiently with the Nylon 66. So it makes sense that you should use it.)

Remington Reports are based on facts documented by the specialists who design and make our products. For more information, write for a copy of our latest catalog: Remington Arms Company, Inc., Dept. 483, Bridgeport, Conn. 06602.

Nylon 66 MB
$64.95*

Remington® DU PONT

Great guns deserve great ammunition. We make both.

*Prices shown are suggested minimum prices. Subject to change without notice. "Remington" and "Kleanbore" are trademarks registered in the U.S. Patent Office; "golden" is a trademark of the Remington Arms Company, Inc.; "Zytel" is a registered trademark of the Du Pont Co. for nylon resins.

More than ten years following Tom Frye's endurance shoot in 1959, Remington executives fanned the flames for sales of the Nylon 66 rifle by bringing up Frye's efforts with a pair of guns that were said to not malfunction during the entire two-week event. Remington Society of America.

"I guess Mr. Kerr had a daughter, and she and Tom wanted to get married. Lee Braun was contacted by Alex Kerr, and the next thing you know Tom was in Montana."[2]

Braun was in charge of the field reps for Remington west of the Mississippi. He also was very close with Alex Kerr, both personally and professionally. The two shot skeet together on many occasions, and Kerr was a multiple national champion. "He handles a shotgun like a precision instrument, [and] he possesses the most beautiful swing in skeet," said Robert Stack, one of the many actors who shot with Kerr.[3] Plus, Kerr's was a prized retail outlet for Remington. The company had an audience with the well-heeled clientele through an agreement with Kerr to sell a Remington-branded "Kerr Skeet Gun."[4] If Kerr was displeased over anything, Braun and Remington would be obliged to solve it.

But it was a rumor, which Heath recognized. "How true that was, I don't know," he said.[5] But it was no rumor that Alex Kerr was uneasy over his daughter marrying a man who was so much older than her. In fact, Tom was two years younger than Mr. Kerr.

"My dad said it would be really tough if he walks down the aisle and gives away his daughter to a man that looks older than him," Carolyn said.

Her father wasn't the only one concerned. More questions about the relationship came from the matron of the family, the person who was hands-on in running the company that built the family fortune. It was Carolyn's grandmother, Ruth Kerr, who regularly attended prayer meetings and choir practice at her Baptist church. Then she'd go to work, where her office had paintings with religious themes on the walls and a Bible that obviously had been well-perused on her desk. Ruth Kerr ran the Alexander H. Kerr & Co. as its president for more than twenty-five years. When *Time* magazine visited her for a profile of the company, the story credited Mrs. Kerr for increasing company revenue eleven fold, and stated that before 1950 more than 100 million Kerr jars were being produced annually.[6]

She was left a widow at age thirty-four, and the wide range in age that existed between her and her husband before his death left an impression on Mrs. Kerr. She was not supportive of Carolyn marrying Tom Frye. Carolyn wanted a family; she wanted to have kids. Tom's commitment to a family, however, didn't look good. He didn't appear the type to want to settle down in a 9-to-5 office work environment. He liked his job as a traveling field rep.[7]

The more Carolyn asked Tom about their future together the more it looked like it would not fit Carolyn's vision. He thought an accident playing baseball when he was growing up in Ohio did something to him that made it highly unlikely he could have children.[8]

But he was willing to be sure. He visited a doctor to see about getting a fertility test. No matter how the tests would turn out, there was a cloud over Tom that would not go away. He admitted he'd been married before, and there was a failed relationship in Denver where he had the bad car accident. After Carolyn painfully told him she could not go on, she said Tom told her he could get the house they owned in Chatsworth sold if he requested a transfer. He liked the West, and a sales region covering a portion of Idaho, Montana, and Wyoming was open. Months went by, and Carolyn was contacted by a girlfriend. "Tom called me," she told Carolyn. "He said 'I really miss her. I've not met anyone like her. I wonder if she would think about it again. Is she seeing anyone?'" Carolyn was. It was the last she would hear from Tom Frye.[9]

Some things about Tom Frye never would change. When he showed up at the Yellowstone Rifle Range at Billings, Montana, in the spring of 1961, he was wearing that same, ever-present grey Remington jacket with the green sleeves. His shooting transcended the brand, for a crowd of about 3,000 rollicked along with the lively show, where Tom blew up watermelons and the like with his powerful guns. "It might have been two hours," one of the spectators said, "but he kept you thoroughly entertained."[10]

At the end of the show, there were plenty in the crowd who accepted Tom's smiling invitation to come to the tables where the guns were displayed and inspect the Remington line.

"Must be great, shooting all you want with the ammo furnished," someone at the table asked him. "Yeh," Tom said as he started to smile again. "But I have to work during the week." Another question would come, and Tom started his response through another slow drawl. "Well . . ."

That table, like one strewn with hundreds of boxes of .22 caliber cartridges and stacks of scorepads nineteen months earlier outside Dayton, Nevada, had a green cloth covering it, white lettering spelling out TOM FRYE REMINGTON ARMS. This was the guy people asked about pointers for the proper shooting technique, but they were finding out there was more to him than that.

Someone in the crowd found out that Tom had shot with movie stars like

Roy Rogers, Clark Gable, and Gary Cooper. One fellow couldn't get over the fact that someone so well-connected to famous people was now there in Billings. Seems "unusually happy about being assigned to Montana," the man thought after he spoke with Tom. "He says he was happy when Remington transferred him from Los Angeles to Montana a year ago and hopes they leave him here." There was also word that Tom was connected to what was reported to be an incredible world record when he shot at 100,000 wooden blocks thrown into the air, and he missed just six. Now, he was performing in thirty exhibitions each shooting season when it wasn't too cold to be outside in his new territory of Montana, Wyoming, and Idaho.[11]

Why was this accomplished shooter, this man who not more than a year ago performed an incredible marathon performance of rifle accuracy that was reported to be a world record, now assigned by Remington to the backcountry when he could have been pushing the product in the limelight of Hollywood? Getting the story straight appeared difficult. From his advertising office at Remington headquarters, Dick Baldwin was telling a version that included no details of Tom's falling out with the daughter of a well-to-do-family. He heard that Tom's transfer came while the ashes were still smoldering from Tom's shoot in Nevada. The Remington bosses were uneasy about Tom going through with a shoot that would break the record of a famed performer with chief rival Winchester—Ad Toepperwein. Now that Tom did it, without their blessing, they appeared to grow more uncomfortable as the accomplishment began to gain notice. Tom's job was hanging in the balance.

"The Associated Press, radio, and even TV . . . talked for weeks about a 52-year-old shooting record broken by a Remington man," Baldwin noted. "Officials at Remington [are] beside themselves. They ignored the performance for six weeks and then finally issued a press release that said, 'Tom Frye did this on his own during vacation.' In other words, 'To our competitors who make red shells, we didn't have anything to do with this.' Winchester chose to ignore the feat, other than issuing a statement that said the blocks Toepperwein shot at were smaller than the ones Frye used.[12]

"Tom's career at Remington was saved, thanks to a few executives who came to his rescue," Baldwin went on, without naming names. "But they thought it best to get him away from the Hollywood crowd, and he was transferred. . . . Their thought was Montana is a big state, with few people and virtually no business. Tom couldn't get in trouble there."[13]

Tom made the best of the situation. He'd met another woman, and this one hailed from his native Ohio. Her name was Sue McClosky. She was the same age as Tom, in fact a month older than him. She already had two children. Wearing dark hair of medium to short length, she moved from Toledo and married Tom in Reno in the summer of 1961.[14]

Tom was an attraction in Montana, and he gathered quite a bit of talk among shooters and sports fans in Billings by killing an antelope, which was recorded by Boone & Crockett, in Natrona County, Wyoming, west of Casper. He also had the boar's head from Hawaii, that trip he took while working for Remington in Southern California, mounted in his home at a corner residential lot west of downtown. He was so busy with his shooting that he estimated he shot 150,000 rounds of .22 ammo each year, 25,000 shotgun shells, and about 15,000 cartridges for centerfire rifles.[15]

The fellow field reps at Remington, who couldn't help but talk and listen to the latest rumors concerning Tom's love life, saw in Sue a perfect mate for Tom. "She's a great person," said Jack Heath, who had started training with Tom when Jack was assigned the Remington sales area that covered Washington State and the portion of Idaho that Tom did not have.[16]

Things looked settled, until more questions came over the shoot at Reno. When a reporter from *SPORT* magazine tracked down Tom in Billings, Tom was taking out jackrabbits with one shot from long range. If he blew their heads off just so, he wouldn't damage the pelts, and he could sell those to coat makers; the meat he took to cat-food canneries. If he didn't like the way his ammunition tore the heads off the long-legged bunnies, Tom would return to his guns bench and remix the loads for his own cartridges.

The reporter followed Tom to his workshop and could tell Tom was trying to focus on getting the mix just so. But the reporter's questions were asking for Tom to get into the specifics of the shooting event, reported to be a world record. News reporters at Reno chronicled a big picture, a plodding storyline of Tom Frye breaking a world record by posting astonishing numbers. One hundred thousand targets and only six missed. The details, largely, were not rendered. If Tom was going to be pressed for the details of the shoot, and if Remington would not show up in his corner, he needed someone else to vouch for him. He would need a man to whom so many other people turned for support. Again, he needed Newt Crumley.

CHAPTER TWENTY-TWO
An Entirely Different Story All Together
Ad's Open Letter to Tom

Ad Toepperwein was having a tough time getting it out of his system. Plinky had been dead for about a year, his son Lawrence for two, and maybe it was time for Ad to put on one last show for Winchester. Actually, Ad thought, retirement had its advantages. Though Ad had trained Dot and Ernie Lind to take over a sort of Wonderful Topperweins show for Winchester, the company was gaining quite a bit of notice from Herb Parsons's show. Parsons had shot for Winchester since 1930, and the constant travel to meet the demand for his performances had worn on him to the point that he collapsed in the summer heat at a show in 1952. Ad, as usual, pecked out a typewritten letter to Herb: "I hope that you are taking thigs [*sic*] as easy as you can. You'll last longer if you do so. I see that the grand [*sic*] American is going on, and I am d—glad that I don't have to be there to listen to all the alibis."[1]

Ad performed his retirement show within a year of Plinky's death in 1945 at the Leon Springs School close to where he grew up. Despite the passage of years, Ad progressed through all his tricks of old. When he told his assistant to grab him by his ankles and turn him upside down so he could shoot at a few more targets, cries literally rang into the air. "What are they about to do to him?" a thought ran through the head of one of the small members of the Toepperwein family. The boy cried and feared for his great-great-uncle's life, the sight of this friendly man's face scrunched upside down while some stranger had a hold of his legs being too much for the innocent thoughts

Photos like this brought scrutiny to the Tom Frye endurance shoot from 1959. The targets in this image were presented much closer to Frye than the 25–30 foot distance noted from the 1907 shooting event performed by Ad Toepperwein. Courtesy of the Nevada State Library, Archives and Public Records.

of an under-ten child. His fears diminished when he saw his distant uncle break targets with his gun just as well as he could if he were standing on his feet. After his show Ad reached into his shipment from Alton, Illinois, with the Red W on the case. He pulled out a rectangular box, and Uncle Ad called it a brick. There were 500 cartridges for a .22 rifle in them. The boys devoured it like candy.[2]

By the time he became an octogenarian, Ad ably attended shooting competitions not far from his home. While there, Colonel Charles Askins took note and reported it in his position as a contributing editor with one of the firearms trade magazines: "Shooters were honored by a visit from Ad Topperwein, that incredible marksman now pushing the far side of 80 whose record of 72,500 wooden blocks fired at with the .22, and only nine misses, still is one of the gunning wonders of the world."[3]

Ad would be asked often about it, his ten days accurately shooting thousands of blocks in 1907 at San Antonio.

"Although all this occurred practically fifty years ago, it is all still very fresh in my memory," Ad said, "and I think these were the most eventful days in my entire life."[4]

"Pushing the far side of 80" brought its challenges. Ad's once piercing eyes were turning glassy. Friends would say their man was becoming hard of hearing. Yet he remained remarkably engaged. He'd wait in his house at Brackenridge Park on weekends, impatiently, before his brother Fred or one of his friends would pick him up and drive him the twenty miles out to Leon Springs and the shooting range at Casa Lometa, the shack. During the week, after he finished his three-mile morning walk, he'd reach out to his old friends from Winchester through his typewriter.

"I have just completed a checkup on our hunting season which has closed recently," the eighty-eight-year-old Ad typed in a February 1958 letter to Jack Boone at Winchester. He cited game department statistics that showed more than 250 deer were killed the first day of the season in a one-hundred mile radius around San Antonio. Ad complimented the .243 cartridge, but he had a thumbs-down report on the high-powered, lever-action Model 88. "Among the reports I have from the late shooting season, I find that the Mod. 88 is not very popular, it lacks the smooth action Winchester rifles are noted for, and the trigger pull is very bad and I am afraid that if this trouble is not corrected, it will interfere with its popularity."[5]

His report was rebutted by Boone: "As to the Model 88—there isn't a damn thing wrong with that rifle. I have number 11 in my gun rack and it works like a charm—like a lever action rifle should when it's handled FAST."[6] The company still had Ad on the payroll, and they kept up his correspondence. For his ninetieth birthday later that year Ad received from Winchester a lever-action Model 92, chambered in .32-20 with the WCF Serial No. 1007286. "Paul Doane did all the work on it for you, Top," company sales service manager E.J. Rudolph wrote, noting that Doane, head of Winchester's repair department,[7] had re-worked a model originally designed by John Browning. "All of us at Winchester are happy to hear of your good health in the golden years of your life," Rudolph wrote on. "Keep that old powder dry, as we want to hear about you on your hundredth birthday."[8]

Ad enjoyed the fact that Colonel Askins would make the short drive from his post at Fort Sam Houston to talk guns. But when Colonel Askins was gone, Ad was back at the typewriter, needling the brass and seeking debate.

"My friend Col. Chas. Adkins [*sic*] is at the present time in Africa after big game," Ad wrote to Jack Boone, who didn't take too kindly to Ad's criticism of the Winchester Model 88. "Among his battery of Winchester rifles he told me that he was taking along a .243 and I expect to see him back here in S.A. in a few weeks and we will see what he has to say about the different Winchester rifles. Besides being a wonderful shot he also is one of the foremost writers on shooting we have today."[9]

Colonel Askins was provocative, to say the least. The leads he wrote to his articles did their job; they attracted readers to his stories and got them talking. To top his article entitled "Are Pistol Champs Alcoholics?" Colonel Askins (a former champion in national pistol competitions) wrote, "I have seen pistol shooters so drunk they could not hit the ground with their hats—but brother, how they could hit the bullseye!"[10] Then there was the lead to his essay wondering why target shooting, as he saw it, was lacking in interest in this country: "Target rifle shooting in the United States is as popular as birth control in India."[11]

Colonel Askins told of killing runners of contraband during his days watching over the Rio Grande as a Border Patrol agent at El Paso. Colonel Askins asked Ad, "Have you ever had to shoot anybody? Or use your extraordinary skill to defend your life or the life of a friend?" Ad remained true to himself, wouldn't boast nor join up with the Colonel Askins bravado: "No, I'd rather shoot at tin cans."[12]

A line of writers followed in for visits. One was Fred Maly, writer of an outdoors column in one of the local newspapers. In December 1959 Maly had heard a shooter by the name of Frye—Tom Frye—had been firing at 100,000 wooden blocks at Reno, Nevada. It sounded unbelievable: This Frye had done it, had beaten Ad Toepperwein's record for shooting at aerial targets—by more than 25,000 targets, and with three fewer misses than Ad back in 1907. To Maly, Ad sounded a resigned note—he had "no regrets"—that his record finally had been broken. He was resigned, but congratulatory.[13] Ad returned to his typewriter five days after Maly informed him, and he wrote his letter of congratulations to Mr. Frye. But he couldn't keep from thinking, even out loud in his letter to Tom Frye, wanting to "know exactly under what conditions and rules you shot this score."

Col. Askins heard about the Frye record as well. The colonel had his contacts. He managed to get possession of photos from the Frye shoot. If he was going to inform Ad, now ninety, as to what was going on in the photos, he'd have to stand next to the hard-of-hearing old man and yell. Ad's eyesight, well wracked by what everyone attributed to cataracts, would cause him to move the images out to his peripheral vision to get a more clear view.

But anything short of blindness could not obstruct the obvious from these photos. It was so obvious as to be downright silly, an embarrassing oversight, or something. It was made out to Ad from the photos that the men tossing blocks into the air for Mr. Frye to shoot were a bit cozy. Ad returned to the typewriter on January 5, 1960:

> It has been announced by the Remington Company that one of their shooting representatives recently shot 100,000 wooden blocks thrown into the air, missing but six. Most wonderful shooting, I would say, and I don't believe he could have hit more if he had set them on a fence post. All shooting with a rifle, pistol or shotgun is judged by distance. This is especially true when shooting a moving object. A score with a shotgun shot at 16 yards does not compare with one shot at twenty. In shooting my block record, which was shot over fifty years ago, I did everything to make it official. It was announced beforehand in all of the newspapers and was witnessed by the public. I had a referee and judge who checked every shot and a separate scorekeeper. The assistant who tossed up the blocks for me stood between 25 and 30 feet in front of me, measured, and tossed the blocks approximately 30 feet straight up in the air. Colonel Charley Askins, noted gun editor who lives in San Antonio, a few days ago received some photographs sent out by Remington. He came to see me the other day just before he set out for his African hunt and told me the pictures he has showed the assistants standing beside the shooter and the blocks were tossed in that manner close to the muzzle of the rifle—all of which makes this an entirely different story. This shooter, if he really shot 100,000 targets as he claimed he did, established more of an endurance test than accuracy. I am giving you this information so you may not form a concrete opinion of this man's wonderful performance. Keep your powder dry.
>
> Sincerely yours, Top.[14]

It did not take much to engage the still amble mind of Ad Toepperwein. And, now, it appeared to be clacking as fast as the lever-action on Ad's favorite rifle. There were rules for this sort of thing. Had been for years. When the first International Clay Pigeon Tournament was conducted in May 1884 in Chicago, one evening session was devoted to the discussion of standard rule making for various shooting competitions. Apparently as a result of that meeting, a prospectus for the National Trap Shooters' Association was published by January.[15]

If that wasn't enough, Ad thought about the intentions of the man who had inspired him, who made endurance shooting what it was. Ad, sitting at his desk, reached over to the middle drawer and slid his wrinkled hand over the dusty handle. He reached in there into the opened drawer and started digging.

"I got the original paperwork right here," he said, reaching, digging, grabbing, "some place." The groping stopped. Eureka. He pulled out a yellowed piece of paper. "Doc Carver told me about the rules right here in San Antonio in 1897," Ad said. "Fact is, he wrote 'em down for me and advised me to follow them exactly if I wanted any marks I made recognized as official."[16]

The "rules" dictated "standard" targets to be used. There was a prescribed distance for the targets, the space from the shooter, and how high they had to travel in the air (both from twenty-five to thirty feet). The presence of a judge, referee, and scorer was mandated.

The words filed by reporters out of Reno had been spare of details, and Ad cautiously waded through the 1960s news cycle before he stated something he felt comfortable to hammer up there for the ages. And his judgment of "This shooter, if he really shot 100,000 targets as he claimed he did," went beyond picking on the details of the Tom Frye shoot. He called into question the entire event. Was there anyone who could rebut that?

While Newt Crumley managed to attract the most swashbuckling, up-and-coming entertainment of the day—Eric Fleming and Clint Eastwood of TV's *Rawhide*—to witness his Tom Frye world-record shooting event at Dayton, Newt had to notice the newspapers in Reno were going ga-ga over the cool speedboat races at Pyramid Lake. Front-page stories and wide photographs, banner headlines, accompanied each day of the races—not the shooting. The enormity of what Tom Frye did under the Holiday Hotel banner just wasn't sinking in, even with many enthusiasts in the shooting crowd. Dale Shaw was a journalist who knew shooting history, and in the early sixties he was ready to record Frye's Holiday Hotel–sponsored event for his latest magazine assignment.

"I have told many people about this phenomenally strange shooting accomplishment," Shaw wrote, "and not a few of them have squinted at me, squinted hard in disbelief. Oddly enough, a lot of people who have never heard of Frye's amazing marathon are shooting nuts."[17]

So, after Dayton, Newt was pursuing other sports sponsorships. He landed on the hydroplane races at Pyramid Lake. In 1961, the event was conducted as the Reno Gold Cup and was considered the world championship of unlimited hydroplane racing under the sanction of the American Power Boat Association.[18]

Russ Schleeh, an Air Force colonel like Newt, was a boat pilot for a crew trying to bring a boat back into competition, named *Maverick*, after it won the national points championship two years earlier. The crew needed a sponsor for a two-race commitment. It would cost a sponsor about $10,000 per race, and Newt climbed aboard in July 1961.[19] "It's my introduction to hydroplane racing," Newt said. "It's a pleasure to work with such good fellows."[20] Colonel Schleeh had set transcontinental flying records and test flew the YB-49 "Flying Wing" during a crash in March 1950 at a dry lake bed that left the prototype aircraft in a heap and Schleeh's back broken. It didn't stop him from trying the hydroplanes that could skip over the water at well more than 100 mph.[21]

Newt had her renamed *Miss Reno*, and when he walked to the end of a dock at Seattle's Lake Washington in his business suit and watched the crew put her in, Newt had a pair of Reno misses—a couple of seventeen-year-old girls—christen the red-colored craft with champagne bottles. But while getting ready for the first racing event at Lake Washington, Schleeh throttled the *Miss Reno* into a crash and caused $1,500 worth of damages. The crew fixed her, and the *Miss Reno* pulled out a hard-fought third-place finish.[22]

Emboldened, Newt looked forward to racing in front of the homefolks in Reno. "I have the highest regard for our crew," he said. "This is a labor of love. Those fellows work all night long, if necessary, to get the boat running right." And, with that, the *Miss Reno* had the fastest heat on opening day at Pyramid Lake.[23] But Schleeh, at his test-pilot, structural-integrity-pushing best, throttled up *Miss Reno* in the second heat. She flipped over and slapped down hard on the water's surface. A five-foot long section of the tail—just enough to have painted onto it NATIONAL CHAMPION from its days as the *Maverick* and Newt Crumley's HOLIDAY logo—went floating off from the rest of the boat.[24] Schleeh was all right, but the *Miss Reno* wasn't racing any time soon. Instead, Newt and his cowboy-hat-wearing buddy, Nevada Lt. Gov. Rex Bell, helped load the jagged piece of tailsection aboard the crew's trailer. They would haul it over to the Holiday Hotel and display it. Newt managed to laugh about it.[25]

Newt headed for something he found more dependable—flying. His latest purchase was a twin-engine Aero-Commander 680, painted maroon and white.[26] He was to officiate a Shriners' ceremony and play golf in Palm Springs, California, and he brought along his wife, Frances, and family friend E.J. Questa, a banker and chairman of Reno's organizing committee for the 1960 Winter Olympics that had been conducted at nearby Squaw Valley, California. Frances, however, left the event early on a commercial flight when she felt pressed to make it back to Nevada in time for her mother's birthday.[27]

Newt got the Aero-Commander airborne with Questa aboard later in the week. Soon, he'd be flying over landscape only a native like Newt would recognize. Tonopah. That was about 230 miles into the flight, and on a typical Saturday afternoon a pilot's voice came through a flight controller's radio like so many routinely would. It was 4:18 in the afternoon, and the pilot just relayed his position and heading for the controller to log. It was confirmed, and minutes passed with the flight controller left to monitor the radio for the next passing pilot. But twelve minutes later, the flight controller heard that voice again. It crackled through the radio in front of him. The pilot of the private plane was noticing icing conditions on his wings. He wanted permission to climb from 15,000 feet to 17,000. Five minutes later, there were no more requests. But the pilot was back on. He told the flight controller he was reversing course. Worse, his reason: "Aircraft out of control due to ice. Attempting return to Tonopah."[28]

It was 4:35 p.m. And that was it. Nothing more was heard. So the Federal Aviation Administration was notified, and a search was initiated.[29] High winds and the coming darkness would halt any progress until the next day, but some things were beginning to be known. The pilot, notifying the ground he had one passenger with him, had filed a flight plan after taking off from Palm Springs, California, about two hours earlier. Despite the darkness and the fact that the airplane was lost out there in the vastness of Nevada, people at Reno's Stead AFB knew who they were looking for once the details made it in. Colonel Crumley owned a maroon and white twin-engine Aero Commander 680. That's what they would look for, once they could get out there.[30]

In a control room at Stead, a map of Nevada was laid out on a table, and a line was penciled from Tonopah to the northeast. A couple of notations were scribbled. Major Jack Thompson sat at the radio console. Major Thompson was assistant wing operations commander at Stead. He reported to wing commander Col. M.C. Barnard, who was standing right there in the control room with base helicopter squadron commander Lt. Col. Carney Francis.[31] But Major Thompson was in charge of this one because Newt Crumley was a friend of his. He flew with Newt during off-duty hours.[32]

The word of Newt missing traveled fast in the Reno community where he was such a well-known community leader. One of the Crumley kids, Peggy, was cheerleading at a high-school basketball game on the night her father was expected back from Palm Springs. She went to a dance afterwards. "Do you know your father is missing?" one of her friends asked her.[33] Reports on the radio stations fueled the talk at the school dance about Peggy's daddy. Newt's wife had the radio on during the drive back from her mother's house at Lovelock. It's how she heard about her husband.

A tip to the search party came from Pine Creek Ranch at Nevada's Monitor Valley.[34] That windy, snowy night turned into an overcast day covering the vast, stark, and desolate spot. Roads that crisscrossed the valley were few. Some routes, which served the ranches and the distant, tiny barns that were widely strung along Monitor's rim, likely could hardly be seen as they dipped and swerved in greenish foothills shrouded by fog way past the scrubby expanse of the valley. As noontime approached, the rescuers got a break in the weather, and they could see something near the 11,807-foot Mount Jefferson.[35] Major Thompson heard the uptick in activity over the radio. From the initial words relayed from the scene, he knew what had happened: "We're waiting confirmation, but I don't think there's much doubt left," Thompson said.[36] He turned back to the radio. "You saw them?" Major Thompson asked. "Outside or inside the plane? Outside . . ." Thompson gave some details, all of them obvious. "The plane was all tore to hell. Our pilot saw both of them. He landed beside the wreckage. It's confirmed." The emotions came, and Major Jack Thompson couldn't hold it back. He got up and left the room. He would do privately what other men would do openly in public just a few days later.[37]

Told of the news, the old family friend Bing Crosby figured bad luck finally kept its grasp on someone who always seemed to slip through. "Newt was quite a sportsman, and quite a businessman," Bing said. "He was an excellent pilot, but he ran into the wrong kind of weather, that's all."[38]

Bob Laxalt, the novelist and instructor at University of Nevada, could not say that he was shocked to hear of Newt dying in a plane crash:

"In this day when people are tucked safely into their little holes, Newt never was. With his restlessness and his courage and his love of doing, he made you remember that it was still possible to be an individual in this world.

"I'm not usually one to believe in ordained things, but in Newt's case, you really begin to wonder whether this is the way it was supposed to be from the beginning, and underneath, you knew it all the time. All the things in his life seemed to add up to a man who was going to be around only a while. And the ironic thing about it all was that he risked his life all over the world, and then came home to die almost where he was born."[39]

When it was time, Frances made one last loving gesture toward her husband as she led the young Crumley family toward the flag-covered casket and touched the roses where Newt was in repose. His young children walked out with their mother from the Episcopal Church, and for the first time in their lives they saw something they could not place. Grown men were crying.[40]

Before Newt had flown to Palm Springs, the Sierra Nevada Sportswriters and Broadcasters Association chose him as Reno's "Sportsman of the Year." Plans for the awards dinner were seen through after the mourning of the crash, and the Crumley boy, eleven-year-old son Newt Jr., managed a smile when presented on stage with the award.[41]

Bob Stoddard, owner of a Reno radio station, was the last speaker to honor Newt that night. And he did it by quoting an inscription at the California state capital building in Sacramento: "Bring me men to match my mountains."[42]

When Dale Shaw wrote his magazine piece for *SPORT*, he seemed to wonder what sort of judgment he could make of the proceedings when Tom Frye was reported to have broken Ad Toepperwein's shooting world record. "Nobody really knows quite what to make about this marksmanship monkeyshines . . . ," Shaw commented. He referred to Tom's work as "Ripley-esque."[43]

Eventually, even Colonel Askins, who alerted Mr. Toepperwein to the photos showing Frye shooting the blocks at close range, appeared to have a difficult time discrediting Frye after considering the fact Tom went well past the Toepperwein mark of 72,500, to 100,000. Colonel Askins wrote a lengthy feature in an issue of *Guns Magazine*, stating of Tom Frye, "Here was a champion unequaled in history—undoubtedly the greatest exhibition marksman alive, perhaps in all history. . . . Not only had he broken every shooting record ever established but he had gone ahead to hang up a new mark the like of which I reckon will stand for all time."[44] Colonel Askins mentioned nothing of the presentation of the targets, their size, and the distance the shooter stood from them. In fact, he was quite complimentary of "this rifleman, this champion." He piled on the superlatives:

> He is, as you might suspect, an athlete, a veritable superman, if you will. He is a big, handsome type with shoulders like Paul Bunyan, a cowboy's trim hips, 16-inch biceps, and a bouncy step to his gait. Six feet and three inches tall and two hundred and five pounds, I'd gladly match him against Cassius Clay any day. He is every inch fighting muscle. He played football in college; could play again today if he was of a mind. He is tough and hard and conditioned. He doesn't touch the filthy weed and abhors demon rum. He doesn't overeat, nor overdrink nor overindulge, nor do anything that is likely to do harm to the razor-sharp coordination which permitted him to aim that pair of little plinking Remingtons more than one hundred thousand times and literally never miss.[45]

Askins did not get around to an interview with Newt Crumley; no reports surfaced with his comments. Newt's attention was elsewhere, with hydroplanes, casino business, regents meetings, family. He also was in the air, until February 1962. A few months after Newt's death, Shaw's article appeared.

In life and death Newt Crumley was known to run an honest game. His family and friends were quick to defend him in the rare case his actions were questioned. His daughter Peggy was growing up, and she remembered a father who was strict and seemingly incapable of pulling a quick one.

"He detested lying, duplicity, cheating, slipperiness—would not tolerate them," Peggy said. "Definitely not his style. But he was a very forceful talker. Around him, things changed."[46]

Under Crumley at the Holiday, Pat Kerrigan worked his way from the floor in the slots area to a chance to lease the hotel gift shop from Newt. "He was a living example of fair play and justice," Kerrigan said. Robert Dill, as public relations and sports director at the Holiday, saw first-hand Newt's involvement in the property's promotional activities. "He was precise in everything he did," Dill said. "He was a perfectionist, but a good-tempered one."[47]

Perhaps time would fill in the blanks that led to Ad Toepperwein's question marks. In the meantime, what could have been suggested? Cheating, or just that the principals were unaware that there existed a nuanced set of "rules" faded even further by the passing of time? The only standards known to exist were the ones that could be found when an old man in Texas opened his desk drawer and found a keepsake from his idol. And those were handwritten.

Dale Shaw continued his *SPORT* magazine interview with Tom, and he sensed the shooter was slightly embarrassed about the record. Shaw pressed with the question that shot out from Dayton, Nevada, and ricocheted off Ad Toepperwein's typewriter: Wasn't it set up too easy? Wasn't that rifle he used significantly lighter than the one used by the record-holder, Ad Toepperwein? The answers came, and the writer reported a rather stunning admission: "Actually Tom Frye says he is not so sure he beat Toepperwein's record in the true sense."[48]

CHAPTER TWENTY-THREE

"Piedras Pintas"

Ad's "Mecca for Shooters of All Ages"

He had reached his ninetieth birthday, and Ad Toepperwein showed proof of his still-sharp mind. He'd get up every morning at 5:30 and shortly commence his daily three-mile walk—before the temperatures in July at San Antonio got up around the 100-degree mark. People who saw him thought he still was "keen and alert." "I just walk to keep fit," Ad said, almost dismissively. "A man doesn't want to get to look[ing] old, just because he is 90."[1]

There was no sign of him cutting back on his walks in 1960. But other things about his life did look like they were entering an estate-planning mode. By 1951 Ad had turned his house at Brackenridge Park into a duplex, with Ad living in two rooms at the back.[2]

His hearing was worse. When he was told that an old friend of his from his childhood home of Boerne came to visit him one day, yet Ad missed him because he couldn't hear the knock up front, Ad got back to his typewriter and knocked out a letter to the friend. "Come and see me sometime whenever you can. AND POUND ON THE DOOR so I can hear you."[3]

Though his brother Fred came by to check on him, Ad lived alone. Otherwise, the place was packed. The world records he told everyone that Plinky had set—and still mostly held—were spelled out and hung over his bed. A few of his were up there, too. He mounted some trophies from some of his old hunting trips onto most of the walls of his sitting room. Where there weren't heads of deer and antlers sticking out of those walls there were heads

The Wonderful Topperweins performed in front of a president (Calvin Coolidge in the 1920s), and here they pose with Nevada Governor Edward Carville after 1940. Collection of Kenneth Toepperwein.

of Indian chiefs, Uncle Sam, and Buffalo Bill shot into metal by the bullets from Ad's very skilled hands and once brilliant eyesight. Pictures he had painted were up there, and poetry, too. But it all made it back to the guns, which were crammed into a large gun case that overpowered that last wall in the sitting room.[4]

If it wasn't poetry, Ad still was churning out thoughts that didn't lack for detail.

"I was might proud and happy to hear about you killing those two bucks with your little 'Hornet' Winchester," he wrote to a distant, pre-teen nephew named Max. ". . . [T]here are very few boys at your age that can do that. But of course you are a Toepperwein and you have to keep up the reputation of the family. I'll bet your dad already transformed those deer into a lot of big sausages, hanging in the smokehouse. I hope that you will come by sometime to see me and tell me all about it. . . . "[5]

Ad was more productive with the paint brush than he was with the gun these days. Like he did with bullets, he eschewed canvas. He stroked his brush against rocks made smooth by Hill Country streams. "What color is

Though the number of shows were reduced because of restrictions during World War II, The Wonderful Topperweins continued to perform often in front of military audiences. Plinky performs the notable stunt by firing a revolver at a target behind her while aiming with a hand mirror. Collection of Kenneth Toepperwein.

that?" Ad would ask, not quite able to make it out as he applied the brushstrokes from one small container before switching to another. "What color is that?" He'd be done, and the Ad Toepperwein artwork was worthy of displaying at his relatives' family house, on one side of the front door a Cowboy, his Indian adversary on the other. Then it was back up to Casa Lometa, "The Shack" as the smiling family insisted on calling it. Shooters formed the line, but Ad couldn't take aim through those cloudy old eyes even as he tried to wear glasses. He'd load his gun anyway and get the feel of the recoil, the smell that came out of the spent casing. "Uncle Ad'ulf shoots his gun into the ground," one of the young boys would notice."[6]

The gatherings brought out the "young businessmen of San Antonio" every weekend. There were lots of young faces. "I like to promote the stuff," Ad said, always thinking forwardly.[7]

The shots rang out, bouncing off that hillside enough to be heard about a half mile away. He'd take time to hug all the kids, boys and girls, to the point that their parents would comment on how sweet Uncle Ad'ulf was. His straight, tall walk, they noticed, was becoming a shuffle of old legs and feet. His mustache that had been clipped so neat for decades was now a tad unkempt. Still, he managed to engage with the future generation and imprint on them his love for shooting with his words and his hand-to-hand touch: "Lemme pull your trigger finger."[8]

". . . I manage to keep up my shooting promotion activities," Ad wrote to Jack Boone at Winchester. "Most of [the people coming to the camp for shooting information] are interested in snap shooting and this kind of shooting burns up a lot of ammunition. When I get a fellow interested in the game I create at the same time a good customer, and a carton of 22 ctgs. does not last very long with this kind of shooting. Several of these boys buy ammunition by the case. It gives me something to do and I only wish I could do more. P.S. It was Daniel Boone who said / You are always a little bit ahead / With a little bit of powder / and a little bit of lead."[9]

Ad preached to them the details: "I would call especial attention to the importance of having a course sight and holding full and low under the bull's-eye rather than using a fine sight and holding fine on the object to be hit," he'd preach. "Greater speed and accuracy can be attained by the former method. A weapon with a four-and-a-half-pound trigger pull is best for fast work and will respond instantly to an average muscular development in your index finger. When you get control of a small-calibre [*sic*] gun you will use it in the field in preference to a shotgun. [For birds] and such game, it is an excellent weapon, and the lack of noise when it is discharged enables you to pluck off a flock a field birds, which would be soon frightened away by the crack of the shotgun."[10]

It was difficult to keep all the shooters away, considering all the talk that the shooting practices were getting in newspapers across the state. Ad, reporters wrote, is a "genial host to a score of sportsmen at his private shooting range called 'Piedras Pintas.' The range is a mecca for shooters of all ages. His correspondence is so heavy that I am amazed how he is able to handle it so well; but for his capable brother, Fred, there is no question [that] he would be swamped with a mountain of unanswered letters."[11]

He was doing his best to caution anyone from using words that he was a passing legend.

"A fellow told me I'm almost to the end of my rope," he said. "But I decided to tie a knot in it and hang on for a while. And while I'm here, I want to help anybody I can in the shooting game."[12]

But Uncle Ad'ulf, they noticed, was becoming scarce. He no longer was seen walking for three miles along the paths of Brackenridge Park. He still was up at 5:30 in the morning, and his checks from Winchester still were getting cashed. Another reporter came out and saw Ad was walking around his half of the duplex. He was counting the steps up to a mile. "He is surprisingly self-reliant," though Fred and his neighbors attend to his needs, the reporter wrote.[13]

Letters from his old typewriter were becoming infrequent, yet he continued to reach out. "Uncle Ad was a colorful, charming, and thoughtful individual," one relative said. "At ninety-two, he never forgot a birthday or holiday of any kind. His memory of people and facts was remarkable."[14]

So many people wanted to know his story, to sit back and let him fill up their notebooks, so they could tell others about it. And, in telling it, his story reminded him of his life's journey, its start, and its fiber:

> I don't think it will be boasting if I say that I was born to be a marksman. I can't think of a moment in my life when I wasn't handling guns, or wanting to. When I was five years old . . . my greatest delight was to hang around my father's gunmaking shop and watch him at work. When I was six he made me a little crossbow and I got pretty expert with it, but that didn't satisfy me for long. I was all of six years old and I wanted a real gun of my own. He finally gave me a big, old muzzle-loading 14-gauge shotgun. Actually I think he gave me the gun in the hopes that its kick would cure me of my hankering to shoot. I had considerable talent for drawing and I guess he wanted me to be an artist.
>
> But far from curing me of my love for firearms, that old shotgun only made it grow stronger. The recoil was tough to take, but by the time I was eight years old I was dropping birds on the wing. That was enough for dad. He gave up then, gave me a new .22 rifle and let nature take its course. At the time of his death in 1879, I was ten years old and rated the best child marksman in the state of Texas. A lot of Texans claimed I was the best in America right then, but you know Texans.
>
> It's hard to tell things like this about yourself because it has got to sound like boasting. But if you want to hear it, I guess that's a risk I'll have to take.[15]

Ad made his noise in life. And, when the pleasant and awesome popping and plinking was done from those shows on the road, he'd sell a bunch of guns, have the ones he didn't sell packed up, and he'd head down the road. He left behind memories, and, reluctantly, some peace and quiet. He had died on March 4, 1962, after enjoying ninety-two birthdays.

Colonel Walter Siegmund, who as director of sales at Winchester had kept in so much contact with Ad, thought of a way to memorialize Ad and Plinky—The Wonderful Topperweins. He commissioned a sculptor named Harvey Botts to fashion a bronze plaque with the shooting records listed under the names of Adolph Toepperwein and Elizabeth Servaty Toepperwein. When it was unveiled on the grounds of the San Antonio Gun Club at Olmos Park, fourteen months after Ad's death, Siegmund read a message from another man born of German heritage in the Texas Hill Country. It came from the seventy-eight-year-old retired Commander of the Pacific Fleet from World War II, Admiral Chester W. Nimitz. His words credited the skill of The Wonderful Topperweins for generating interest throughout the nation in marksmanship.[16]

Other tributes came, some elegant, some as boisterous as those weekends at The Shack. "If there are rifle or shotgun ranges in the Promised Land," came words from the *Dallas Morning News*, "then Ad and Plinky doubtlessly are wowing the saints, just as they did mortal man when they hung up records that have lasted a half a century or more."[17]

Col. Charles Askins dipped his irascible pen into a salty inkwell to provide some perspective into Ad's career: "Topperwein and his contemporaries flourished in what is now nostalgically referred to as 'the good old days.' It should be explained for the benefit of those who were not there during those halcyon days that amusement was limited to more simple things. Hippies, teeny-boppers, love-ins, LSD, pot, pornographic movies, go-go clubs and topless parties were either completely unknown or were woefully underrated as a means for innocent amusement."[18]

The house at Brackenridge Park, once secluded along the creek and the shade from the oaks, was taken over by a motor hotel that had been built along busy Broadway Avenue. When the motel proprietor went through the property to repair it and leave it standing, he said cartridges, shells, and other things from the shooting careers of the legendary Ad and Plinky Toepperwein were found.[19]

But, by that time, not any guns. Some were willed to friends. Others were donated to Winchester, which moved its collection to the Buffalo Bill Historical Center in Cody, Wyoming.

Some went up for sale during an auction benefitting the arms and armor collection of the Metropolitan Museum of Art at New York. In fact, an entire trunk used by The Wonderful Topperweins was brought out for bids. It creaked open, and inside were playbills and posters, hats and wardrobe; it contained two Model 63 Winchester .22 rifles. David Marmet, a writer who would churn out scripts for plays and movies such as *Glengarry Glen Ross* and *The Postman Always Rings Twice*, marveled over what the auctioneer claimed about the rifles. One, Marmet wrote, "was warranted to be one of the battery with which Ad shot 43 million two-inch cubes out of the air." Ad's profiles of an Indian chief, George Washington, a turkey, and other images shot into metal reminded Marmet of one Toepperwein "drawing" he once saw "in the shop of a celebrated gunsmith in Louisiana."

Marmet continued:

> So I sat amazed as, one after one, beautiful Edwardian artifacts came out of the trunk; mementos of shooting, and show business, and, in short, the dream material of another time. . . . I think I was one of the only people in the audience who knew of the Topperweins . . . and so the bidding did not go very high. The trunk went cheap . . . [and] some years later I saw, at an antiques show, a pin-back button promoting the Topperweins, and I bought it.[20]

He found that pin, but no guns. There was a time when Ad would leave five guns at the shop of the Cline Brothers. One of the Clines was considered a protégé of Ad's, and he was an award-winning pistol shooter himself. The brothers had a shop off South Alamo Street, and at the back there were repairs done on anything from bird cages to wagons. When Ad returned from his Winchester tours with Plinky, that shop was Ad's first stop from the road to drop off the guns that needed attention. "He was always amazed that the guns never got lost in all the clutter that covered the benches, floor and hanging from the ceiling joists," said his relative, the publisher Fritz Toepperwein. "He'd drop off five guns and pick up five, and he trusted them like no other."[21]

Ad's life passed. His guns, his shooting, always were standouts from the clutter.

CHAPTER TWENTY-FOUR

The Empty Trophy Room

The Irrepressible Days of Tom Frye

Despite how his shooting in Nevada might be viewed, Tom Frye would not go off quietly to Montana or anyplace where he "couldn't get in trouble," as some at Remington hoped. Tom got back onto the competitive shooting circuit, and a youngster captured his imagination. Tom watched a teenager named Eugene Clawson shoot at competitions in Montana, and he told the young man he could stay in Remington's sales and service building on the grounds of the Grand American Handicap in Ohio so that Eugene could afford to compete in the event in 1963. It also marked Tom's strongest return to the Grand after missing the event in 1958 due to his car-accident-related back surgery and in '59 as well.

He marked his comeback by wearing a cowboy hat, western tie, and boots. His shooting vest was emblazoned with Indian emblems, tomahawk pins, and other rather loud regalia, more than twenty pins and badges in all. This did not follow a dress code the organizers of the Grand American envisioned for their professional and industry shooters. Tom would not adhere. Eugene saw his traveling partner transformed. This low-keyed forty-seven-year-old man, who only seemed uneasy on the 24-plus-hour trip when his back tightened up in that car seat, now was stirred up.[1]

At his turn on the firing line, Tom went out and looked over the traps with incredible focus. He ran up eight hundred straight hits at one point. By

While he lived at Billings, Montana, Tom Frye expanded his version of "bullet drawings." He fired from about twenty feet and managed neat, block lettering of local companies and also shot the images of popular cartoon characters. Collection of Dean Dunlap.

the end of it he had won his second North American Clay Target championship to go along with the one he won thirteen years earlier. He won the nation's high average all-around for professionals with a .9394 percentage on doubles, handicaps, and singles on 3,650 targets. He won the professional doubles high average with .9266 on six hundred targets.[2]

"He wanted to make a point that he wasn't going to be pushed around by anyone," Clawson related. "Tom's always very reserved, yet kind of a swashbuckler, because he lets his actions do the talking."[3]

Jimmy Robinson, the hunting and shooting columnist for *Sports Afield*, took it upon himself to single-handedly pick the All-America trapshooting team every year. Jimmy studied what he saw at the Grand. It became trapshooting's answer to Ben Hogan's return to golf following his head-on collision with a bus. Six years following his car crash in Denver, Tom Frye got another *Sports Afield* patch signifying his selection to the All-America team. This one came with a word added to it. Captain.

Tom headed back to his routine on the sales route, and he took time to include hands-on testing of the new offerings from the Remington line. When he and his neighboring field rep Jack Heath got their hands on the XP-100, a bolt-action pistol that was introduced by Remington in 1963, they headed for a target. Jack sat down at a bench with iron sights. He shot a grouping that he could place a dime over to cover all the holes in the target. Not bad. Tom sat down and fired. "That's a grouping you could put in a peanut, and that's the peanut you removed from the shell," Jack said. "Fifty yards away. Holy shit."[4]

Soon, however, Jack noticed something about Tom when he shot at the metal sheets to draw his Indian heads and other characters. The Indian chief with the war bonnet took more than two hundred and thirty shots to complete, and he could do it in less than seven minutes.[5] He struggled through them. "He would take a deep breath, hold it, and go bang-bang-bang-bang as long as he could hold the breath," Jack said. It was before 1965, and Tom's breathing was affected by a heart attack. He hadn't even turned fifty.[6]

When Tom returned home, his corner lot in Billings reflected the mix of personalities between him and his wife, Sue. She had her memberships in the gun clubs, and Tom . . . did what?

"I grow pansies," Tom said. His visitors were rather impressed with the flowers in the backyard, their "strange and exotic coloring" and that they were "larger than usual." To get back there, people had to walk through rooms where a "huge buffalo head" loomed prominently, and there was the stuffed Hawaiian boar as well. But out from the pansies would emerge a "husky the size of a pony who sticks his muzzle in your lap and makes strange sounds" while looking for a pat on his back.[7]

In that house on the corner lot, heart troubles would come back. It was not Tom's. On an October night, about a month from birthday No. 50, Sue had a heart attack. It killed her. Tom faced life alone again.[8]

Tom could try to get away from the empty house, and he fell back on things that had worked before: shooting, and hanging out with celebrities who enjoyed his shooting. In September 1966 he was at Lander, Wyoming, for the One-Shot Antelope Hunt. There were four "state" teams, and each had its governor. Montana's was Gov. Tim Babcock, and Tom was listed as part of the team. Also participating in the shoot were astronauts Gordon Cooper, Deke Slayton, and Frank Borman; Dodgers owner Walter O'Malley; Donald Douglas Jr. of Douglas Aircraft; opera star Lauritz Melchoir; and Tom's old shooting pal Roy Rogers.[9]

Tom drove through his territory in a station wagon with an oversized Peters shotgun shell mounted onto the roof of the car. He also had a personalized, Montana vanity license plate he put on the car. ONE SHOT.[10]

The horn blew, but Tom Frye did not come out. It blared again. Still, no Tom. Honk! Honk!

The group of field reps for Remington Arms Company was in the car, ready to head out for another day of work at the grounds of the Grand American Handicap at Vandalia, Ohio, but they couldn't raise Tom from his motel room. One of the junior reps was told to go and knock on Tom's door, "find out what the hell he's doing that would take him so long." Considering that Tom had a professional shooter's ear—he guessed his on-the-job hazards of continual bangs and pops caused a hearing loss of about sixty percent[11]—maybe the only way for him to hear that the group was waiting for him would be for someone to beat on the door. But, considering Tom's heart problems, would they get a response at all?

A closed hand knocked against the door. Tom finally opened it. He was going to need a little bit more time. He had just gotten the Remington shooting vest, the company uniform of a white shirt and gray gabardine slacks, back from the cleaners. He was sticking the last few of the more than twenty pins through the gray lapels and breast of the vest. He'd grab his cowboy hat. Now, the rep from the West was ready to go.[12]

But when he got there he'd still have trouble hearing. Grits Gresham, the outdoors writer who hosted television's The *American Sportsman* on ABC, once noted that going to the "Grand" and walking along the mile-long path to view all the trap ranges was like being in the middle of a popcorn popper that never stopped popping.[13] Though Tom missed the Grand in 1958–59 because of his car accident, more than two thousand shotgunners did attend one of those years, and 1.75 million shells were used during the nine-day event. Close to two hundred thousand were used during practice on the grounds. With each shell containing about one-and-an-eighth ounce of shot, it meant a total of seventy tons of pellets were propelled into that Ohio field.

Tom would walk along wearing his Remington blazer, and the people who remembered how he hit eight hundred consecutive in 1963 would stop him and ask for pointers. Tom would smile, but if questions were coming and bouncing around him, people noticed he didn't give the extensive answer they might have been looking for. How do you do it, Tom? "It takes concentration," he'd often say.[14]

When he got away from the bang-bang of the trap field in a one-on-one conversation, Tom could be very insightful when he spoke about his shooting philosophy. Like all the great shooters before him—the Oakleys, the Toepperweins—he shot with both eyes open.

"The principle," Tom would start, "is not that you keep one eye for aligning your sights and the other eye for judging distance." That's when he'd actually put the gun in the person's hands and tell him or her to give it a try. "You see, one eye works with the other to feed the brain divergent images—two separate images; the closer the target, the greater the angle between the lines of vision of the two eyes and the bigger the difference between the images. The brain senses this difference, and in return gives you a sense of depth in your vision, the third dimension. Well, if you squint you lose this, a terrible loss when it comes to hitting a moving target which must be led. Look at it this way: can you imagine trying to drive a car with one eye shut?" If it still didn't work, Tom could use another visual to nudge the shooter toward stereoscopic shooting. "Here, cover your eye and look at that beef herd over yonder. See how the scene flattens out? If you didn't know the size of the cattle, you wouldn't know how far off they were."[15]

Tom's personal touch came out when he needed it. Remington's offices at Bridgeport, Connecticut, noticed it, and headquarters seemed glad Tom was still around, making an impact in an out-of-the-way place.

"He got to know every trapshooter by name," the Remington ad executive Dick Baldwin said. "Tom added new accounts, increased Remington's business. . . ."[16]

He was soft-spoken, but the times he would pipe up came when he spoke of his own shooting. He bragged, some shooters back in Ohio felt, of hitting one hundred pair of targets in doubles back at Fennwood Shooting Park. He wanted to show people in Montana that he could do it.

"Tom had a big ego, and he wanted to get the management of the shoot at Helena to make a larger event so he could do 100 doubles," the Montana teen-age shooter Eugene Clawson noted. "He got them to run 100 'birds' instead of 50, and he hit all of them."[17]

He looked to push the edge in competition, and he felt the need to polish an exciting addition to his show. It was an incendiary inspired trick, similar to what Herb Parsons had done during his shows for Winchester and Bob Allen and his son Matt would perform in their shows. Tom was beginning to perform shows through the Bureau of Indian Affairs. But he needed a large plot of land away from any buildings to pull off his new stunt with a high-powered, centerfire rifle. Tom knew of a wheat field outside of Billings, but the farmer envisioned a bunch of cars driving out to the show and running over his crop. Tom convinced him he could keep the cars parked away from the wheat. The farmer went along with it, and all was going well into the show's finale. Tom grabbed the .30-06 caliber centerfire rifle and aimed it one hundred yards away at a 50-gallon drum filled with gasoline. He had it perched over a lighted candle. Bam, the .30-06 round hurtled over to the drum and punctured it so that the dripping gas hit the flame of the candle. A skin-warming flash jumped away from the impressive explosion. A board of fireworks stayed in place once the drum exploded, and it went off in the colors and shape of an American flag. Great stuff, even in a sort of stiff, harvest-time Chinook wind. But the farmer was enraged. The cars didn't get a hold of his crop, but Tom's trick was pushed by the wind and burned forty acres worth of wheat. Tom put the bill on an expense account and sent it to Bridgeport. "How do I hide forty acres of wheat on the expense account?" Tom's boss at Remington wondered.[18]

Tom returned to his home in Billings and tried to create things to do in a house where Sue no longer was living. He had built bird coops in his backyard. He began breeding pigeons and found a competitive outlet with it. He had his birds judged by the National Pigeon Association, and in 1971 he was issued a Master Breeder Award of Pure-Bred Pigeons for his work with Giant Homers. Recipients of the award had to have been active in showing their birds for at least ten years.[19]

Invariably, these stocky, squatty birds would have a splotch of white above the beak. A collection of gray feathers, hinting of the shade of Tom's eyes, often were specked with markings of black. But brilliant colors, purple and emerald, could flare along their necks like an opal brooch. Color patterns with auburn, almond, and blond would flare from the matings Tom chose. The artistic hand he shared with his sisters could bang out cartoon characters with the bullets he fired onto a sheet of metal, but the color he blended from that pigeon coop fascinated him.

His mornings could be quiet. The regulars at the Country Kitchen Café on Grand Avenue, the long drive that ran due west from the edge of downtown Billings, noticed Tom in there almost every morning. Gravy would cover the biscuits on his plate.[20]

Sometimes they would be served to him by a pretty blond waitress. Jan Dunlap started working as a waitress at restaurants in Billings because it's where her mother worked.[21]

Jan could greet diners with a cheerful, wide, and toothy smile. Her fine, bright hair with strawberry tones rolled out lightly into waves. She often cut that hair short. Perhaps, in the time after Sue's death and in between some other failed relationships—people around Billings and in the shooting industry had heard Tom had been married six or seven times—Tom and Jan exchanged glances and talked.[22]

It didn't bother Jan's father, Clyde Dunlap, that Tom was fifty-seven and about twenty-six years older than Jan. She had been married before and had two small children.

"He's a man's man," Clyde said,[23] and in 1972, Tom and Jan traveled over to Wyoming, not far from Casper, and married.

During company meetings and sales updates at Remington, it was becoming clear that the sales of the Nylon 66 .22 rifle were suffering. The "plastic gun" needed a boost. Dick Baldwin wondered from his ad office what he could do.

He remembered that Tom Frye was persona non grata in the eyes of Remington management when the subject of the 1959 wooden-block shooting record was broached.

"It's high time we told the world what Tom did with his little rifle," Baldwin told his bosses.[24]

They went along with it, and by the early seventies full-page ads began running in outdoors periodicals and shooting-industry trade magazines. The pictures of Tom sitting atop those 100,000 wooden blocks came back to life. His smile shone once again out from under that shooting helmet. Baldwin got company permission to keep running the ad. It went on for two years. Remington was pleased that an additional sixty thousand Nylon 66 rifles sold. Total sales of the rifles were climbing toward one million and looked to be sure to exceed it, a landmark most guns could not reach. Baldwin saw the company finally extended its gratitude toward Tom. It took Remington twelve years, but he was paid a bonus that exceeded his annual salary of the year he set the record. "Better late than never," Baldwin thought.[25]

As early as 1959, Tom sensed his place as a shooting exhibitioner and field rep was not secure. He told people at the Holiday Game Ranch near Dayton at the completion of his record that gun companies were cutting back on the shooting teams they would employ. "Times have changed," he slowly said.[26]

Some of the Remington field reps cast a suspicious eye toward the corporate men coming over from the parent company at Du Pont. The reps felt the expenses were being hawked over.[27] Remington was checking into the performance of its field reps. Jack Heath, the Remington rep who Tom trained and worked in the neighboring region at Washington and Idaho, heard that the sales department was concerned over the performance of reps in Nebraska, Minnesota, and Montana. He'd heard that the rep in Minnesota had multiple heart attacks and that he wanted Remington to pay his wife when she drove him along his route. That wasn't going to happen. Remington began "retiring" reps. By 1973, Tom Frye was retired from Remington, by Remington, and he was fifty-seven years old.[28]

Jack got a phone call from the Western sales director for Remington. "I've known Tom for twenty years," Jack heard from the other end of the line. "Tom took it hard. All the guys did."[29]

∘∘∘

People still admired the Indian heads. In fact, Tom believed they were the most popular of his rifle drawings with bullets. He'd tell people they were the easiest because they require about two hundred and five shots from his .22 rifle. But Tom wouldn't stop with Indian heads. He'd shoot a wolf that resembled Wile E. Coyote. Images of owls and roadrunners made it onto his metal canvas. They could take eight hundred and fifty shots from close to twenty feet. "The only outline I use," Tom said, "is the one in my head."[30]

Tom had business cards printed with the depiction of the bullet holes forming the Indian head profile. A tomahawk was similarly designed onto the cards, which read Western Shooting Shows. He was hustling business. He was going to keep shooting, even if he had to work a steady job and go do it on the weekends. He sold cars. He was a sporting goods buyer for a large chain of department stores in Montana, which advertised Tom's shooting shows to generate more business.

He'd show Remington he still could shoot. In the spring after Remington released him, Frye had a pump shotgun fitted with a specially designed magazine to handle eight shells. He landed an engagement at a convention of the Midwest Game Law Enforcement Officers at Helena. He wanted to pull off a stunt he told people would break a world record held by Winchester exhibition shooter Herb Parsons. First, he took out an automatic shotgun and had eight clay targets hurled into the air. "The trick is to get the targets to spread out so [I] can get off eight distinct shots," Tom directed his hurlers. Up they went, and he got all of them before they fell to the ground. Parsons, throwing his own targets, had been able to hit seven, Tom told everyone. Tom then reached for the pump shotgun. Eight more clays were airborne, and Tom pumped away and erased them all from the sky.[31]

When it was printed in the newspaper, Tom made sure some of his friends got a copy. "Appreciated getting the results of your super shooting," wrote astronaut Deke Slayton, who Tom knew through the One-Shot Antelope Hunt at Lander, Wyoming.[32]

Tom's break as an independent shooter finally came. Tom got a spot on television's *Mike Douglas Show*. When he traveled to Miami Beach in January 1975 for the show he was caught in a lineup of popular stars. Paul Williams, the diminutive pianist and singer/songwriter with the thin, pale yellow hair, was there. So, too, Gabe Kaplan from the *Welcome Back Kotter* hit TV show. Once the sky was clear after commercial actor Mason Reese took a turn at the controls of the Goodyear Blimp, Tom started firing at an arrangement of targets. Mike Douglas and guest host Robert Goulet tossed silver dollars up high, and Tom's hits on them with his rifle could be heard dinging in the air. He shredded cabbages with a shotgun and shot .22 bullets through aluminum to capture an image of Goulet. He then handed a shotgun to Goulet. A target went into the air and Goulet managed to hit it. Quitting? "While I'm ahead," Goulet said.[33]

It was a success, yet public figures catch their share of hecklers and detractors. Tom's appeared after a notice printed in the newspaper announced an upcoming exhibition also mentioned his Nevada endurance shoot. A reader who identified himself as S.D. Bradford wrote to the editors of the *Billings Gazette* and openly questioned the math of Tom's 100,000 blocks shot over two weeks back in 1959. Tom wasn't letting anything go by without a fight, so he wrote back because "it merits a direct answer from the shooter in order to give . . . the facts," his response read. "It took 13 days of shooting and 10 to 11 hours daily to complete this due to TV celebrities, officials and other guests taking up time for pictures, autographs and television coverage of the event. There were hundreds present to watch. Coverage in newspapers has been quite extensive since October 1959, plus many magazine articles."[34]

His firing by Remington, some people close to him thought, was affecting his health. "He's going downhill," his brother-in-law Luke Dunlap said. Luke said Tom remained bitter about the retirement, that Tom believed he did a load of work that benefitted Remington through the sale of the Nylon 66 alone, "and they treated him like this."[35]

Tom was uncomfortable at night. It got to the point that Tom slept in a downstairs room so as not to disturb Jan with his tossing and turning. Tom would go to the doctor for checkups on his heart, but relatives thought he wasn't following their instructions.

It still didn't keep him from shooting, as he was getting more imaginative with his rifle drawings. He shot images of *Sesame Street*'s Bert and Ernie, and he shot out a Boeing 737 with wide holes for the row of windows that ran down the fuselage. He also spelled out, in neat block lettering still shot from paces away with his .22, FRONTIER. The airline's executives accepted it and displayed it in the terminal of their home base at Stapleton Airport in Denver at some point after he shot it in November 1980.

During his travels between his district and Washington, D.C., Montana congressman Ron Marlenee noticed the bullet-hole drawing. Rep. Marlenee attended Tom's shows and enjoyed following the sequence of stunts when

Tom started by throwing a coin into the air and hitting it with rifle fire before the coin could make it to the ground. Then he'd add a coin. Rep. Marlenee was clapping hard when Tom finished the sequence at five coins. "That's remarkable shooting," the congressman told Tom. Others wanted to speak with Tom following the shoot, but many of Tom's replies to questions, Rep. Marlenee noticed, were "Yep" and "Nope." When the congressman would campaign and tell his constituents he would protect their rights to bear arms, he did it at some of Tom's shows. Rep. Marlenee commented about the bullet drawing of the airline jet hanging in the airport. "Can you take that to President Reagan?" Tom asked the congressman.[36]

When Rep. Marlenee spoke at Tom's shows, he could have done it while Tom was catching his breath. As a sixty-one-year-old performer, Tom could not hide his gray hair with his cowboy hat. His face appeared drawn. His friends wondered if he could make it through his shows. Tom wondered, too.

"Basil," he told his hunting buddy and landlord, "if I can get through this day, I will be lucky."[37]

Tom's spirits jumped one day after the mailbox was opened. The letter read:

> THE WHITE HOUSE
> WASHINGTON
> Aug. 17, 1982
>
> Dear Mr. Frye:
>
> Congressman Ron Marlenee has recently passed along the inscribed print of the "Frontier 737" jetliner which you wanted me to have. You were thoughtful to give me the first of this limited-edition work depicting your impressive marksmanship. As an admirer of western memorabilia, I can certainly appreciate your special remembrance. Many thanks for sharing your special talent with me.
>
> With my best wishes for your continued success,
>
> Sincerely,

There was no typewritten name at the bottom. It was simply signed: Ronald Reagan.[38] The president never gave the metal artwork to anyone else.[39]

If there was any question over Tom's ability at this stage in his life, he could show them this letter. He also touted his listing in the Guinness Book of World Records, which recognized the two weeks he spent in Nevada, shooting at more than 100,000 wooden blocks thrown into the air and hitting all but six with his .22 caliber Nylon 66.

Less than two months later, Tom felt the chest pain again. It was time to go to the hospital, again. Tom made it into the passenger side of his car. Jan's little sister Coni hurried into the back. They knew the way, and Jan knew the procedure when they arrived at St. Vincent's Hospital on October 12, 1982. She parked and went in to get Tom admitted. But Coni looked at Tom and sensed something different.

"I always want you to tell your sister," Tom said, "that she's the love of my life. I always want her to know that."

"Tom, you're going to be fine," Coni answered.

Tom said nothing more. But Coni could not get the way he looked at her out of her mind. By the end of the day, Coni and her sister left Tom. The heart attacks happened enough times before that perhaps he felt he could fight through it again. He told them he would be OK.

Two days later, Tom Frye was dead.

A man's hands grabbed down onto the cold box to pick it up and move it. It was time to carry it onward, to lay it to rest in a new place. Rich Trang grabbed enough of the freezer that he could get it away from the wall of the garage and get it on its way to the new home that he and his wife, the former Jan Dunlap and widow of Tom Frye, had acquired. If Rich hadn't known better, he could have thought at first glance that what he saw lying there from underneath that freezer were the remnants from insects molting. There were hundreds of them down there on this now uncovered part of the garage floor. Brown. No, brass. Of course, they were spent casings ejected from the .22 rifle Tom had shot to draw his Indian chiefs, 737s, and the happy eyes and smiles of Wile E. Coyote, Bert, and Ernie.[40]

There was another room at the house that measured about fifteen feet by six feet. Really an expanded closet, it became a guns room for Tom. He had it stuffed full of guns, so many that he could not hang them all in racks along the walls. It was a piece of shooting history, for in there was a .270 Winchester single-shot rifle engraved for him by the fellowship of hunters associated with Tom at the One-Shot Antelope Hunt at Lander, Wyoming, a number of the Nylon 66 rifles, revolvers, Colts, .357 Magnums, shotguns of uncommon designs. Among the Nylon 66 rifles, Jan took pains to make sure she had one Tom had used in his October 1959 record shoot in Nevada. At first, Tom had returned two to Remington, but requested that one be returned to him. Jan had it, and it would be donated to the McCracken Research Library at Cody, Wyoming. The other, without the serial number, stayed in a Remington collection at Ilion, New York.[41] Jan left Billings for Las Vegas, Nevada. Tom's room full of guns was empty.

Jack Heath, Tom's fellow field rep, was an encyclopedia of the Remington collection. He thought about Tom Frye and flipped through his records and saw that more than one million Nylon 66 rifles—1,336,373 exactly—were manufactured in seven different variations. Heath wonders: "How much Tom shooting all those blocks added to the sales, I don't know."[42]

His story was beginning to fade. But outdoors writers would bring it up from time to time. One article from a scribe in Alton, Iowa, finished with a sentence about Tom Frye firing at the 100,000 targets and missing only six outside Reno, Nevada: "That sentence provoked considerable interest among the readers, as there were a number of inquiries concerning it, especially wanting to know more details on such an astounding feat."[43]

Dick Baldwin knew about it. He knew Tom, he had watched Tom's career for so many years from his advertising office at the Remington headquarters. When he left the company, Baldwin was the museum director for the Trapshooting Hall of Fame. In the fall of 2000, Dick Baldwin rose to a podium and he gave the speech for Tom Frye's induction into the Hall. He filled it with the best stories he knew of Tom, tales of the maverick career that bounced through the halls at Remington. But he recognized the emptiness that accompanied so much of Tom's career.

"Tom Frye has been dead almost 20 years now," Baldwin said, "and I can assure you that if he were here tonight, he would have entertained you much better than I. Unfortunately, he had no living relatives that we were aware of who could appear on his behalf this evening."[44]

Tom was from Ohio. It was in Ohio where Tom first started firing at those targets in the sky. So many of them went down right there outside the Hall of Fame in Vandalia, Ohio. Tom's accurate shot made them vanish. Finally, Tom's name reappeared, back home.

NOTES

Chapter 1

1. Born with the name Toepperwein, the spelling was later adjusted to Topperwein for the stage. For all future instances of Toepperwein within this text, the original spelling with an extra 'e' will be used, unless quoted or promotional material uses a different spelling.
2. James B. Trefethen, "King of the Riflemen," *True: The Man's Magazine* (undated), 32, 101.
3. Norman Wiltsey, "Ad Topperwein . . . A Shooting Legend," *Guns & Ammo* (October 1961), 72.
4. Hank Wieand Bowman, *Famous Guns From the Winchester Collection* (Greenwich, CT: Fawcett Publications, 1958), 129.
5. Colonel Charles Askins, "Adolph Toepperwein, Exhibition Shooter," *American Rifleman* 134, no. 2 (February 1986), 72.
6. Bowman, *Famous Guns From the Winchester Collection,* 129.
7. Ernie Pyle, *Home Country* (New York: William Sloane Associates, 1947), 38.
8. Ibid.
9. Jaroslav Lugs, *The History of Shooting* (Feltham, Middlesex, England: Spring Books, 1968), 172.
10. Wiltsey, "Ad Topperwein . . . ," 75.

Chapter 2

1. Dale Shaw, "Master Marksman," *SPORT* (June 1962), 43.
2. Chris H. Sheerin, "Newton Hunt Crumley, 1911–1962," *Northeastern Nevada Historical Quarterly* 79, no. 1 (Winter 1979), 12.

3. Shaw, "Master Marksman," 43.
4. Dean Dunlap, telephone interview.
5. Shawn R. Hall, "A History of Elko, Nevada," *Northeastern Nevada Historical Society Quarterly* 95, no. 3 140–43.
6. Radio documentary, National Public Radio (Elko, NV: Deep West Radio production, Western Folklife Center, 2008).
7. United Press, "Three Nevada Men," March 31–April 1, 1936; "Crumley Party Is Unharmed," *Nevada State Journal*, April 1, 1936.
8. *Nevada State Journal*, May 24, 1959.
9. Sheerin, "Newton Hunt Crumley," 12.

Chapter 3

1. Greta Nissen, "Old Marksman; Leading Quiet Life," *San Antonio Light*, June 24, 1951.
2. Ernie Pyle, *Home Country*, 38.
3. Harold V. Ratliffe, Associated Press, "Ad Topperwein Now Teaching Kids," *San Antonio Express and News*, July 15, 1956.
4. "Tep On Shooting; San Antonio Boy Creates a Sensation in New York," *San Antonio Daily Light*, September 7, 1898.
5. Joann Toepperwein, interview.
6. Wiltsey, "Ad Topperwein . . . ," 47.
7. Ibid., 46.
8. Colette Kohler, telephone interview.
9. Fred Maly, "Angling Around," *San Antonio Light*, December 14, 1959.
10. "Ad" Topperwein, "FOR YOUR INFORMATION," open letter, January 5, 1960, obtained courtesy the collection of Tony Sapienza; "The Toepp Guns Of All Times," http://www.showmanshooter.com/html/toepperwein.html.

Chapter 4

1. "A Printer's Error," *San Antonio Light*, March 15, 1896.
2. Art Gogan, "A 'Doc' Carver Gun," *Man At Arms* (Number One, 2001), 32.
3. Larry McMurtry, *The Colonel and Little Missie: Buffalo Bill, Annie Oakley, and the Beginnings of Superstardom in America* (New York: Simon & Schuster, 2005), 123.
4. Raymond W. Thorp, *Spirit Gun of the West: The Story of Doc W.F. Carver* (Glendale, CA: The Arthur H. Clark Company, 1957), 108; Thorp cites the *London Sportsman*, March 26, 1879.
5. *New York Times*, July 6, 1878.
6. Clayton E. Cramer, *Armed America: The Story of How and Why Guns Became as American as Apple Pie* (Nashville, TN: Nelson Current, 2006), 236.

7. *Americans and Their Guns: The National Rifle Association story—through nearly a century of service to the nation*; compiled by James B. Trefethen (Harrisburg, PA: Stackpole Company, 1967), 62.
8. Charles Askins, "World's Greatest Shooter," *Guns Magazine* (November 1967), 33.
9. Jaroslav Lugs, *The History of Shooting* (Feltham, Middlesex, England: Spring Books, 1968), 172.
10. Thorp, *Spirit Gun of the West,* 79.
11. Ad Topperwein and Norman B. Wiltsey, "World's Greatest Sharp Shooter," *Guns and Hunting* (October 1961), 12–14.
12. *Reminiscences of Gottfried Christian Daniel Toepperwein and A Brief History By His Son Lucian Ferdinand Toepperwein*, Translated by Flora Wertheim (Boerne, Texas: Highland Press, 1984), 85.
13. "United States, Civil War Soldiers Index." *FamilySearch* (https://www.familysearch.org: accessed 24 June 2011), entry for E. A. Toepperwein, Confederate Private; Citing Civil War Records, FHL microfilm 880,050; United States Federal Archives and Records Center, Washington D.C., United States.
14. "One of the World's Greatest Shots Born at Boerne," *Boerne Star*, August 18, 1949.
15. Garland Perry, *Historic Images of Boerne and Kendall Country, Texas*, Sesquicentennial Edition 1849–1999 (Boerne, Texas: Perry Publications, 1998), 202.
16. Trefethen, *Americans and Their Guns*, 111.
17. Louis B. Engelke, "The Old Schuetzen Verein was a way of life for 60 years," *San Antonio Express-News Sunday Magazine*, October 12, 1975, 8–9 (published as a reprint from *San Antonio Express*, December 3, 1950).
18. *A History of Kendall County, Texas: Rivers, Ranches, Railroads, Recreation*; compiled and edited by the Kendall County Historical Commission (Dallas, Texas: Taylor Publishing Company, 1984), 226.
19. *Boerne Star*, August 18, 1949.
20. Perry, *Historic Images of Boerne,* 140.
21. Lt. Col. William S. Brophy (USAR, Ret.), *Marlin Firearms: A History of the Guns and the Company that Made Them* (Harrisburg, PA: Stackpole Books, 1989), 5–6.
22. Emil E.A. Toepperwein, 1875. Improvement in Magazine Fire-Arms. US Patent 167,712, filed July 24, 1875, and issued September 14, 1875.
23. Ibid.
24. Brophy, *Marlin Firearms,* 147.
25. David D. Smits, "The Frontier Army and the Destruction of the Buffalo: 1865–1883," *The Western Historical Quarterly* 25, no. 3 (Autumn 1994), 314.
26. *The Cedar Rapids (Iowa) Evening Gazette*, "The Evil Spirit: He Rests in the City for a Few Days on His Way West—A Chat with Dr. Carver," (January 11, 1888), 4.

27. D. Jean Smith, *Medicine Creek Journals: Ena and the Plainsmen* (North Platte, NE: The Old Hundred and One Press, 2003), 100; *Lincoln County Advertiser*, October 12, 1872, Carver Collection, Nebraska State Historical Society.
28. Don Russell, *The Wild West: A History of the Wild West Shows* (Fort Worth, TX: Amon Carter Museum of Western Art, 1970), 10.
29. Nellie Snyder Yost, *Buffalo Bill: His Family, Friends, Fame, Failures, and Fortunes* (Chicago: Sage Books, 1979), 75.
30. Russell, *The Wild West,* 289. Russell cites Nate Salsbury, "The Origin of the Wild West Show," *The Colorado Magazine*, XXXII, no. 3 (July 1955), 205–8.
31. Thorp, *Spirit Gun of the West*, 215.
32. Louis S. Warren, *Buffalo Bill's America: William Cody and the Wild West Show* (New York: Alfred A. Knopf, 2005), 231. Warren cites Don Russell, *The Lives and Legends of Buffalo Bill* (Norman: University of Oklahoma Press, 1960), 297.
33. Russell, *The Wild West,* 10.
34. Laura Browder, *Her Best Shot: Women and Guns in America* (Chapel Hill, NC: The University of North Carolina Press, 2006), 86.
35. "Great Shooting Feat," *New York Times*, January 4, 1878.
36. Captain A.H. Bogardus, Trapshooting Hall of Fame, http://www.traphof.org/People-Stories/captain-a-h-bogardus.html.
37. Thorp, *Spirit Gun of the West,* 95.
38. Shirl Kasper, *Annie Oakley* (Norman: University of Oklahoma Press, 1992), 11.
39. Thorp, *Spirit Gun of the West,* 96–97.
40. Kasper, *Annie Oakley,* 15.
41. *The American Field*, March 31, 1883.
42. James B. Trefethen, "King of the Riflemen," *True: The Men's Magazine* (undated, circa 1957), 102.
43. Fritz Toepperwein, Ad Topperwein biography manuscript, unpublished (provided courtesy of Kenneth Toepperwein).
44. Chris Hersch, *The Texas Gun Trade: A Guide to the Guns Made or Sold in the Lone Star State, 1780–1899* (Woonsocket, RI: Mowbray Publishers, 2008), 171.
45. Regina Adam, email via Bettie Edmonds, archivist, Genealogical & Historical Society of Kendall County (Texas), August 2, 2011.
46. Ad Topperwein, letter to M.B. Allen, June 7, 1947.
47. Fritz Toepperwein, Ad Topperwein biography manuscript, unpublished.

Chapter 5

1. "Our Industry: Background," www.ooga.org.
2. Ron Chernow, *Titan: The Life of John D. Rockefeller, Sr.* (New York: Random House, 1998), 284–88.
3. US Census, 1920.

4. Carolyn Mulne, telephone interview.
5. Dick Baldwin, "The Road to Yesterday," *Trap & Field* (September 2002).
6. *Americans and Their Guns*, compiled by James B. Trefethen (Harrisburg, PA: Stackpole Books, 1967), 138–41.
7. *Billings Gazette*, June 28, 1964.
8. Addison Bragg, "Billings man makes shooting history," *Billings Gazette*, April 23, 1971.
9. Coni Wein, telephone interview.
10. Dean Dunlap, telephone interview.
11. *Blue & Gold*, Findlay High School yearbook of 1935 (provided by Hancock County Historical Museum, Mark H. Donaldson Jr., accessionist, September 1, 2011), 49.
12. *Billings Gazette*, June 28, 1964. "My father was a good field shot," Tom Frye said. "He started me (as a 16-year-old amateur)."
13. Military Personnel Records, Thomas R. Frye (Request No. 1-9984628676), National Personnel Records Center, St. Louis, Mo.
14. Official website of Oilers Athletics (http://athletics.findlay.edu/sports/fball/football_records/Football_Records.pdf); *The Argus* (Findlay College annual), 1936–37.
15. *The Ohio State Patrol: The First 75 Years: A History of Service, 1933–2008* (Columbus: The Ohio State Highway Patrol, 2008), 12.
16. Ibid., 21, 23, 133.
17. Ibid., 22.
18. Thomas R. Frye enlistment during February 1942, serial number 15110032, at Lockbourne AAB, Columbus, Ohio; Box 0185, Film Reel Number 2.42, accessed September 2, 2011 (www.fold3.com).
19. *The Flying Wheel* (Columbus: Ohio State Highway Patrol, August 1942), 3.
20. Military Personnel Records, Thomas R. Frye.
21. Tom Frye, Trapshooting Hall of Fame, http://www.traphof.org/Inductees/Frye-Tom.html
22. Bob Allen, *Shooter: An Autobiography; the Life and Times of Bob Allen* (Austin: Nortex Press, 2001), 89.
23. Ibid., 340.
24. *Billings Gazette*, June 28, 1964.
25. D. Lee Braun, Trapshooting Hall of Fame inductees, http://www.traphof.org/Inductees/Braun-D.-Lee.html.
26. James Joseph, "Greatest Shot of Them All," *Guns & Ammo*, *The Best of Guns & Ammo*, 1958–1962 (originally appeared in *Guns & Ammo*, February 1960), 56–61.
27. Dale Shaw, "Master Marksman," *SPORT* (June 1962), 81.

Chapter 6

1. Dean K. Boorman, *The History of Winchester Firearms* (New York: The Lyons Press, 2001), 70.
2. Theodore Roosevelt, *Hunting Trips of a Ranchman; Hunting Trips on the Prairie and in the Mountains* (New York: The Review of Reviews Company, G.P. Putnam's Sons, 1885), 39, https://archive.org/details/huntingtripsranch04roosrich.
3. Herbert G. Houze, *Winchester Repeating Arms Company, Its History and Development from 1865 to 1981* (Iola, WI: Krause Publications, 1994), 170.
4. Harold F. Williamson, *Winchester: The Gun That Won the West* (Washington, DC: Combat Forces Press, 1952), 198.
5. Ibid., 131, 198.
6. Raymond W. Thorp, *Spirit Gun of the West: The Story of Doc W.F. Carver* (Glendale, CA: Arthur H. Clark Company, 1957), 151.
7. Judith Berg Sobre, *San Antonio on Parade: Six Historic Festivals* (College Station: Texas A&M University Press, 2003), 7.
8. Dick Baldwin, "The Fabulous Toepperweins," *Trap and Field*, nos. 11, 12 (2006).
9. S.C. Gwynne, *Empire of the Summer Moon: Quanah Parker and the Rise and Fall of the Comanches, the Most Powerful Indian Tribe in American History* (New York: Scribner, 2010), 82–87.
10. Berg Sobre, 10, 20.
11. Richard F. Selcer, *Legendary Watering Holes: The Saloons That Made Texas Famous* (College Station, Texas: Texas A&M University Press, 2004), 63–64.
12. Paul Adams, "The Unsolved Murder of Ben Thompson, Pistoleer Extraordinary," *Southwestern Historical Quarterly* XLVIII, no. 3 (January 1945), 324.
13. G.R. Williamson, *Texas Pistoleers: The True Story of Ben Thompson and King Fisher* (Charleston, SC: The History Press, 2010), 17.
14. Adams, 328.
15. New York passenger lists, ancestry.com.
16. Twelfth Census of the United States, June 1, 1900.
17. "'Tep' Goes East: San Antonio's Crack Rifle-Shot Leaves for New York Monday," *San Antonio Daily Light*, July 30, 1898.
18. Baldwin, *Trap and Field*, nos. 11, 12 (2006).
19. "A New Athletic Club," *San Antonio Daily Light*, June 23, 1896.
20. "A Night Of Sport: Some Clever Exhibitions Given in the Bexar Athletic Club Rooms," *San Antonio Daily Light*, October 23, 1896.
21. Charles Merritt Barnes, *Combats and Conquests of Immortal Heroes* (San Antonio: Guessaz & Ferlet Company, 1910), 169. The text refers to Adolph Toepperwein as a "natural born artist . . . [he] literally shoots likenesses with his rifle . . . an all-around genius, painting in oil or water colors, burning on wood or leather."

22. Baldwin, *Trap and Field,* nos. 11, 12 (2006).
23. *San Antonio Daily Light*, June 7, 1897.
24. "A Great Feat By Ad. Toepperwein: The Crack Rifle Shot Breaks His Own World's Record," *San Antonio Daily Express*, August 23, 1897. Charles Askins, "World's Greatest Shooter," *Guns Magazine*, November 1967, 32. Col. Askins wrote that Annie Oakley hit 943 out of 1,000 with a .22 rifle.
25. "Fowling and Fowlers," *San Antonio Sunday Light*, February 6, 1898.
26. "Through The Years," *San Antonio Light*, July 14, 1969.

Chapter 7

1. Don Miller, "Afloat and Afield," *Elyria Chronicle-Telegram*, April 26, 1955.
2. Grand American Handicap Champions, Trapshooting Hall of Fame, http://www.traphof.org/grand-american-handicap-champions.html.
3. *Hamilton Journal–The Daily News*, July 10, 1949.
4. Cliff Doughman, Trapshooting Hall of Fame, http://www.traphof.org/Inductees/Doughman-Cliff.html.
5. *Hamilton Journal–The Daily News*.
6. "Howard Otto Elected Chairman of League's Junior Rifle Training," *Sandusky Register-Star-News*, April 2, 1954.
7. Fred Waldock, Jr., telephone interview, February 13, 2012.
8. "Cliff Doughman, Trapshooting Hall of Fame," http://www.traphof.org/Inductees/Doughman-Cliff.html.
9. *Hamilton Journal–the Daily News*, August 19, 1953; *European Stars & Stripes*, August 23, 1953.
10. *Billings Gazette*, June 28, 1964.
11. "Record Wreckers," *Sandusky Register-Star-News*, August 31, 1954; Bob Allen, *Shooter: An Autobiography . . .*, 252.
12. Waldock, telephone interview.
13. "Frye Honored at Fennwood for His Help," *Sandusky Register-Star News*, March 27, 1957.
14. *Lima News*, August 24, 1956.
15. "Tom Frye Wins Top Pro Honor," *Sandusky Register-Star News,* August 27, 1956.
16. Carolyn Mulne, telephone interview, February 3, 2012.

Chapter 8

1. Dick Baldwin, "Road to Yesterday: The Fabulous Topperweins, Part I," *Trap & Field*, November 2006.
2. Norman B. Wiltsey, "The West's Greatest Marksman," *Real West* (Vol. XI, Number 65, November 1968), 16–17.

3. Baldwin, "Road to Yesterday," November 2006.
4. Fritz Toepperwein, Ad Topperwein biography manuscript (unpublished), provided courtesy of Kenneth Toepperwein.
5. K. D. Kirkland, *America's Premier Gunmakers: Winchester* (East Bridgewater, MA: World Publications Group, Inc., 2007), 25.
6. W.H. Depperman, "Texas Triggerman," *Collier's*, June 8, 1946; Baldwin.
7. "George Walker Returns With a List of Attractions For The Season," *Galveston Daily News*, August 6, 1891.
8. Judith Berg Sobre, *San Antonio on Parade: Six Historic Festivals* (College Station: Texas A&M University Press, 2003), 7.
9. "San Antonio's Representative," *San Antonio Daily Light*, January 29, 1895.
10. Berg Sobre, 9.
11. Fred Mosebach, "Memories of Grand Opera House Thrill Old Theater Fans," *San Antonio Express*, June 16, 1935, 8C.
12. "Home-Grown Booster is 'Tep,' San Antonio's Crack Rifle Shot Famous throughout Country," *San Antonio Express*, January 20, 1925.
13. Ad Topperwein and Norman B. Wiltsey, "World's Greatest Sharpshooter," *Guns and Hunting* (October 1961), 14.
14. *San Antonio Daily Light*, July 30, 1898.
15. Office of Historic Preservation, City of San Antonio, http://www.sanantonio.gov/historic/Districts/Cattleman_Square.aspx.
16. Baldwin, "Road to Yesterday," November 2006. *Sporting Life*, 27.1, March 28, 1896, 19, http://library.la84.org/SportsLibrary/SportingLife/1896/VOL_27_NO_01/SL2701019.pdf.
17. Toepperwein, Ad Topperwein biography manuscript (unpublished).
18. Dan Klepper, "The Outdoorsman: Ad to Celebrate Birthday No. 90," *San Antonio Express and News*, October 16, 1959.
19. Albert F. McLean, Jr., *American Vaudeville as Ritual* (Lexington, KY.: University of Kentucky Press, 1965), 20–21.
20. D. Travis Stewart, *No Applause—Just Throw Money: The Book That Made Vaudeville Famous* (New York: Faber and Faber, 2005), 114.
21. Bernard Sobel, *A Pictorial History of Vaudeville* (New York: Bonanza Books, 1961), 67, 69–70. Sobel. Also reference in Groucho Marx, *Groucho and Me* (New York: Bernard Greis Associates, 1959).
22. Fritz Toepperwein, "Duck Soup," Ad Topperwein biography manuscript, unpublished (provided courtesy of Kenneth Toepperwein).
23. Topperwein and Wiltsey, *Guns and Hunting*.
24. Baldwin, "Road to Yesterday," November 2006.
25. "Through the Years: September 2, 1898," *San Antonio Light*, September 2, 1978.
26. *San Antonio Express*, January 20, 1925.

27. Topperwein and Wiltsey, *Guns and Hunting*.
28. Baldwin, "Road to Yesterday," November 2006.
29. "Tep on Shooting; San Antonio Boy Creates a Sensation in New York," *San Antonio Daily Light*, September 7, 1898. The article quotes another article that Adolph Toepperwein was credited with writing for the *New York Journal* at some point previously.
30. Ibid.
31. Ibid.
32. *San Antonio Express*, January 20, 1925.
33. Toepperwein, "Duck Soup."
34. Greta Nissen, "Old Marksman; Leading Quiet Life," *San Antonio Light*, June 24, 1951.
35. *San Antonio Daily Light*, September 7, 1898.
36. Undated photo cutline, Ken Toepperwein collection.
37. "Expert Marksman," *Portsmouth Herald*, January 21, 1899.
38. "Done With A Rifle: The Head of an Indian Shot Out with One-Hundred and Fifty-Two Bullets," *Reno Evening Gazette*, February 21, 1899.
39. Baldwin, "Road to Yesterday," November 2006.
40. Wiltsey, "Ad Topperwein," *Guns & Ammo*, October 1961, 47.

Chapter 9

1. "Frye Honored at Fennwood for His Help," *Sandusky Register-Star News*, March 27, 1957.
2. *Ogden Standard-Examiner*, April 8, 1957.
3. Carolyn Mulne, telephone interview.
4. Lynn Parsons, M.D., "My Personal Hero: Roy Rogers and the Crew," Burton Blog, April 4, 2010, http://www.burtonblog.com/view.cfm?post=3835.
5. Roy Brooks, telephone interview, January 7, 2012; Brooks, "The Glory Years of Skeet At Pacific Rod & Gun Club," Pacific Rod & Gun Club website (http://prgc.net/our-famous-shooters/).
6. Harold S. Smith Sr., Trapshooting Hall of Fame, http://www.traphof.org/Inductees/Smith-Sr.-Harold-S.html.
7. Roger Butterfield, "Elko County, Nevada," *LIFE* (April 18, 1949), 101.
8. Shawn Hall, *Preserving the Glory Days: Ghost Towns and Mining Camps of Nye County, Nevada* (Reno: University of Nevada Press, 1981), 61; Hall, *Old Heart of Nevada: Ghost Towns and Mining Camps of Elko County* (Reno: University of Nevada Press, 1998), 132; Al W. Moe, *Nevada's Golden Age of Gambling*, Revised and Expanded Edition (Puget Sound Books, 2001), 51.
9. Kay McDonald, "The Goldfield Hotel," *The D C Bee*; The Newsletter of the Nevada Historical Society Docent Council 18, no. 9 (May 2007), 4.

10. "Noted Gold Field Food for Flames," *Frederick (Md.) News*, July 7, 1923.
11. Benjamin J. Crumley, Correspondence, 1861–1878, 1865–1866. University Special Collections, University of Nevada, Reno, Library. http://innopac.library.unr.edu/record=b1703361~S0.
12. "J. Grant Crumley Is Dead On Coast," *Reno Evening Gazette*, September 17, 1940.
13. "Millionaire Miner Killed," *New York Times*, August 23, 1901.
14. "Pink Pajama Kid Is Good Booster," *Reno Evening Gazette*, December 10, 1914.
15. Angel Strong Smits, "Sam Strong: Cripple Creek's Notorious Millionaire," *Wild West*, http://www.historynet.com/sam-strong-cripple-creeks-notorious-millionaire.htm.
16. "Nellie Lewis Fainted When She Heard of Millionaire Sam Strong's Death," *Newark Daily Advocate*, August 24, 1901.
17. "Gen. Tarsney Tarred And Feathered," *New York Times*, June 24, 1894.
18. Peggy Drake, "Belmont," (unpublished manuscript).
19. Chris H. Sheerin, "Newton Hunt Crumley, 1911–1962," *Northeastern Nevada Historical Quarterly* 79, no. 1, (Winter 1979), 12.
20. Ibid.
21. "Nevada Football Players Take to Air and Fly to Los Angeles for Contest," *Reno Evening Gazette*, November 8, 1929.
22. Ibid.
23. Ibid.
24. Washoe Pete, "Loose Leaf: From the Journal," *Nevada State Journal*, April 5, 1934.
25. Dale Shaw, "Master Marksman," *SPORT Magazine*, June 1962, 43.
26. James Joseph, "Greatest Shot of Them All," *Guns & Ammo, The Best of Guns & Ammo 1958–1962* (originally appeared in *Guns & Ammo*, February 1960), 59.
27. Mulne, telephone interview.
28. Joseph, "Greatest Shot of Them All," *The Best of Guns & Ammo, 1958–1962* (originally appeared in *Guns & Ammo*, February 1960), 59.
29. Ibid.

Chapter 10

1. *Official Catalogue and Guide Book to the Pan American Exposition* (Buffalo, NY: Charles Ahrhart, 1901), 175–76, http://panam1901.org/documents/original_sources/guidebook_ahrhart.PDF.
2. Mark Bennitt, *Bennitt Illustrated Souvenir Guide Pan American Exposition* (Buffalo, NY: The Goff Company, 1901), 57–58; http://babel.hathitrust.org/cgi/pt?id=nnc1.ar52097595;seq=7;size=125;view=image;page=root;orient=0.
3. Dick Baldwin, "Road to Yesterday: The Fabulous Topperweins, Part I," *Trap & Field*, November 2006.

4. Harold F. Williamson, *Winchester: The Gun That Won the West* (Washington, DC: Combat Forces Press, 1952), 183. Williamson cites *New Haven Courier-Journal*, April 28, 1930.
5. Baldwin. "Road to Yesterday," November 2006.
6. Mark Gado, "The Assassination of President William McKinley," http://www.trutv.com/library/crime/terrorists_spies/assassins/mckinley/5.html.
7. Baldwin, "Road to Yesterday," November 2006.
8. Ibid.
9. Laura Browder, *Her Best Shot: Women and Guns in America* (Chapel Hill, NC: The University of North Carolina Press, 2006), 70.
10. Texas City Directories, San Antonio, Texas, 1891–1893, ancestry.com; the 1910 US Census shows the Toepperwein address as 231 Starr Street, San Antonio, Texas.
11. Baldwin, "Road to Yesterday," November 2006.
12. "Mrs. Ad. Toepperwein Tells Why She Took Up Trapshooting . . . ," *San Antonio Light*, July 8, 1917.
13. Wiltsey, "Ad Topperwein," 47.
14. "Tep on Shooting; San Antonio Boy Creates a Sensation in New York," *San Antonio Daily Light*, September 7, 1898.
15. Baldwin, "Road to Yesterday," November 2006.
16. *San Antonio Light*, July 8, 1917.
17. Ibid.
18. *San Antonio Daily Light*, September 7, 1898.
19. Baldwin, "Road to Yesterday," November 2006.
20. *San Antonio Daily Light*, September 7, 1898.
21. Baldwin, "Road to Yesterday," November 2006.
22. *San Antonio Daily Light*, September 7, 1898.
23. Fritz Toepperwein, Ad Topperwein biography manuscript, unpublished (provided courtesy of Kenneth Toepperwein).
24. Baldwin, "Road to Yesterday," November 2006.
25. *San Antonio Daily Light*, September 7, 1898.
26. Baldwin, "Road to Yesterday," November 2006.
27. *San Antonio Light*, July 8, 1917.
28. Ernie Pyle, "Home Country," reprinted in *Omnibook Magazine* (September 1947), 37.

Chapter 11

1. Todd Larson, "Fishing for History: The History of Fishing and Fishing Tackle; 52 Trade Houses Part 3: The Kerr Sports Shop of Beverly Hills," April 20, 2011, http://fishinghistory.blogspot.com/2011/04/52-trade-houses-part-3-kerr-sport-shop.html.

2. Roy Anderson, "From A To Z: Frye Doesn't Miss Hollywood," *Billings Gazette*, May 16, 1961.
3. Photograph obtained courtesy of G.A. "Luke" Dunlap.
4. Anderson "From A To Z: Frye Doesn't Miss Hollywood."
5. Chand Sultana, Ph.D., letter to Mr. Michael A. Shull, March 20, 2013, 1–4, http://www.laparks.org/environmental/pdf/chatsworth/draftRem.pdf.
6. *The Daily Inter Lake*, Kalispell, MT, October 7, 1960.
7. Carolyn Mulne, telephone interview; Anderson, "From A To Z: Frye Doesn't Miss Hollywood."
8. Gene Clawson, telephone interview.
9. Ken Berger, telephone interview; Mulne, telephone interview.
10. Janice Pine, email interview.
11. Chris H. Sheerin, "Newton Hunt Crumley, 1911–1962, *Northeastern Nevada Historical Society Quarterly* 79, No. 1, (Winter 1979), 2–5, 12–15.
12. Shawn R. Hall, "A History of Elko, Nevada," *Northeastern Nevada Historical Society Quarterly* (Issue 95-3), 140–43.
13. Hall, *Preserving the Glory Days: Ghost Towns and Mining Camps of Nye County, Nevada*, 61; Hall, *Old Heart of Nevada: Ghost Towns and Mining Camps of Elko County,* 132; Moe, 51.
14. Thomas A. DeLong, *Pops: Paul Whiteman, King of Jazz* (Piscataway, NJ: New Century Publishers, 1983), 202–4.
15. David W. Toll, "Silver Circuit stars' fees force big risk for casino, not customer," *Elyria Chronicle Telegram*, September 29, 1968.
16. Ross Firestone, *Swing, Swing, Swing: The Life & Times of Benny Goodman* (New York: W.W. Norton & Company, 1993), 70; Ian Carr, Digby Fairweather and Brian Priestly, et al., *Jazz, The Rough Guide* (London: Rough Guides, Ltd., 1995), 386.
17. Radio documentary, National Public Radio (Elko, NV: Deep West Radio production, Western Folklife Center, 2008).
18. Toll, *Elyria Chronicle Telegram*, September 29, 1968.
19. Radio documentary, NPR (Elko, NV, Deep West Radio production, Western Folklife Center, 2008).
20. Hall, *Northeastern Nevada Historical Society Quarterly*, 142–43.
21. *Bakersfield Californian*, April 27, 1959.
22. Jim Day, "Pipefuls," *Bakersfield Californian*, January 26, 1960.
23. Berger, telephone interview.
24. Robert Stack (with Mark Evans), *Straight Shooting* (New York: Macmillan Publishing Co., Inc., 1980), 35.
25. Jack Heath, telephone interview, May 25, 2011.
26. Mulne, telephone interview.

27. Ibid.
28. *Bakersfield Californian*, April 27, 1959.
29. "Shooting Exhibit Planned," *Bakersfield Californian*, April 22, 1959.

Chapter 12

1. "Tep On Shooting; San Antonio Boy Creates a Sensation in New York," *San Antonio Daily Light*, September 7, 1898.
2. *San Antonio Express*, October 21, 1940.
3. Harold F. Williamson, *Winchester: The Gun That Won The West* (Washington, DC: Combat Forces Press, 1952), 183.
4. K.D. Kirkland, *Winchester: America's Premier Gunmaker* (East Bridgewater, MA: World Publications Group, Inc., 2007), 20, 24.
5. S.M. Purcell, "The Preacher's New Gun," *San Antonio Express and News*, August 16, 1970, 8D.
6. Dick Baldwin, "Road to Yesterday," November 2006.
7. "Toepperwein Breaks Record," *The LeMars Globe-Post*, September 24, 1902.
8. "Winchester Greaseless Bullet Smokeless Powder Cartridges," *Sporting Life* 40, no. 13 December 13, 1902), 16.
9. "Famous Shots Coming To The International," *San Antonio Light*, September 8, 1907.
10. *San Antonio Daily Light*, April 12, 1904.
11. *San Antonio Light*, September 8, 1907.
12. Fritz Toepperwein, Ad Topperwein biography manuscript, unpublished, provided courtesy of Kenneth Toepperwein.
13. Duncan Barnes, George R. Watrous, James C. Rikhoff, Thomas H. Hall and Pete Kuhlhoff, *The History of Winchester Firearms, 1866–1980, 5th ed.*, (Tulsa, OK: Winchester Press, 1966), 57.
14. Baldwin; *San Antonio Light*, September 8, 1907.
15. Larry McMurtry, *The Colonel and Little Missie: Buffalo Bill, Annie Oakley, and the Beginnings of Superstardom in America* (New York: Simon & Schuster, 2005), 8.
16. Charles Askins, "World's Greatest Shooter," *Guns Magazine* (November 1967), 33.
17. James B. Trefethen, *Americans and Their Guns: The National Rifle Association Story through nearly a century of service to the nation* (Harrisburg, PA: Stackpole Books, 1967), 108.
18. Bruce N. Canfield, "The Foreign Rifle: US Krag-Jorgensen," *American Rifleman* (October 2010), 86–89, 126, 129.
19. Trefethen, *Americans and Their Guns*, 132–33.
20. "Held Her Own With Experts; Mrs. Elizabeth Toepperwein Of This City

Qualifies For Marksmen's Reserve; Opened Their Eyes; Her Shooting One of the Features of Sea Girt Meet—Title Confirmed by War Department," *San Antonio Light*, July 16, 1906.

21. Trefethen, *Americans and Their Guns*, 133
22. *San Antonio Light*, July 16, 1906.
23. Laura Browder, *Her Best Shot: Women and Guns in America* (Chapel Hill: The University of North Carolina Press, 2006), 70. Browder cites Henry Brewer, letter to Major Leonard A. Horner, September 6, 1917, file 67.1, Winchester Arms Collection Archives.
24. *Sporting Life* (May 13, 1905) 23, http://library.la84.org/SportsLibrary/SportingLife/1905/VOL_45_NO_09/SL4509023.pdf.
25. *Sporting Life* (May 13, 1905) 23, http://library.la84.org/SportsLibrary/SportingLife/1905/VOL_45_NO_22/SL4522023.pdf.
26. "Winchester Experts in the South," *Sporting Life* (April 20, 1907), 23 (courtesy of Kenny Ray Estes, Amateur Trapshooting Association Hall of Fame).
27. *Sporting Life* (August 24, 1907), 31, http://www.la84foundation.org/SportsLibrary/SportingLife/1907/VOL_49_NO_24/SL4924031.pdf.
28. Browder, *Her Best Shot*, 67, 70.
29. "San Antonio In The State Shoot," *San Antonio Gazette*, July 27, 1908.
30. James C. Goldbaum, "Women's Work: Mrs. Ad. Topperwein Wins Texas State Shoot, *Sporting Life* (August 15, 1908), 30 (courtesy of Kenny Ray Estes, Amateur Trapshooting Association Hall of Fame).
31. Forest W. McNeir, *Forest McNeir of Texas* (San Antonio: The Naylor Company, 1956), 220.
32. Ibid.
33. Edmund Goes, "Die amerikanischen Kunstschutzen Adolph Topperwein und Seine Frau," *Schuss und Waffe III* (1909/1910, No. 23), 478–79.
34. "Feats of Marksmanship; Remarkable Skill of Adolph Topperwein of Texas," *Frederick (Md.) Daily News*, April 24, 1906.
35. Jaroslav Lugs, *The History of Shooting*, (Feltham, Middlesex, England: Spring Books, 1968), 185.
36. Browder, *Her Best Shot*, 71.
37. Ibid., 72.
38. McNeir, *Forest McNeir of Texas*, 220.
39. David Mamet, "First Person: The Buttons on the Board," *Arts & Antiques*, November 1992, 33.

Chapter 13

1. Photograph, undated, provided from the collection of Dean Dunlap, February 21, 2010.

2. Gerard Colby Zilg, *Du Pont: Behind the Nylon Curtain* (Englewood Cliffs, N.J.: Prentice-Hall, Inc., 1974), 8–14, 19–20, 291.
3. "Discovery: 1927, Wallace Carothers," http://www2.dupont.com/Phoenix_Heritage/en_US/1927_detail.html.
4. John Gyde and Roy Marcot, "The Remington Nylon 66; A new concept in rifles, back then," *American Rifleman*, http://www.americanrifleman.org/ArticlePage.aspx?id=1797&cid=9.
5. Ibid.
6. "Outdoor Beat," *Nevada State Journal*, March 1, 1959.
7. Jack Heath, telephone interview.
8. "Hall of Fame Banquet," *Trap & Field* 176, no. 11 (November 2000), 54.

Chapter 14

1. William A. Cook, *The Louisville Grays Scandal of 1877: The Taint of Gambling at the Dawn of the National League* (Jefferson, NC: McFarland, 2005), 164.
2. "Great Shooting Feat," *New York Times*, January 4, 1878.
3. "The Evil Spirit: He Rests in the City For a Few Days on His Way West—A Chat With Dr. Carver," *The Cedar Rapids Evening Gazette* (January 11, 1888), 4.
4. Norman B. Wiltsey, "World's Greatest Marksman," *V.F.W. Magazine* (January 1963), 37.
5. "2 Complete Game Victories by 1 Pitcher in 1 Day," www.baseballalmanac.com.
6. Raymond Thorp, *Spirit Gun of the West: The Story of Doc W.F. Carver* (Glendale, CA: Arthur H. Clark Company, 1857), 151.
7. Ibid., 148.
8. Ibid., 148–50.
9. *The Cedar Rapids Evening Gazette* (January 11, 1888).
10. Ibid.
11. If Doc Carver shot Winchesters chambered for a .38 bullet, it's likely he fired the Model 1886 Repeating Rifle. According to Duncan Barnes, George R. Watrous, James C. Rikhoff, Thomas R. Hall and Pete Kuhlhoff, *The History of Winchester Firearms, 1866–1980, 5th ed.* (Tulsa, Okla.: Winchester Press, 1966), 30, the M/86 was the most advanced of the company's rifles to be chambered for the .38, and that came in June 1887 with the production of the 38–56 W.C.F. However, the Model 1873 Repeating Rifle appeared in .38 by 1880.
12. Thorp, 175–76.
13. Ibid., 174.
14. Ibid., 173–76.
15. *The Cedar Rapids Evening Gazette* (January 11, 1888), 4.
16. Wiltsey, "The West's Greatest Marksman," *Real West* XI, no. 65 (November 1968), 16.

17. *Dunkirk Evening Observer*, October 10, 1890.
18. *Sporting Life* 26, no. 7, (November 9, 1889), 12.
19. *Oak Park Vindicator*, November 27, 1896; exact copy and art appeared in *Logansport (Ind.) Journal*, November 29, 1896.
20. *Sporting Life* 28, no. 1, (September 26, 1896), 18.
21. "Good With Guns: Rollo O. Heikes and Capt. B.A. Bartlett in the City; Exhibition of Fancy Shooting at the Driving Park Today," *Logansport Journal*, December 3, 1896.
22. Col. Charles Askins, "Adolph Toepperwein, Exhibition Shooter," *American Rifleman* (Volume 134, No. 2, February 1986), 72.
23. Joan Crosby, NEA wire service, "Success Elements Consist Of Diving Horse, Steel Pier," *Victoria Advocate*, August 31, 1967.
24. Grand American Handicap Champions, Trapshooting Hall of Fame, http://www.traphof.org/grand-american-handicap-champions.html.
25. "Beat His Record," *San Antonio Daily Light*, February 14, 1898.
26. Norman Wiltsey, "Ad Topperwein . . . A Shooting Legend," *Guns & Ammo* (October 1961), 74.
27. "Famous Shots Coming To The International," *San Antonio Light*, September 8, 1907.
28. "A Free Exhibition; Captain A.H. Hardy Will Do Some Shooting on Saturday," *Hutcheson Daily News*, April 11, 1906.
29. *Beatrice Daily Sun*, December 27, 1905.
30. *Iola Daily Register*, March 10, 1906.
31. Ad Topperwein, letter to Ernie and Dot Lind, July 8, 1947.
32. R.V. Sutliffe, "Retail Sales Promotion Activities," *Winchester Record*, undated. The article contends, without providing a date or further documentation, that Ad Topperwein shot at 10,000 thrown targets and hit 9,999.
33. "Expert Shot Is After Own Record," *San Antonio Light*, September 16, 1907.
34. Ad Topperwein, personal notebook, from the collection of John Stein, accessed April 5, 2012.
35. "Breaks 19,990 But Misses Ten; Remarkable Work of Ad. Toepperwein at 20,000 Flying Targets Completed," *San Antonio Light*, September 21, 1907.
36. Wiltsey, *Guns & Ammo*, 72, 73.
37. Ryan Vogt, "Web Exclusives: Texas History 101," *Texas Monthly*, September 2005, http://www.texasmonthly.com/2005-09-01/texashistory.php.
38. Paula Allen, "Roosevelt Avenue named after Teddy—not FDR," *San Antonio Express-News*, January 16, 2011.
39. Fred Maly, "Outdoors: Ad Toepperwein . . . Legend Lives On," *San Antonio Light*, undated, collection of Kenneth Toepperwein.
40. "Toepperwein Recalls His Greatest Feat; Blockbuster Tells Of World Record,"

publication unidentified, circa December 1947 (found in vertical files, Patrick Heath Public Library, Boerne, Texas).

41. Wiltsey, *Guns & Ammo.*
42. Wiltsey, *V.F.W. Magazine*, 36.
43. Barnes et al. 57–58.
44. Harold F. Williamson, *Winchester: The Gun That Won the West* (Washington, DC: Combat Forces Press, 1952), 171.
45. "Tep On Shooting; San Antonio Boy Creates a Sensation in New York," *San Antonio Daily Light*, September 7, 1898.
46. "New World's Rifle Record," *Lawrence Jeffersonian-Gazette*, November 20, 1907.
47. *Fort Wayne Journal-Gazette*, December 8, 1907.
48. Wiltsey, *Guns & Ammo*, 72.
49. James Joseph, "Greatest Shot of Them All," *Guns & Ammo, The Best of Guns & Ammo, 1958–1962* (originally appeared in *Guns & Ammo*, February 1960), 57.
50. "Extraordinary Rifle Shooting," *Lawrence (Kan.) Jeffersonian-Gazette*, November 26, 1907.
51. Topperwein, letter to Ernie and Dot Lind.
52. Wiltsey, *Guns & Ammo*, 73.
53. James B. Trefethen, "King of the Riflemen," *True: The Man's Magazine* (undated), 32, 101.

Chapter 15

1. James B. Trefethen, "King of the Riflemen," *True: The Man's Magazine* (undated), 32, 103.
2. Ibid.
3. S.M. Purcell, "Toepperwein Best in Half Century," *Austin American-Statesman*, undated, appears in Toepperwein family scrapbook provided by Joann Toepperwein.
4. Norman B. Wiltsey, "Rifleman In Retrospect," *Frontier Times* (August–September 1964), 59.
5. Trefethen, "King of the Riflemen," 103–4.
6. "Tep on Shooting," *San Antonio Daily Light*, September 7, 1898.
7. Ibid.
8. "Tops With Winchester," *Winchester Record* (undated; found in scrapbook from the collection of Joann Toepperwein), 129.
9. Temperature readings and other references to weather were made through front page reports on the *San Antonio Light* and several magazine articles where Ad Toepperwein was interviewed.
10. *Winchester Record* (undated, Toepperwein scrapbook).
11. Trefethen, "King of the Riflemen," 101.

12. Ernie Pyle, "Home Country," *Omnibook* (New York: William Sloan Associates, 1947), 38.
13. Trefethen, "King of the Riflemen," 104.
14. Ibid.
15. Norman Wiltsey, "Ad Topperwein . . . A Shooting Legend," *Guns & Ammo* (October 1961), 74.
16. Wiltsey, *Frontier Times*, 59.
17. Ibid.
18. Ibid.
19. Ibid.
20. "Is Completing His Great Target Run: Adolph Toepperwein, World Famed Marksman, Making Phenomenal Mark," *San Antonio Light*, December 22, 1907; and Kenneth Foree, "Outdoors: Greatest Gun Team In History Reunited," *Dallas Morning News*, undated (referenced from letter from Mrs. W. Roy Hastings to H. Ben Decherd of *Dallas Morning News*, March 12, 1962, and found in the collection of Kenneth Toepperwein).

Chapter 16

1. "Ad" Topperwein, *Snap Shooting* (New Haven, CT: Winchester Repeating Arms Company, 1939), 7, 8.
2. Ibid., 8, 9.
3. Ernie Pyle, "Home Country," *Omnibook* (New York: William Sloan Associates, 1947), 38.
4. Ibid., 9.
5. Norman B. Wiltsey, "World's Greatest Marksman," *V*F*W Magazine* (January 1963), 37.
6. Pyle, "Home Country," 38.
7. Topperwein, 8.
8. Larry McMurtry, *The Colonel and Little Missie: Buffalo Bill, Annie Oakley, and the Beginnings of Superstardom in America* (New York: Simon & Schuster, 2005), 122.
9. Norman B. Wiltsey, "The West's Greatest Marksman," *Real West* X1, no. 65 (November 1968), 73.
10. "Tops With Winchester," Winchester Record (undated; found in scrapbook from the collection of Joann Toepperwein), 130.
11. Norman B. Wiltsey, "Rifleman In Retrospect," *Frontier Times* (August–September 1964), 59.
12. Jaroslav Lugs, *The History of Shooting* (Feltham, Middlesex, England: Spring Books, 1968), 186.

13. D.E. Whitla, "Grand Champion," *Field & Stream* (February 1943), reprinted version found in "Life and Times of 'Ad' Adolph Toepperwein," compiled in 1993 by Georgia L. Toepperwein and provided by Joann Toepperwein.
14. Ibid.
15. Wiltsey, "Ad Topperwein . . . A Shooting Legend," *Guns & Ammo* (October 1961), 74.
16. Trefethen, "King of the Riflemen," *True;* 104.
17. Ibid.
18. Duncan Barnes, George R. Watrous, James C. Rikhoff, Thomas H. Hall and Pete Kuhlhoff, *The History of Winchester Firearms, 1866–1980, 5th ed.*, (Tulsa, OK: Winchester Press, 1980), 57–58.
19. "Is Completing His Great Target Run: Adolph Toepperwein, World Famed Marksman, Making Phenomenal Mark," *San Antonio Light*, December 22, 1907.
20. Trefethen, "King of the Riflemen," 104; Wiltsey, *Guns & Ammo*, 74.
21. Trefethen, "King of the Riflemen," 104.
22. Wiltsey, *Guns & Ammo*, 75.
23. *San Antonio Light*, December 22, 1907.
24. Trefethen, "King of the Riflemen," 104.
25. Wiltsey, *Guns & Ammo*.
26. "Toepperwein Recalls His Greatest Feat; Blockbuster Tells Of World Record," publication unidentified, circa December 1947 (found in vertical files, Patrick Heath Public Library, Boerne, Texas).
27. Trefethen, "King of the Riflemen," 104.
28. Kenneth Foree, "Outdoors: Greatest Gun Team In History Reunited," *Dallas Morning News*, undated (referenced from letter from Mrs. W. Roy Hastings to H. Ben Decherd of *Dallas Morning News*, March 12, 1962, and found in the collection of Kenneth Toepperwein).
29. Trefethen, "King of the Riflemen," 104.
30. Charles Askins, "World's Greatest Shooter," *Guns Magazine* (November 1967), 78.
31. Trefethen, "King of the Riflemen," 104.
32. Dan Klepper, "The Outdoorsman: Ad to Celebrate Birthday No. 90," *San Antonio Express and News*, October 16, 1959.
33. "Great Rifle Record Is Now In History: Ad. Toepperwein Fires 72,000 Shots In 10 Days With 9 Misses—High Run 14,540," *San Antonio Light*, December 23, 1907, 6.
34. Wiltsey, *Frontier Times*.
35. "A Record That Is A Record," *Sporting Life* 50, no. 19 (January 19, 1908), 16.

Chapter 17

1. Dale Shaw, "Master Marksman," *SPORT* (June 1962), 43.
2. Ibid.
3. "Plane Crash Victim Was Known Here: Newton H. Crumley Made Many Trips To Local Airport," *Cumberland (Md.) Evening Times*, February 13, 1962.
4. "Nevada Aviator 'Bails Out' Of Plane and Is Not Hurt," *Reno Evening Gazette*, April 4, 1934.
5. Associated Press, "Elko Flier Hurt In Auto Mishap After Air Escape," *Reno Evening Gazette*, April 6, 1934.
6. Chris H. Sheerin, "Newton Hunt Crumley, 1911–1962, *Northeastern Nevada Historical Society Quarterly* 79, no. 1 (Winter 1979), 4.
7. Associated Press, "Authorities Fear All Are Dead on Nevada Mountain," December 24, 1934; "Bodies of 4 Elko Air Crash Victims Found in Canyon," *Nevada State Journal*, December 25, 1934.
8. "Pilot Crumley, Two Passengers Missing," *Nevada State Journal*, March 31, 1936.
9. United Press, "Three Nevada Men In Plane Long Overdue," March 31–April 1, 1936; "Crumley Party Is Unharmed," *Nevada State Journal*, April 1, 1936.
10. Janice Pine, email interview, March 13, 2012.
11. Sheerin, "Newton Hunt Crumley, 1911–1962," 4.
12. Roger Butterfield, "Elko County," *LIFE* 26, no. 16 (April 18, 1949), 99.
13. Associated Press, "Snow-Bound Livestock Getting Hay," March 22, 1952.
14. Associated Press, "Shipwrecked Family Is Flown to Safety After Crash Into Reef," February 20, 1953.
15. Ibid.
16. "Newton Crumley Helped Strengthen Gaming Law," *Reno Evening Gazette*, February 12, 1962.
17. Sheerin, "Newton Hunt Crumley, 1911–1962," 12.
18. Butterfield, 101.
19. Sheerin, "Newton Hunt Crumley, 1911–1962," 12.
20. Dwayne Kling, *The Rise of the Biggest Little City: An Encyclopedic History of Reno Gaming* (Reno, NV.: University of Nevada Press, 2000), 34.
21. Jennifer Sweeney, "Vacant hotels hold keys to Reno's heritage," *Nevada Outpost*, http://www.jour.unr.edu/outpost/community/archives/com.sweeney.renoheritage.html).
22. Bob Laxalt, letter, undated; from the collection of Peggy Drake.
23. Addison Bragg, "Billings man makes shooting history," *Billings Gazette*, April 23, 1971.
24. Laxalt, letter, undated; from the collection of Peggy Drake.
25. Sheerin, "Newton Hunt Crumley, 1911–1962," 2–5, 12–15

26. *Bakersfield Californian*, July 30, 1953.
27. Matt Allen, telephone interview, April 4, 2012.
28. *Billings Gazette*, June 28, 1964.
29. *Reno Evening Gazette*, August 24, 1959.
30. Ty Cobb, "Inside Stuff," *Nevada State Journal*, April 16, 1959.
31. Shaw, "Master Marksman," *SPORT* (June 1962), 43.
32. "Hall of Fame Banquet," *Trap & Field* 176, no. 11 (November 2000), 54.
33. Ken Berger, telephone interview, January 23, 2011.
34. *Trap & Field* (November 2000).
35. Sheerin, "Newton Hunt Crumley, 1911–1962," 12.
36. Shaw, "Master Marksman," *SPORT*, June 1962, 43.

Chapter 18

1. Peggy Drake, telephone interview, October 13, 2011.
2. Chris H. Sheerin, "Newton Hunt Crumley, 1911–1962," *Northeastern Nevada Historical Society Quarterly* 79, no. 1 (Winter 1979), 2–5, 12–15.
3. Drake, telephone interview.
4. "Holiday Employees Feel Great Personal Loss in Death of Boss Newton Crumley," *Reno Evening Gazette*, February 12, 1962.
5. "Tom Frye Memorial," undated, obtained via collection of Dean Dunlap.
6. Charles Askins, "World's Greatest Shooter," *Guns*, November 1967, 76.
7. "Inside Stuff," *Nevada State Journal*, October 3, 1959.
8. Drake, telephone interview.
9. "Hall of Fame Banquet," *Trap & Field* 176, no. 11 (November 2000), 54.
10. James Joseph, "Greatest Shot of Them All," *Guns & Ammo*, *The Best of Guns & Ammo, 1958–1962* (originally appeared in *Guns & Ammo*, February 1960), 56–61.
11. Joseph, "Greatest Shot of Them All," 61.
12. Ibid., 57.
13. Askins, "World's Greatest Shooter," 77.
14. Joseph, "Greatest Shot of Them All," 57, 58.
15. Ibid., 61.
16. *Nevada State Journal*, October 7–9, 1959.
17. "Many Attend Rifle Shoot Grind Today," *Nevada State Journal*, October 10, 1959.
18. *Nevada State Journal*, October 10, 1959, and October 16, 1959.
19. Photo, courtesy of University of Nevada archives.
20. Marc Eliot, *American Rebel: The Life of Clint Eastwood* (New York: Harmony Books, 2009), 42–45, 49–51.
21. Carolyn Mulne, telephone interview.

22. "Tom Frye Sets New Mark with Rifle; He's Still at It," *Reno Evening Gazette*, October 15, 1959.
23. "Nearly In," *Nevada State Journal*, October 14, 1959.

Chapter 19

1. Dale Shaw, "Master Marksman," *SPORT*, June 1962, 81.
2. Carolyn Mulne, telephone interview.
3. Shaw, "Master Marksman," 81.
4. "One of Thousands," *Nevada State Journal*, October 13, 1959.
5. Shaw; Mulne; Coni Wein, telephone interview, October 12, 2009.
6. James Joseph, "Greatest Shot of Them All," *Guns & Ammo, The Best of Guns & Ammo, 1958–1962* (originally appeared in *Guns & Ammo*, February 1960), 56–61.
7. Joseph, "Greatest Shot of Them All," 56.
8. Ibid.
9. Reno, NV, Population Growth, CensusScope, http://www.censusscope.org/us/m6720/chart_popl.html.
10. Joseph, "Greatest Shot of Them All," 57.
11. Shaw, "Master Marksman," 81.
12. Ibid.
13. Joseph, "Greatest Shot of Them All," 56–61.
14. Ibid., 59.
15. "Frye Approaches 100,000-Target Shooting Goal," *Nevada State Journal*, October 16, 1959.
16. Joseph, "Greatest Shot of Them All," 58; Shaw, "Master Marksman," 81, 82.
17. Joseph, "Greatest Shot of Them All": Shaw, "Master Marksman," 82.
18. Joseph, "Greatest Shot of Them All."
19. Ibid., 59.
20. Ibid.
21. Luke Dunlap, telephone interview, December 20, 2012.
22. Charles Askins, "World's Greatest Shooter," *Guns Magazine*, November 1967, 78.
23. Ibid.
24. Ad Topperwein, letter to Mr. Tom Frye, December 19, 1959.

Chapter 20

1. D. E. Whitla, "Grand Champion," *Field & Stream*, February 1943, 4.
2. Dean K. Boorman, *The History of Winchester Firearms* (New York: The Lyons Press, 2001), 76.

3. Dick Baldwin, "Road To Yesterday: The Fabulous Topperweins, Part 2," *Trap & Field*, December 2006.
4. *San Antonio Light*, July 17, 1908.
5. D.H. Eaton, *Trapshooting: The Patriotic Sport* (Cincinnati: Sportsmen's Review Publishing Co., 1921), 371.
6. "Woman Makes Fine Record In Trap Shooting," *San Antonio Daily Express*, July 18, 1908.
7. "Woman Most Expert Shot In The World," *Oakland Tribune*, January 10, 1915.
8. "Mrs. Topperwein of San Antonio Heads List," *The Decatur* (Ill.) *Review*, May 9, 1916.
9. "Mrs. Topperwein's Record: Complete Details Show Texas Woman Gave Most Wonderful Performance in History of Trap Shooting," *Sporting Life* 68, no. 13, (November 25, 1916), 23.
10. Ibid.; Baldwin, "Road to Yesterday: The Fabulous Topperweins, Part 2."
11. *Sporting Life*.
12. Baldwin, "Road to Yesterday: The Fabulous Topperweins, Part 2."
13. Mrs. A.D. Topperwein, ATA Trapshooting Hall of Fame, http://www.traphof.org/Inductees/Topperwein-Mrs.-A.-D.html.
14. Eaton, *Trapshooting: The Patriotic Sport*, 372.
15. *Washington Post*, January 7, 1917.
16. Laura Browder, *Her Best Shot: Women and Guns in America* (Chapel Hill, N.C.: The University of North Carolina Press, 2006), 70. Browder cites Henry Brewer, letter to Major Leonard A. Horner, September 6, 1917, file 67.1, Winchester Arms Collection Archives.
17. Laura Browder, *Her Best Shot*, 70. Browder cites L.A. Horner, letter to Henry Brewer, September 8, 1917, file 67.1, Winchester Arms Collection Archives.
18. "Local 'Crack-Shot' Teaches Fliers How To Wing The Boches," *San Antonio Light*, August 22, 1918.
19. *San Antonio Evening News*, February 17, 1919.
20. "Toepperwein Makes Perfect Score in Muny Traps Event," *San Antonio Evening News*, September 13, 1922.
21. Frost Woodhull, "Folklore Shooting," from James Frank Dobie, editor, Texas Folklore Society, *Southwestern Lore* (Denton, TX: University of North Texas Press, 1931), 2; via digital images (http://texashistory.unt.edu/ark:/67531/metadc38867/: accessed May 14, 2012), University of North Texas Libraries, The Portal to Texas History, http://texashistory.unt.edu; crediting UNT Press.
22. *San Antonio Express*, October 22, 1940.
23. "Topperwein Shoots Before Texas 'Cops,'" *The Winchester Herald*, undated (circa July 1925); "Home-Grown Booster is 'Tep,' San Antonio's Crack Rifle Shot Famous Throughout Country," *San Antonio Express*, January 20, 1925.

24. Peter P. Carney, "President Coolidge Applauds Topperwein's Skill at Pemberton Shoot," undated.
25. Ibid.
26. Woodhull, "Folklore Shooting," 11; Baldwin, "Road to Yesterday: The Fabulous Topperweins, Part 2."
27. "Winchester and the Topperweins at Atlantic City," *Winchester Record*, undated.
28. Pat Mosher, Director, Gonzales County Historical Commission, email interview, October 5, 2011.
29. Alton Pagel, interview, October 11, 2011.
30. *San Antonio Express*, October 22, 1940.
31. Chief of Police Owen W. Kilday, San Antonio, Texas (as told to Lawrence Topperwein), "Man Trap: The Red Riddle of Lawrence Rea," *True Detective Mysteries* 29, no. 5 (February 1938), 34.
32. Fritz Toepperwein, Ad Topperwein biography manuscript, unpublished.
33. "L. Toepperwein Is Injured in Fall," *San Antonio Light*, May 17, 1936.
34. Woodhull, "Folklore Shooting," 4.
35. Wanda K. Jackson, telephone interview.
36. Gerard Colby Zilg, *Du Pont: Behind the Nylon Curtain* (Englewood Cliffs, N.J.: Prentice-Hall, Inc., 1974), 265.
37. Duncan Barnes, George R. Watrous, James C. Rikhoff, Thomas H. Hall and Pete Kuhlhoff, *The History of Winchester Firearms, 1866–1980, 5th ed.*, (Tulsa, Okla.: Winchester Press, 1980), 94.
38. Ad Topperwein, letter to Henry Brewer, August 7, 1944.
39. Judith N. McArthur, "GLADNEY, EDNA BROWNING KAHLY," *Handbook of Texas Online* (http://www.tshaonline.org/handbook/online/articles/fgl11), accessed May 15, 2012. Published by the Texas State Historical Association.
40. "In the Anacacho Room," *San Antonio Express*, February 20, 1942.
41. Joann Toepperwein, interview, May 12, 2011.
42. Colette Kohler, telephone interview.
43. Fritz Toepperwein, Ad Topperwein biography manuscript, unpublished.
44. Dick Baldwin, "Long, Long Ago," from *Trapshooting with D. Lee Braun and the Remington Pros: America's masters of the shotgun tell you the secrets of professional marksmanship*, edited by Robert Campbell (New York: Benjamin Company, Inc., 1969), 46.
45. Norman Wiltsey, "Ad Topperwein . . . A Shooting Legend," *Guns & Ammo*, October 1961, 72.
46. "Shoot Victory 'Biggest Yet,'" *San Antonio Light*, November 15, 1933.
47. Woodhull, "Folklore Shooting," 1–2.
48. *Winchester Record*, undated, collection of Kenneth Toepperwein.
49. "Rationing Affects Toepperweins Tour," *Winslow (Ariz.) Mail*, July 2, 1943.

50. Topperwein, letter to Henry Brewer.
51. "Toepperweins in Michigan," *San Antonio Light and Gazette*, August 5, 1909.
52. Colonel Charles Askins, "Miracle Shooter," *Guns Magazine*, July 1956, 63.
53. George Carmack, "Fastest gun in the West," *San Antonio Express-News*, June 25, 1983.
54. "World's Champion Shooter Dies," *San Antonio Light*, January 28, 1945.
55. Ad Toepperwein notebooks, collection of John Stein.
56. Baldwin, "The Road to Yesterday: The Fabulous Topperweins, Part 2."
57. Video cassette, *Showman Shooter, Featuring Herb Parsons* (also includes rare video of Ad and Plinky Toepperwein), provided by Jerry Parsons, PhD.
58. Wiltsey, *Guns & Ammo*, October 1961, 47.
59. Photograph, undated, Kenneth Toepperwein collection.
60. Ed Pugsley, letter to Mr. A. Topperwein, May 10, 1945.

Chapter 21

1. "10,000 Crowd Into Park for Fish, Game Barbecue," *Bakersfield Californian*, April 25, 1960.
2. Jack Heath, telephone interview.
3. Robert Stack (with Mark Evans), *Straight Shooting* (New York: Macmillan Publishing Co., Inc., 1980), 36.
4. Hall of Fame History and Criteria, California Skeet Shooting Association, http://www.calskeet.com/HOFhistory.html; Todd Larson, "52 Trade Houses Part 3: The Kerr Sport Shop of Beverly Hills," Fishing for History: The History of Fishing and Fishing Tackle, April 20, 2011, http://fishinghistory.blogspot.com/2011/04/52-trade-houses-part-3-kerr-sport-shop.html.
5. Heath, telephone interview.
6. "Corporations: The Lord Helps Those . . . ," *Time*, February 21, 1949, http://www.time.com/time/subscriber/article/0,33009,805089-1,00.html.
7. Carolyn Mulne, telephone interview.
8. Coni Wein, telephone interview.
9. Mulne, telephone interview.
10. G.A. "Luke" Dunlap, telephone interview.
11. Roy Anderson, "From A to Z: Frye Doesn't Miss Hollywood," *Billings Gazette*, May 16, 1961.
12. "Hall of Fame Banquet," *Trap & Field* 176, no. 11 (November 2000), 54.
13. Ibid.
14. *Billings Gazette*, October 8, 1961.
15. Anderson, "From A to Z: Frye Doesn't Miss Hollywood."
16. Heath, telephone interview.

Chapter 22

1. Ad Topperwein, letter to Herb Parsons, August 21, 1953.
2. Charles Toepperwein, telephone interview, October 4, 2011.
3. "Shooting News," *Guns Magazine*, June 1956, 6.
4. "Tops With Winchester," *Famous Guns From the Winchester Collection*, compiled by Hank Wieand Bowman (Greenwich, CT: Fawcett Publications, 1958), 131.
5. Ad Topperwein, letter to Jack Boone, February 18, 1958.
6. J.T. Boone, letter to Mr. Ad Topperwein, March 6, 1958.
7. Ned Schwing, *Winchester's Finest: The Model 21* (Iola, WI: Gun Digest Books, 2005), 54.
8. E.J. Rudolph, letter to Mr. Ad Topperwein, October 30, 1958.
9. Topperwein, letter to Boone.
10. Colonel Charles Askins, "Are Pistol Champs Alcoholics?" *Guns Magazine*, January 1956, 24.
11. Colonel Charles Askins, "What's Wrong with Target Rifle Shooting," *Guns Magazine*, March 1956, 34–35.
12. Colonel Charles Askins, "Miracle Shooter," *Guns Magazine,* July 1956, 63.
13. Fred Maly, "Angling Around," *San Antonio Light*, December 14, 1959.
14. "The Toepp Guns of All Times," A compilation of articles written by Norman Wiltsey for *Guns & Ammo*, October 1961, Col. Charles Askins for *American Rifleman*, February 1981, From "Famous Guns of the Winchester Collection" (1958), http://www.showmanshooter.com/html/toepperwein.html.
15. Trapshooting Hall of Fame and Museum, "History of Organized Shooting in America: Timeline," www.traphof.org/history.htm.
16. Norman Wiltsey, "Ad Topperwein . . . A Shooting Legend," *Guns & Ammo*, October 1961, 72.
17. Dale Shaw, "Master Marksman," *SPORT*, June 1962, 43.
18. "Fleet Hydroplanes Race at Pyramid Lake in Gold Cup," *Reno Evening Gazette*, August 22, 1961.
19. "'Miss Reno' to Compete in Gold Cup Race," *Reno Evening Gazette*, July 26, 1961.
20. "Crumley Receives 'Thank You' Cup," *Reno Evening Gazette*, September 6, 1961.
21. David Tremayne, "Russ Schleeh—The Shanty Man," The Hydroplane and Raceboat Museum, http://www.thunderboats.org/history/history0303.html.
22. "Miss Reno Qualifies—Damaged in Mishap," *Nevada State Journal*, August 6, 1961.
23. Ty Cobb, "Inside Stuff," *Nevada State Journal*, September 7, 1961.
24. *Reno Evening Gazette*, September 6, 1961.
25. *Reno Evening Gazette*, August 29, 1961; *Nevada State Journal*, August 31, 1961.
26. Peggy Drake, telephone interview, October 13, 2011.

27. Drake, *Belmont*, unpublished essay dated November 11, 1996.
28. "Nevada Joins in Tribute to Late Crumley, Questa," *Nevada State Journal*, February 13, 1962, 1.
29. "Hotelman Newt Crumley Pilot of Missing Plane," *The Oakland Tribune*, February 11, 1962, 4A.
30. "Newton Crumley Rites Scheduled for Today," *Nevada State Journal*, Reno, Nev., February 13, 1962, 13.
31. "Long Wait as Search Began—Then Came Final Word," *Reno Evening Gazette*, February 12, 1962.
32. *San Francisco Chronicle*, February 12, 1962.
33. Drake, telephone interview.
34. Associated Press, "Crash Kills Prominent Reno Men," *Pasadena Independent*, February 12, 1962.
35. "Newt Crumley, Banker Killed in Plane Crash," *San Francisco Chronicle*, February 12, 1962, 6.
36. *Nevada State Journal*, February 13, 1962.
37. *Reno Evening Gazette*, February 12, 1962.
38. "Tributes Paid to Nevadans Crumley, Questa," *Reno Evening Gazette*, February 13, 1962, 5.
39. Bob Laxalt, letter, undated; from the collection of Peggy Drake.
40. Drake, telephone interview.
41. "Athlete of Year Dinner Attracts Big Attendance," *Nevada State Journal*, February 20, 1962, 10.
42. *Nevada State Journal*, February 20, 1962, 10.
43. Shaw, "Master Marksman," 82.
44. Charles Askins, "World's Greatest Shooter," *Guns Magazine*, November 1967, 78.
45. Ibid.
46. Drake, e-mail interview, September 10, 2009.
47. "Holiday Employees Feel Great Personal Loss in Death of Boss Newton Crumley," *Reno Evening Gazette*, February 12, 1962.
48. Shaw, "Master Marksman," 82.

Chapter 23

1. Keith Ozmore, "Texas Outdoors: His Eyes Dim At 91, but Ad Still Can Hit," United Press International, July 26, 1960; Harold V. Ratliffe, Associated Press, "Ad Topperwein Now Teaching Kids," *San Antonio Express and News*, July 15, 1956.
2. Greta Nissen, "Leading Quiet Life," *San Antonio Light*, June 24, 1951.

3. Ad Topperwein, letter to Adolph Phillips, November 16, 1958 (circa).
4. Nissen, *San Antonio Light*.
5. Ad Topperwein, letter to Max Toepperwein, November 19, 1951 (obtained courtesy Darla Toepperwein Bacon).
6. Charles Toepperwein, telephone interview, October 4, 2011; Dan Klepper, "The Outdoorsman: Ad to Celebrate Birthday No. 90," *San Antonio Express and News*, October 16, 1959.
7. Ratliffe, Associated Press, "Ad Topperwein Now Teaching Kids," *San Antonio Express and News*.
8. Joann Toepperwein, interview.
9. Ad Topperwein, letter to Jack Boone, February 18, 1958.
10. "Tep on Shooting; San Antonio Boy Creates a Sensation in New York," *San Antonio Daily Light*, September 7, 1898.
11. Ray J. Montambo, letter to Sales Manager, Winchester Repeating Arms Co., March 7, 1958.
12. Dan Klepper, "I'm Game: Ad Ties a Knot in the Rope," undated article, provided by the scrapbook of Joann Toepperwein.
13. "Friends to Put on a Show for Toepperwein," *San Antonio Light*, October 15, 1961.
14. Kenneth Foree, "Outdoors: Greatest Gun Team In History Reunited," *Dallas Morning News*, undated (referenced from letter from Mrs. W. Roy Hastings to H. Ben Decherd of *Dallas Morning News*, March 12, 1962, and found in the collection of Kenneth Toepperwein).
15. Ad Topperwein and Norman B. Wiltsey, "World's Greatest Sharp Shooter," *Guns and Hunting*, October 1961, 12, 14.
16. Fred Maly, "Toepperweins Immortalized," *San Antonio Light*, May 19, 1963.
17. Foree, *Dallas Morning News*.
18. Charles Askins, "World's Greatest Shooter," *Guns Magazine*, November 1967, 74.
19. George Carmack, "Weekend Visit: Fastest gun in the West," *San Antonio Express-News*, June 25, 1983.
20. David Mamet, "First Person: The Buttons on the Board," *Arts & Antiques*, November 1992, 33.
21. Fritz Toepperwein, Ad Topperwein biography manuscript, unpublished.

Chapter 24

1. Eugene Clawson, telephone interview, December 7, 2011.
2. "Frye Named Team Captain," *Billings Gazette*, May 23, 1964.
3. Clawson, telephone interview.
4. Jack Heath, telephone interview, May 25, 2011.

5. James Joseph, "Greatest Shot of Them All," *Guns & Ammo, The Best of Guns & Ammo, 1958–1962* (originally appeared in *Guns & Ammo*, February 1960), 56–61.
6. Heath, telephone interview.
7. *Billings Gazette*, June 28, 1964.
8. "Mrs. T. Frye Heart Victim," *Billings Gazette*, October 8, 1965.
9. *Helena Independent Record*, September 2, 1966.
10. Coni Wein, telephone interview.
11. Joseph, "Greatest Shot of Them All," 56–61.
12. Ken Berger, telephone interview.
13. Grits Gresham, "Shootin' in Style: The life and times of Bob Allen," *Guns & Ammo*, http://archives.gunsandammo.com/content/shootin-in-style.
14. Addison Bragg, "Billings man makes shooting history," *Billings Gazette*, April 23, 1971.
15. Dale Shaw, "Master Marksman," *SPORT*, June 1962, 43.
16. "Hall of Fame Banquet," *Trap & Field* 176, no. 11 (November 2000), 54.
17. Clawson; *Billings Gazette*, June 28, 1964.
18. *Trap & Field*, 54.
19. "Master Breeder," National Pigeon Association, www.npausa.com/awards/master_breeder.htm.
20. Rich Trang, email interview.
21. Wein, telephone interview.
22. Wein; *Trap & Field*.
23. Dean Dunlap, telephone interview.
24. *Trap & Field*.
25. Ibid.
26. Joseph, "Greatest Shot of Them All."
27. Berger, telephone interview.
28. Heath; Mark Henckel, "Tom Frye still shooting world records," *Billings Gazette*, July 14, 1974.
29. Heath, telephone interview.
30. Bragg, "Billings man makes shooting history," *Billings Gazette*.
31. Henckel, "Tom Frye still shooting world records," *Billings Gazette*.
32. Deke Slayton, letter to Tom Frye, September 1974, image obtained from the collection of G.A. "Luke" Dunlap.
33. "Off the firing line . . . ," *Trap & Field* 151, No. 3, (March 1975), 60.
34. "The shooting facts," *Billings Gazette*, June 27, 1976.
35. G.A. "Luke" Dunlap, telephone interview.
36. Ron Marlenee, telephone interview.
37. Tom Frye Memorial, unpublished, provided from the collection of Dean Dunlap.

38. President Ronald Reagan, letter to Tom Frye, August 17, 1982, provided by the personal collection of Dean Dunlap.
39. Kary Charlebois, Archivist, The Reagan Presidential Library and Museum, email interview, May 21, 2010.
40. Trang, telephone interview.
41. Dean Dunlap, telephone interview, September 22, 2011.
42. Heath, telephone interview.
43. Lambert Hollinga, "Sports N' Hobbies: Rifle Marksmanship," *Alton Democrat*, May 2, 1973.
44. "Hall of Fame Banquet," *Trap & Field* 176, no. 11 (November 2000), 54.

SOURCES

Books

Allen, Bob. *Shooter: An Autobiography: The Life and Times of Bob Allen*. Austin: Nortex Press, 2001.

Baldwin, Dick. "Long, Long Ago." In *Trapshooting with D. Lee Braun and the Remington Pros: America's Masters of the Shotgun Tell You the Secrets of Professional Marksmanship*, 46. New York: Benjamin Company, Inc., 1969.

Barnes, Charles Merritt. *Combats and Conquests of Immortal Heroes*. San Antonio: Guessaz & Ferlet Company, 1910.

Barnes, Duncan, George R. Watrous, James C. Rikhoff, Thomas H. Hall, and Pete Kuhlhoff. *The History of Winchester Firearms, 1866–1980*. 5th edition. Tulsa: Winchester Press, 1980.

Bennitt, Mark. *Bennett Illustrated Souvenir Guide Pan American Exposition*. Buffalo, NY: The Goff Company, 1901.

Boorman, Dean K. *The History of Winchester Firearms*. New York: The Lyons Press, 2001.

Bowman, Hank Wieand. *Famous Guns from the Winchester Collection*. Greenwich, CT: Fawcett Publications, 1958.

Braun, D. Lee. *Trapshooting with D. Lee Braun and the Remington Pros: America's Masters of the Shotgun Tell You the Secrets of Professional Marksmanship*. Edited by Robert Campbell. New York: Benjamin Company, Inc., 1969.

Brophy, Lt. Col. William S. (USAR, Ret.). *Marlin Firearms: A History of the Guns and the Company that Made Them*. Harrisburg, PA: Stackpole Books, 1989.

Browder, Laura. *Her Best Shot: Women and Guns in America.* Chapel Hill, NC: The University of North Carolina Press, 2006.

Bryant, Howard. *The Last Hero: A Life of Henry Aaron.* New York: Pantheon Books, 2010.

Carr, Ian, Digby Fairweather, and Brian Priestly, et al. *Jazz: The Rough Guide*. London: Rough Guides, Ltd., 1995.

Chernow, Ron. *Titan: The Life of John D. Rockefeller, Sr.* New York: Random House, 1998.

Cook, William A. *The Louisville Grays Scandal of 1877: The Taint of Gambling at the Dawn of the National League*. Jefferson, NC: McFarland, 2005.

Cramer, Clayton E. *Armed America: The Story of How and Why Guns Became as American as Apple Pie*. Nashville, TN: Nelson Current, 2006.

DeLong, Thomas A. *Pops: Paul Whiteman, King of Jazz.* Piscataway, NJ: New Century Publishers, 1983.

Dobie, Frank James, ed. *Southwestern Lore*. Texas Folklore Society. Denton, TX: University of North Texas Press, 1931.

Eaton, D. H. *Trapshooting: The Patriotic Sport.* Cincinnati: Sportsmen's Review Publishing Co., 1921.

Eliot, Marc. *American Rebel: The Life of Clint Eastwood.* New York: Harmony Books, 2009.

Fainaru-Wada, Mark, and Lance Williams. *Game of Shadows: Barry Bonds, BALCO, and the Steroids Scandal That Rocked Professional Sports.* New York: Thomson Gale, large-print edition, 2006.

Firestone, Ross. *Swing, Swing, Swing: The Life & Times of Benny Goodman.* New York: W. W. Norton & Company, 1993.

Gwynne, S. C. *Empire of the Summer Moon: Quanah Parker and the Rise and Fall of the Comanches, the Most Powerful Indian Tribe in American History.* New York: Scribner, 2010.

Hall, Shawn. *Old Heart of Nevada: Ghost Towns and Mining Camps of Elko County.* Reno, NV: University of Nevada Press, 1998.

———. *Preserving the Glory Days: Ghost Towns and Mining Camps of Nye County, Nevada.* Reno, NV: University of Nevada Press, 1981.

Hersch, Chris. *The Texas Gun Trade: A Guide to the Guns Made or Sold in the Lone Star State, 1780–1899.* Woonsocket, RI: Mowbray Publishers, 2008.

Houze, Herbert G. *Winchester Repeating Arms Company: Its History and Development from 1865 to 1981.* Iola, WI: Krause Publications, 1994.

Kasper, Shirl. *Annie Oakley.* Norman, OK: University of Oklahoma Press, 1992.

Kassen, John F. *Rudeness & Civility: Manners in Nineteenth-Century Urban America.* New York: Hill and Wang, 1990.

Kendall County Historical Commission. *A History of Kendall County, Texas: Rivers, Ranches, Railroads, Recreation.* Dallas, TX: Taylor Publishing Company, 1984.

Kirkland, K. D. *Winchester: America's Premier Gunmaker.* East Bridgewater, MA: World Publications Group, Inc., 2007.

Kling, Dwayne. *The Rise of the Biggest Little City: An Encyclopedic History of Reno Gaming.* Reno, NV: University of Nevada Press, 2000.

Lugs, Jaroslav. *The History of Shooting.* Feltham, Middlesex, England: Spring Books, 1968.

Martin, Judith. *Common Courtesy: In Which Miss Manners Solves the Problem That Baffled Mr. Jefferson.* New York: Athenium, 1985.

Marx, Groucho. *Groucho and Me.* New York: Bernard Greis Associates, 1959.

McCloskey, John, and Julian Bates, MD. *When Winning Costs Too Much: Steroids, Supplements, and Scandal in Today's Sports.* Lanham, MD: Taylor Trade Publishing, 2005.

McLean, Albert F., Jr. *American Vaudeville as Ritual.* Lexington, KY: University of Kentucky Press, 1965.

McMurtry, Larry. *The Colonel and Little Missie: Buffalo Bill, Annie Oakley, and the Beginnings of Superstardom in America.* New York: Simon & Schuster, 2005.

McNeir, Forest W. *Forest McNeir of Texas.* San Antonio: The Naylor Company, 1956.

Moe, Al W. *Nevada's Golden Age of Gambling.* Revised edition. Puget Sound Books, 2001.

Official Catalogue and Guide Book to the Pan American Exposition. Buffalo, NY: Charles Ahrhart, 1901, http://panam1901.org/documents/original_sources/guidebook_ahrhart.PDF.

The Ohio State Patrol: The First 75 Years: A History of Service, 1933–2008. Columbus, OH: The Ohio State Highway Patrol, 2008.

Parsons, M. D., H. Lynn, and Jerry M. Parsons, PhD. *Showman Shooter: The Life and Times of Herb Parsons.* Dallas, TX: Taylor Publishing, 2009.

Perry, Garland. *Historic Images of Boerne and Kendall County, Texas,* Sesquicentennial edition 1849, 1999. Boerne, TX: Perry Publications, 1998.

Russell, Don. *The Lives and Legends of Buffalo Bill.* Norman, OK: University of Oklahoma Press, 1960.

———. *The Wild West: A History of the Wild West Shows.* Fort Worth, TX: Amon Carter Museum of Western Art, 1970.

Schwing, Ned. *Winchester's Finest: The Model 21.* Iola, WI: Gun Digest Books, 2005.

Selcer, Richard F. *Legendary Watering Holes: The Saloons That Made Texas Famous.* College Station, TX: Texas A&M University Press, 2004.

Smith, D. Jean. *Medicine Creek Journals: Ena and the Plainsmen.* North Platte, NE: The Old Hundred and One Press, 2003.

Sobel, Bernard. *A Pictorial History of Vaudeville.* New York: Bonanza Books, 1961.

Sobre, Judith Berg. *San Antonio on Parade: Six Historic Festivals.* College Station, TX: Texas A&M University Press, 2003.

Stack, Robert, with Mark Evans. *Straight Shooting*. New York: Macmillan Publishing Co., Inc., 1980.

Stewart, D. Travis. *No Applause—Just Throw Money: The Book That Made Vaudeville Famous*. New York: Faber and Faber, 2005.

Thorp, Raymond. *Spirit Gun of the West: The Story of Doc W. F. Carver*. Glendale, CA: Arthur H. Clark Company, 1857.

Topperwein, "Ad." *Snap Shooting*. New Haven, CT: Winchester Repeating Arms Company, 1939.

Trefethen, James B., ed. *Americans and Their Guns*. Harrisburg, PA: Stackpole Books, 1967.

Warren, Louis S. *Buffalo Bill's America: William Cody and the Wild West Show*. New York: Alfred A. Knopf, 2005.

Weintraub, Robert. *The House That Ruth Built: A New Stadium, the First Yankees, and the Redemption of 1923*. New York: Little, Brown and Company, 2011.

Wertheim, Flora, trans. *Reminiscences of Gottfried Christian Daniel Toepperwein and a Brief History by His Son Lucian Ferdinand Toepperwein*. Boerne, TX: The Highland Press, 1984.

Williamson, G. R. *Texas Pistoleers: The True Story of Ben Thompson and King Fisher*. Charleston, SC: The History Press, 2010.

Williamson, Harold F. *Winchester: The Gun That Won the West*. Washington, DC: Combat Forces Press, 1952.

Yost, Nellie Snyder. *Buffalo Bill: His Family, Friends, Fame, Failures, and Fortunes*. Chicago: Sage Books 1979.

Zilg, Gerard Colby. *Du Pont: Behind the Nylon Curtain*. Englewood Cliffs, NJ: Prentice-Hall, Inc., 1974.

Articles

Adams, Paul. "The Unsolved Murder of Ben Thompson, Pistoleer Extraordinary," *Southwestern Historical Quarterly* XLVIII, no. 3 (1945): 324.

Askins, Colonel Charles. "Adolph Toepperwein, Exhibition Shooter," *American Rifleman* 134, no. 2 (February 1986): 72.

———. "Are Pistol Champs Alcoholics?" *Guns Magazine*, January 1956, 24.

———. "Miracle Shooter," *Guns Magazine*, July 1956, 63.

———. "What's Wrong with Target Rifle Shooting," *Guns Magazine*, March 1956, 34–35.

———. "World's Greatest Shooter," *Guns Magazine*, November 1967, 74.

Baldwin, Dick. "Road to Yesterday: The Fabulous Topperweins, Part 1 and Part 2," *Trap & Field*, December 2006.

Brooks, Roy. "The Glory Years of Skeet at Pacific Rod & Gun Club." Pacific Rod & Gun Club, http://prgc.net/our-famous-shooters/.

Butterfield, Roger, "Elko County," *LIFE*, April 18, 1949, 99.

Canfield, Bruce N. "The Foreign Rifle: US Krag-Jorgensen," *American Rifleman*, October 2010, 86, 89, 126, 129.

Carney, Peter P. "President Coolidge Applauds Topperwein's Skill at Pemberton Shoot," *Winchester Record*, undated.

Crosby, Joan. NEA wire service, "Success Elements Consist of Diving Horse, Steel Pier," *Victoria (Texas) Advocate*, August 31, 1967.

Depperman, W.H. "Texas Triggerman," *Collier's*, June 8, 1946.

Gado, Mark. "The Assassination of President William McKinley," http://www.trutv.com/library/crime/terrorists_spies/assassins/mckinley/5.html.

Goes, Edmund. "Die amerikanischen Kunstschutzen Adolph Topperwein und Seine Frau," *Schuss und Waffe III* no. 23 (1909/1910): 478–79.

Goldbaum, James C. "Women's Work: Mrs. Ad. Topperwein Wins Texas State Shoot," *Sporting Life*, August 15, 1908, 30 (courtesy of Kenny Ray Estes, Amateur Trapshooting Association Hall of Fame).

Gresham, Grits. "Shootin' in Style: The Life and Times of Bob Allen," *Guns & Ammo*, http://archives.gunsandammo.com/content/shootin-in-style.

Gogan, Art. "A 'Doc' Carver Gun," *Man at Arms*, no. 1 (2001): 32.

Gyde, John, and Roy Marcot, "The Remington Nylon 66: A New Concept in Rifles, Back Then," *American Rifleman*, http://www.americanrifleman.org/ArticlePage.aspx?id=1797&cid=9.

"Hall of Fame Banquet: Brad Dysinger, Tom Frye Inducted at Annual Ceremony during Grand," *Trap & Field* 176, no. 11, November 2000, 54–56.

Hall, Shawn R. "A History of Elko, Nevada," *Northeastern Nevada Historical Society Quarterly* 95, no. 3, 140–43.

Hollinga, Lambert, "Sports N' Hobbies: Rifle Marksmanship," *Alton (Iowa) Democrat*, May 2, 1973.

Joseph, James, "Greatest Shot of Them All," *Guns & Ammo, The Best of Guns & Ammo, 1958–1962* (originally appeared in *Guns & Ammo*, February 1960), 56–61.

Kilday, Chief of Police (San Antonio, Texas) Owen W. "Man Trap: The Red Riddle of Lawrence Rea," as told to Lawrence Toepperwein. *True Detective Mysteries* 29, no. 5 (February 1938): 34.

Klepper, Dan. "I'm Game: Ad Ties a Knot in the Rope," undated article, provided by the scrapbook of Joann Toepperwein.

———. "The Outdoorsman: Ad to Celebrate Birthday No. 90," *San Antonio Express and News,* October 16, 1959.

Larson, Todd. "52 Trade Houses Part 3: The Kerr Sport Shop of Beverly Hills," Fishing for History: The History of Fishing and Fishing Tackle, April 20, 2011, http://fishinghistory.blogspot.com/2011/04/52-trade-houses-part-3-kerr-sport-shop.html.

Mamet, David. "First Person: The Buttons on the Board," *Arts & Antiques* (November 1992), 33.

McArthur, Judith N. "GLADNEY, EDNA BROWNING KAHLY," *Handbook of Texas Online* (http://www.tshaonline.org/handbook/online/articles/fgl11), published by the Texas State Historical Association.

McDonald, Kay. "The Goldfield Hotel," *The D C Bee*; The Newsletter of the Nevada Historical Society Docent Council 18, no. 9 (May 2007): 4.

"Off the Firing Line . . . ," *Trap & Field* 151, no. 3, (March 1975): 60.

Ozmore, Keith. "Texas Outdoors: His Eyes Dim at 91, but Ad Still Can Hit," United Press International, July 26, 1960.

Parsons, Lynn. "My Personal Hero: Roy Rogers and the Crew," Burton Blog, April 4, 2010, http://www.burtonblog.com/view.cfm?post=3835.

Purcell, S.M. "The Preacher's New Gun," *San Antonio Express and News*, August 16, 1970.

———. "Toepperwein Best in Half Century," *Austin American-Statesman*, undated, appears in Toepperwein family scrapbook provided by Joann Toepperwein.

Pyle, Ernie. "Home Country," excerpted from *Omnibook* (New York: William Sloan Associates, 1947), 38.

Scovill, Dave. "The Winchester Model 1886," *Rifle Magazine's The Legacy of Lever Guns*, Winter 2000, 12–13.

Shaw, Dale. "Master Marksman," *SPORT*, June 1962, 43.

Sheerin, Chris H. "Newton Hunt Crumley, 1911–1962," *Northeastern Nevada Historical Society Quarterly* 79, no. 1 (Winter 1979): 2–15.

Smits, Angel Strong. "Sam Strong: Cripple Creek's Notorious Millionaire," *Wild West*, http://www.historynet.com/sam-strong-cripple-creeks-notorious-millionaire.htm.

Smits, David D. "The Frontier Army and the Destruction of the Buffalo: 1865–1883," *The Western Historical Quarterly* 25, no. 3 (Autumn 1994), 314.

Stone, Lary. "Has Time for Change Arrived at Safeco Field?" *Seattle Times*, June 16, 2012.

Sweeney, Jennifer. "Vacant Hotels Hold Keys to Reno's Heritage," *Nevada Outpost*, http://www.jour.unr.edu/outpost/community/archives/com.sweeney.renoheritage.html.

Topperwein, Ad, and Norman B. Wiltsey, "World's Greatest Sharp Shooter," *Guns and Hunting*, October 1961, 12–14.

"Topperwein Shoots before Texas 'Cops,'" *The Winchester Herald*, undated (circa July 1925).

Trapshooting Hall of Fame and Museum, "History of Organized Shooting in America: Timeline," www.traphof.org/history.htm.

Trefethen, James B. "King of the Riflemen," *True: The Man's Magazine*, undated, 104.

Tremayne, David. "Russ Schleeh—The Shanty Man," The Hydroplane and Raceboat Museum, http://www.thunderboats.org/history/history0303.html.

Vogt, Ryan. "Web Exclusives: Texas History 101," *Texas Monthly*, September 2005, http://www.texasmonthly.com/2005-09-01/texashistory.php.

Whitla, D. E. "Grand Champion," *Field & Stream*, February 1943, 4.

Wiltsey, Norman. "Ad Topperwein . . . A Shooting Legend," *Guns & Ammo*, October 1961, 72.

———. "Rifleman in Retrospect," *Frontier Times* 59 (August–September 1964).

———."The West's Greatest Marksman," *Real West* X1, no. 65 (November 1968): 73.

———. "World's Greatest Marksman," *V.F.W Magazine*, January 1963, 37.

General References

Allen, Matt. Telephone interview by author, April 4, 2012.

baseballalmanac.com

Berger, Ken. Telephone interview by author, January 23, 2012.

Blue & Gold, Findlay High School yearbook of 1935 (provided by Hancock County Historical Museum, Mark H. Donaldson Jr., accessionist, September 1, 2011).

Boone, J.T. Letter to Mr. Ad Topperwein, March 6, 1958.

Brooks, Roy. Telephone interview by author, January 7, 2012.

California Skeet Shooting Association, http://www.calskeet.com/HOFhistory.html.

CensusScope, http://www.censusscope.org/us/m6720/chart_popl.html.

Charlebois, Kary. Archivist, The Reagan Presidential Library and Museum, email interview by author, May 21, 2010.

Clawson, Eugene. Telephone interview by author, December 7, 2011.

Crumley, Benjamin J. Correspondence, 1861–1878, 1865–1866. University Special Collections. University of Nevada, Reno, Library. http://innopac.library.unr.edu/record=b1703361~S0.

"Discovery: 1927, Wallace Carothers," http://www2.dupont.com/Phoenix_Heritage/en_US/1927_detail.html.

Drake, Peggy. Telephone interview by author, October 13, 2011.

Drake, Peggy, *Belmont*, unpublished essay dated November 11, 1996 (provided by Peggy Drake).

Dunlap, Dean. Telephone interview by author, September 22, 2011, October 20, 2011.

Dunlap, G.A. "Luke." Telephone interview by author, December 20, 2011.

Genealogical & Historical Society of Kendall County (Texas), Bettie Edmonds, archivist *FamilySearch* (https://www.familysearch.org), United States, Civil War Soldiers Index, United Stated Federal Archives and Records Center, Washington, DC, United States.

Findlay: The University of Findlay (findlay.edu).

Frye, Tom. Unpublished memorial, provided from the collection of Dean Dunlap.

Heath, Jack. Telephone interview by author, May 25, 2011.

Jackson, Wanda K. Telephone interview by author, October 18, 2011.

Kohler, Colette. Telephone interview by author, July 13, 2011.

Laxalt, Bob. Letter, undated; from the collection of Peggy Drake.

Marlenee, Ron. Telephone interview by author, January 23, 2012.

Montambo, Ray J. Letter to Sales Manager, Winchester Repeating Arms Co., March 7, 1958.

Mosher, Pat. Director, Gonzales County Historical Commission, email interview by author, October 5, 2011.

Mulne, Carolyn. Telephone interview by author, February 3, 2012.

National Personnel Records Center, St. Louis, Mo.

National Pigeon Association. "Master Breeder," www.npausa.com/awards/master_breeder.htm.

National Public Radio. Radio documentary (Elko, NV, Deep West Radio production, Western Folklife Center, 2008).

Nebraska State Historical Society (Carver Collection).

Ohio Oil and Gas Association, ooga.org.

Pagel, Alton. Interview by author, October 11, 2011.

Pine, Janice. Email interview by author, March 13, 2012.

Pugsley, Ed. Letter to Mr. A. Topperwein, May 10, 1945.

Reagan, Ronald. Letter to Tom Frye, August 17, 1982, provided by the personal collection of Dean Dunlap.

Rudolph, E.J. Letter to Mr. Ad Topperwein, October 30, 1958.

San Antonio, City of. Office of Historic Preservation, http://www.sanantonio.gov/historic/Districts/Cattleman_Square.aspx

Slayton, Deke. Letter to Tom Frye, September 1974, image obtained from the collection of G. A. "Luke" Dunlap.

Showman Shooter: Dedicated to the Memory of the Great Herb Parsons, "Ad Toepperwein Articles," June 1, 2008, http://www.showmanshooter.com/html/toepperwein.html.

Showman Shooter, Featuring Herb Parsons (video cassette; also includes rare video of Ad and Plinky Toepperwein), provided by Jerry Parsons, PhD.

Sultana, Chand. Letter to Mr. Michael A. Shull, March 20, 2013, 1–4, http://www.laparks.org/environmental/pdf/chatsworth/draftRem.pdf.

Texas City Directories, San Antonio, Texas, 1891–1893, ancestry.com.

The Argus (Findlay College annual), 1936–1937.

Toepperwein, Ad. Handwritten notebooks, collection of John Stein.

———. "FOR YOUR INFORMATION," open letter, January 5, 1960, obtained courtesy the collection of Tony Sapienza.

———. Letter to M.B. Allen, June 7, 1947.

———. Letter to Jack Boone, February 18, 1958.

———. Letter to Mr. Tom Frye, December 19, 1959.

———. Letter to Ernie and Dot Lind, July 8, 1947.

———. Letter to Herb Parsons, August 21, 1953.

———. Letter to Adolph Phillips, November 16, 1958 (circa).

———. Letter to Max Toepperwein, November 19, 1951 (obtained courtesy Darla Toepperwein Bacon).

Toepperwein, Charles. Telephone interview by author, October 4, 2011.

Toepperwein, Fritz. Ad Topperwein biography manuscript, unpublished, obtained courtesy of Kenneth Toepperwein.

Toepperwein, Joann. Interview by author, May 12, 2011.

Trang, Rich. Email interview by author, November 23, 2011.

Trapshooting Hall of Fame, http://www.traphof.org/Inductees/.

University of Nevada archives, http://knowledgecenter.unr.edu/univarch/default.aspx.

US Census, http://www.archives.gov/research/census/.

US Patent Office, http://www.uspto.gov/patents-application-process/search-patents.

Vertical files, Patrick Heath Public Library, Boerne, Texas.

Waldock Jr., Fred. Telephone interview by author, February 13, 2012.

Wein, Coni. Telephone interview by author, October 12, 2009.

Winchester Repeating Arms, winchesterguns.com/products/catalog/.

Winchester Record, undated, collection of Kenneth Toepperwein.

Woodhull, Frost. "Folklore Shooting," from James Frank Dobie, editor, Texas Folklore Society, *Southwestern Lore* (Denton, TX: University of North Texas Press, 1931), University of North Texas Libraries, The Portal to Texas History, http://texashistory.unt.edu; crediting UNT Press.

Newspapers and Journals

The American Field

Associated Press

Austin American-Statesman

Bakersfield Californian

Beatrice Daily Sun

Billings Gazette

Boerne Star

Cedar Rapids Evening Gazette

Collier's Magazine

The Colorado Magazine

Cumberland Press
Dallas Morning News
Decatur Review
Dunkirk Evening Observer
Elyria Chronicle Telegram
Fort Wayne Journal Gazette
Frederick Daily News
Galveston Daily News
Guns Magazine
The Daily News-Journal
Helena Independent Record
Hutcheson Daily News
Iola Daily Register
The Daily Inter Lake
Lawrence Jeffersonian-Gazette
LeMars Globe-Post
LIFE
Lima News
Lincoln County Advertiser
Logansport Journal
Nevada State Journal
Newark Daily Advocate
New York Times
Northeastern Nevada Historical Society Quarterly
Oakland Tribune
Oak Park Vindicator
Ogden Standard-Examiner
Pasadena Independent
Portsmouth Record
Reno Evening Gazette
San Antonio Daily Express
San Antonio Evening News
San Antonio Express-News
San Antonio Gazette
San Antonio Light
Sandusky Register-Star News
San Francisco Chronicle
Seattle Times
Sporting Life
Texas Monthly

The Flying Wheel (Ohio State Highway Patrol)
Time
United Press
Victoria Advocate
Washington Post
Winchester Herald
Winchester Record
Winslow Mail

INDEX

Page numbers in *italics* indicate illustrations or tables

ABOUT THE AUTHOR

Tim Price is a freelance journalist who has written for the *New York Times*, the Associated Press, NBA.com, PGATour.com, and many other outlets. He also co-authored the book *Texas Sports Trivia*.